AMERICA'S WHITE
WORKING-CLASS WOMEN

WOMEN'S STUDIES:
FACTS AND ISSUES
(VOL. 2)

GARLAND REFERENCE LIBRARY
OF THE HUMANITIES
(VOL. 260)

Volume 2

Women's Studies:
Facts and Issues

AMERICA'S WHITE WORKING-CLASS WOMEN
A Historical Bibliography

Susan Estabrook Kennedy

GARLAND PUBLISHING, INC. • NEW YORK & LONDON
1981

Library of Congress Cataloging in Publication Data

Kennedy, Susan Estabrook.
   America's white working-class women.

   (Women's studies : facts and issues ; v. 2) (Garland
reference library of the humanities ; v. 260)
   Includes indexes.
   1. Working class women—United States—History—
Bibliography.   I. Title.   II. Series.   III. Series: Gar-
land reference library of the humanities ; v. 260.
Z7963.E7K45   016.3055′6   80-8593
ISBN 0-8240-9454-9   AACR2

Printed on acid-free, 250-year-life paper
Manufactured in the United States of America

For
Thelma Sara Biddle

CONTENTS

INTRODUCTION

Modern consciousness of the presence and impact of women in American life has accelerated the growth of the field of Women's Studies. Similarly, interest in the working classes has encouraged scholarly activity in that area. Now the two categories are beginning to touch in efforts to give needed attention to working-class women in American history.

Working-class women have a rich history which has been documented and even analyzed, although working-class women themselves are only now being recognized by the larger community as members of a socioeconomic and class-gender group with its own varieties of changing needs, interests, objectives, problems, and priorities.

The classification "America's white working-class women" draws upon concepts of nationality, race, socioeconomic status, and gender; but it also speaks of persons who possess historical experiences which are unique to themselves and which constitute more than the sum of those separate components. The complexities of American social and political history, of being caucasians, of membership in the working class or classes, and of being female indicate a myriad of spheres, activities, perceptions, and prescriptions. And adequate scholarly study of America's white working-class women must draw upon but transcend each of those categories, often examining separate components which become a check upon one another.

When categories become complex, they seem almost to invite misconceptions; and terms need careful definition. In the case of working-class women, for example, aristocrats and the bourgeoisie are clearly ruled out, but what of "working women"? Are they necessarily "working class"? The answer should be just as clear: not all employed females are working-class women; and conversely, many working-class women have never earned wages. For women, as for men, "work" and "working class" are not interchangeable concepts. Similarly, with class lines, sociologists are now using refined categories such as lower middle class and upper lower class, while working-class people often describe themselves in class terms which bear no relation to their income or their lifestyle. I have elsewhere described the working-class woman as living "somewhere between the terrors of poverty and the security of the middle class" (item 22), a condition dictated either by her own presence in that socioeconomic realm or by her attachment to a male who is so described. Moreover, in much of American history, the American white working-class woman has often been seen in the process of becoming something other than the American white working-class woman. Such externally dictated goals frequently stood in the way of that woman's acquiring any strongly articulated sense of herself as part of the working class, just as her commitment to family and community may have prevented her from developing a formal sense of herself as a politicized woman.

Despite these fascinating difficulties, historians will find white working-class women involved in the American experience almost from the beginnings of settlement. It should amuse quantifiers to learn that 50 percent of the initial female immigrant population from England to North America fell into the category of working-class women—or, rather, working-class *woman*, since one of the two women who arrived at Jamestown in 1608 came as maidservant to the other. She soon married a laborer, thereby perpetuating her working-class status, since a colonial wife's socioeconomic position derived in law from that of her husband.

Availability of land and fluidity of social movement in the colonial period, especially the seventeenth century, make it difficult to identify and trace white working-class women of that era. But a constant flow of indentured servants from England and the Continent, as well as a stream of refugees from the enclosures and urban overpopulation indicate a steady replenishment of that part of the population.

Toward the end of the eighteenth century, the beginnings of organized efforts to promote manufacturing introduced not only industrialization, with its class implications for the bourgeoisie and the proletariat, but new opportunities and limitations for women, particularly working-class women. Early manufacturers hired the daughters of yeomen farmers, as much to acquire a docile and inexpensive labor force as to remove the threat that farmers might lose their sons to the new world of the factory.

The "mill girls of New England" represent the first large and clearly identifiable group of white working-class women in America. But they saw themselves as, and largely were, only temporary members of that group. The daughters of solid farmers who had fought the American Revolution, these young women first entered the factories in response to attractive wages, independence, and in some cases intellectual ambitions. As residents of the boarding houses of the Waltham System, they lived and worked away from their families, earning higher pay than they could have commanded as dairymaids or school teachers, and enjoying one another's companionship and self-education. They intended to remain in the mills only part of each year and only until they returned home to marry back into the society which had produced them.

Deteriorating wage rates and working conditions as well as more attractive employment alternatives elsewhere led native-born women to abandon the mills in the 1840s. But their brief career had established a set of assumptions which would be applied to their successors (without much consideration for accuracy) for more than a century. American society chose to conclude that women sought employment by choice rather than from necessity, that they intended to work only temporarily and hence had no concern for long-term skills or employment considerations, that they would leave their jobs to marry men who could provide economic security, that they neither possessed nor needed industrial skills for the simple machine-tending tasks they performed, and that lacking skills, they did not deserve decent wages, which they apparently did not need in any case, thus closing the circular reasoning and with it the trap for working working-class women.

As the native-born women quitted the factories, immigrant families flowed into the job vacuum. Working-class men could not command adequate wages to maintain their families, despite Victorian middle-class prescriptions that families ought not to exist until the husband-father could sustain them economically. The same set of cultural dictates influenced the way working-class wives cooperated in solving this financial dilemma. Since industrialization had removed the work place from the dwelling place, and since the middle-class American way clearly relegated the wife-mother to the household, many mature working-class women of the nineteenth century vigorously denied that they "worked." Instead, they kept house (often under severely primitive conditions), provided all domestic services for their families, and still found "invisible" ways of supplementing family income such as taking lodgers or doing laundry or sewing on a piece-rate basis. Indeed, such families sent children out to work rather than mothers; young, single women might find employment outside the home and contribute their wages, or most of them, to the parental household, while older, married women hid the earning activities which they undertook in addition to their housekeeping duties.

If American white working-class women of the middle and late nineteenth century were surreptitious about their earning activities, most showed even less tendency to reveal any consciousness of class or gender. A few women distinguished themselves by forming or joining trade union groups where women who did participate frequently proved themselves among the most faithful and most militant members. And some supported class-oriented political groups, particularly Eastern European Jewish young women who had been exposed to both unionism and political radicalism before they emigrated. But these women then faced monumental barriers because of their sex, ranging from Victorian fastidiousness which cringed at men and women attending gender-mixed union meetings to male trade unionists' fears that the growing presence of unskilled women in the workforce would undermine the wages of skilled men.

Those groups which might have appealed to such women on gender or class lines either ignored them or stumbled over problems of reconciling the two sets of objectives. Political feminists Susan B. Anthony and Elizabeth Cady Stanton, for example, could provide a home for the Working Women's Association while they conducted their suffrage campaign, but they advised women to place gender issues above class solidarity when they urged would-be female printers to act as strike-breakers in order to learn the skills of that trade. Conversely, at the turn of the century, the Socialist Party produced some pro-woman and gender-free appeals and attempted to recruit female members; but women never achieved integrated policy-making power within the group and women's programs were among the first to be abandoned when financial resources dried up.

Social feminists occasionally tried to bridge class differences. At the beginning of the twentieth century, groups like the Union Label League and the National Consumers League urged women to buy only those goods produced in unionized shops, an effort to support both the principle of trade union organization and union-negotiated improvements in wages and working conditions. The National Women's Trade Union League and its local chapters attempted to create a cross-class alliance to bring women workers into unions. Progressive investigators gathered impressive quantities of data about the lives of working-class women which they used to bolster arguments for reforms ranging from sanitation to a living wage which would enable a man to support his family on his own earnings to adequate housing facilities for young working-class women who had to live away from their families.

Significant difficulties developed, however, over internal vs. external definitions of problems and solutions for working-class women. Reformers urged self-help programs, such as education and unionization, but were sometimes disappointed by the response and, therefore, turned to outside protections for working-class women, such as regulation of industry and public welfare legislation. Meanwhile, working-class women themselves had greater success with educational efforts conceived along lines more responsive to their own needs. But their leaders often cooperated in the movement toward protection. Even trade unionists, particularly those associated with the American Federation of Labor, believed that working-class women could not or would not take care of themselves, and that society should assume the obligation of defending them from inequities of life and labor.

For working-class women, both world wars represented opportunities to advance in skills and pay when they joined the workforce—opportunities which were rapidly withdrawn almost before peace was restored. Few working-class women could afford to follow their middle-class counterparts back into the household; instead, they retreated back into lower-status, lower-paying, unskilled occupations.

By the 1950s and 1960s, however, working-class men were finding means for supporting families without women-produced income, sometimes working second and third jobs, sometimes benefitting from strengthening unionization which increased wages and benefits. For the first time in a century and a half, white working-class women could define themselves as house-wives in fact as well as in theory. Sociologists concluded that such women subordinated themselves to home and family and speculated that the women's liberation movement, which prodded middle-class women out into the workforce, only added to the sense of threat and betrayal which working-class women were experiencing from the move to the suburbs and rapid social change.

At the same time, however, working-class women emerged within their own perspective, defining themselves as working-class women who were satisfied and proud of that status. Participating in grass-roots political and social movements to preserve their neighborhoods, joining women's caucuses within unions, educating their children in working-class values, they appeared across the nation with a sense of their own identity which they confirmed as legitimate in its own right. Coincidentally, scholars and policy-makers have become aware of America's white working-class women as a significant minority group with its own history.

Attempts to collect and reconstruct the history of these persons at first encountered certain frustrations. If women have been "hidden from history," working-class women have been doubly obscured. On reexamination, however, a rich body of literature already exists, one to which contemporary analysts are adding major contributions.

Relatively few working-class women of the past left their own published records. Throughout much of their history, white working-class women in America had neither the time nor the energy left over from living their lives to write about them; nor did they have the strong sense of self-identity which would encourage large numbers of them to record and preserve their attitudes and activities. But, occasionally, a working-class woman appears in person, in a bit of dialogue in response to a surveyor, in a grandmother's stories, or in rare autobiographies. The mill girls of Lowell and its sister communities sometimes described their lives in the *Lowell Offering* (items 168, 176, 185) and other factory magazines. Several immigrant women recorded or told their stories to friendly observers; Rosa Cavaleri so entranced settlement workers in Chicago with her story that Marie Hall Ets transcribed her tales in *Rosa: The Life of an Italian Immigrant* (item 81), and Rose Cohen produced a hymn of praise to Americanization in *Out of the Shadow* (item 77), while unidentified Jewish immigrants told the Pittsburgh Section of the National Council of Jewish Women the lore which became *By Myself, I'm a Book!* (item 100). Some women, successful in trade union activities, later wrote autobiographies, such as Rose Schneiderman's *All for One* (item 313), Mary Anderson's *Woman at Work* (item 291), Rose Pesotta's *Bread Upon the Waters* (item 310), Agnes Nestor's *Woman's Labor Leader* (item 309), and Stella Nowicki's "Back of the Yards" (item 349). Oral history projects and collections such as the Rosie the Riveter reunions or the Summer 1977 issue of *Frontiers* or Nancy Seifer's *Nobody Speaks for Me!* (item 866) indicate the wealth of information still available. But for the more distant past, searchers must often employ intended or accidental accounts compiled by outside observers.

Much of the literature is polemical, the work of feminists, reformers, and other advocates of a variety of solutions to the problems and conditions of working-class women. Some of these works are best characterized by their passion, others by their substance. In particular, the periods 1900 to 1920 and 1960 to 1980 produced significant factual research, often gathered and analyzed in the interest of reform. The earlier era was the day of the great Progressive surveys, during which independent and government interviewers attempted to compile descriptive and statistical materials which could bolster the argument for self-help or for extending protection. The National Women's Trade

Union League, for example, issued a monthly magazine, *Life and Labor*, which aired the tragedies and triumphs of the lives of women workers in industry. Between 1910 and 1913, the federal government issued a nineteen-volume *Report on Conditions of Woman and Child Wage-Earners in the United States* which included the *History of Women in Trade Unions* by John B. Andrews and W.D.P. Bliss (item 196) and the *History of Women in Industry in the United States* by Helen Sumner (item 136), compilations which collected much of the available data about the nineteenth century. At the same time, the Russell Sage Foundation and other organizations sponsored and conducted surveys of neighborhoods, occupations, and similar topics. More recently, reformers, academics, and policy-makers have gathered information to press for social responses to the needs of working-class women. Nancy Seifer's *Absent from the Majority* (item 865) offers not only descriptive data but policy suggestions; Pamela Roby's *The Poverty Establishment* (item 863) raises essential questions about the distribution of resources; and Barbara Wertheimer and Anne Nelson's *Trade Union Women* (item 973) examines the presence and participation of female members of union locals. Throughout the century, since its founding in 1920, the Women's Bureau of the United States Department of Labor has gathered, digested, and publicized information about various aspects of women's working life in an effort to establish standards for equal pay, efficient production, and regulatory laws; their *Handbook on Women Workers* (item 899) goes beyond the work place to provide information on lives, homes, families, and community concerns.

Other segments of the literature are prescriptive. Throughout the nineteenth and much of the twentieth centuries in the United States, an aggressive white middle class attempted to spread the beliefs which underlay its own lifestyle and value system, particularly as those ideas related to the proper role and fulfillment of women. Behavioral norms for female factory workers, for example, were spelled out by the Rev. James Porter's *The Operative's Friend, and Defence: or, Hints to Young Ladies, Who Are Dependent on Their Own Exertions* (item 180). In a more recent and perverse illustration of these directives, wartime writings sought to lure working-class and other women out of their traditional domestic situations for temporary employment during the military emergency; after each war, however, the cult of domesticity reasserted itself. Susan B. Anthony II, for example, asked women to go *Out of the Kitchen—Into the War* (item 977) in 1943, but Susan M. Hartman has amply documented "Prescriptions for Penelope: Literature on Women's Obligations to Returning World War II Veterans" (item 798).

In the last generation, psychologists, political scientists, and market analysts, as well as sociologists, have begun to publish studies of working-class women. Lee Rainwater and his colleagues produced *Workingman's Wife* (item 830) in 1969, Mirra Komarovsky published *Blue Collar Marriage* (item 820) in 1962, and MacFadden-Bartell Corporation continued its market research into the 1970s with *Working-Class Women in a Changing World* (item 837), only a few examples of growing numbers of symposia, research projects, and academic analyses from social scientists. In a number of cases, the research serves commercial interests; in others, it is directed toward labor force participation or trade union activism. But, regardless of objective, it marks a recent attempt to identify, examine, and speculate upon the lifestyles, needs, and priorities of working-class women.

Historians are now joining that research effort, drawing together work in women's studies, working-class studies, and minority studies as well as the tools which have been developed for social history to produce historical analyses of working-class women in America. The kind of rigorous philosophical and methodological explorations which Gerda Lerner (items 37 and 152) and William Chafe (items 139 and 793) have brought to the general field of the History of Women have not yet found parallels within the narrower field of the History of Working-Class Women in America, although such essays as "Women in American Society" by Ann Gordon, Mari Jo Buhle, and Nancy Schrom Dye (item 39) and Susan Kleinberg's "The Systematic Study of Urban Women" (item 43) open that area to investigation. As yet, the most fruitful work is monographic.

Little attention has thus far been given to working-class women in the Colonial period, probably because of difficulties in delineating class lines and the necessity to explore beyond traditional sources of information. But Roger Thompson's *Women in Stuart England and America* (item 53) analyzes many of the factors which affected their lives, and Frances Manges' "Women Shopkeepers, Tavernkeepers, and Artisans in Colonial Philadelphia" (item 57) introduces the subject of women's work lives in that period, as does Gary B. Nash's analysis of "The Failure of Female Factory Labor in Colonial Boston" (item 60).

America's white working-class women are more identifiable with the coming of industrialization. As Gerda Lerner pointed out in "The Lady and the Mill Girl" (item 152), economic changes had enormous consequences for women of both the middle and the lower classes. Susan E. Hirsch's examination of Newark in the early nineteenth century (item 149), Libby Zimmerman's exploration of Lynn, Massachusetts, over a longer period (item 157), and Amy Srebnick's discussion of New York in the 1850s and 1860s (items 119 and 155) focus on women during the period of industrialization, while the continuing impact of industrialization, technology, and urbanization on the lives of working-class women can be seen in Susan J. Kleinberg's study of Pittsburgh between 1870 and 1900 (items 69 and 150).

The aspect of the early factory system which has intrigued a number of historians is the Waltham System, perhaps for the richness of surviving and newly rediscovered information. Lise Vogel has brought several documents into print (items 187, 188, and 189), and Philip S. Foner's collection of the writings of the mill girls themselves (item 169) provides a useful basic literature. Networking in women's living and employment situations under the Waltham System has been studied by Helena Wright in "The Uncommon Mill Girls of Lowell" (item 191), by Sandra Adickes in "Mind Among the Spindles" (item 158), by Richard P. Horowitz in "Architecture and Culture: The Meaning of the Lowell Boarding House" (item 171), and most extensively by Thomas Dublin in *Women at Work: The Transformation of Work and Community in Lowell, Massachusetts, 1826–1869* as well as in a number of articles (items 162–65). The mill communities of New England also provide the base for studies of the transition from native-born to immigrant labor, such as H.M. Gitelman's "The Waltham System and the Coming of the Irish" (item 170), Steven J. Dubnoff's "The Family and Absence from Work" (item 166), and Charles Chauncey Buell's "The Workers of Worcester" (item 116).

Ethnicity has attracted considerable attention, some of which extends to the lives of women. Among the many recent works are Janice Reiff Webster's study of the Americanization of Scandinavian women in Seattle (item 105) and *The Jewish Woman in America* by Charlotte Baum, Paula Hyman, and Sonya Michel (item 76). The interest in this subject at scholarly meetings has resulted in collections of papers such as *Immigrants in Industrial America: 1850–1920*, edited by Richard L. Ehrlich (item 79). Some works have traced the ethnic woman beyond the initial period of immigration, such as Miriam Cohen's (items 240 and 241) and Maxine Seller's (item 328) discussions of Italian-American women and Hanita Frymer-Blumfield's consideration of ethnic identity among Jewish women (item 797).

In particular, students of ethnic women have been interested in the interplay between home and work in their lives, questioning whether industrialization and urbanization disrupted family life. Studies of the Irish in Buffalo by Mary Catherine Mattis (item 94) and the Italians in the same city by Virginia Yans-McLaughlin (items 106–10), as well as the examination of Italian, Jewish, and Slavic immigrant women in Pittsburgh by Corinne Azen Krause (item 93) argue that ethnic family and cultural arrangements survived the adjustments of industrialization. Tamara Hareven and her collaborators (items 70, 248–51) claim further that in New England communities, family and kin networks actually aided adjustment to industrialization, while Laurence A. Glasco, dealing with Buffalo's Irish and Germans and native-born whites (item 85), sees the work activities of immigrant women as easing their adjustment to America. In addition, recent studies examine the important economic roles of both single and married immigrant women within their families. Judith Smith's researches in Providence, Rhode Island (item 103), Carol Groneman's on New York City (items 87 and 88), and Barbara Klaczynska's on Philadelphia (items 366 and 367) all show women earning—single women openly and married women covertly.

Perhaps because records are fuller and more accessible on the activities of women outside the household than within it, considerable attention has been paid to the employed white working-class woman. During the nineteenth century, a major form of employment was domestic service, which David M.

Katzman has examined in *Seven Days a Week* (item 388), while a common and growing form of earning in the twentieth century has been white-collar work, which Elyce J. Rotella traces in general for the period 1870 to 1930 (item 434) and Margery Davies examines with particular attention to clerical workers for the same period (items 423 and 424).

But the most dramatic involvement of working-class women who earn outside their homes has been in the factory labor force; and historians have given most attention to the efforts of such women to achieve organization and self-determination. Daniel J. Walkowitz, for example, has analyzed the interplay between industrial capitalism and family objectives in Cohoes, New York (items 113 and 114), and Judith A. McGraw has shown women industrial workers in the Berkshires as active shapers of their own life and work experiences (item 131). Some studies of union activities have included women in passing, such as dissertations by Joyce Shaw Peterson on automobile workers before unionization (item 598), David Gurowsky on the International Ladies Garment Workers Union (item 556), and John Norten Schacht on communications workers (item 609). Where women workers were active in union and other worker-protest movements, their militancy has attracted attention. As Dolores Janiewski shows in "Making Common Cause," needlewomen demanded fair treatment and public support for it as early as the 1830s (item 206), evidence of an articulate activism which Mary H. Blewett further documents in her study of the Haverhill shoe workers of 1895 (item 197).

Although some women distinguished themselves by their labor militancy, women workers generally did not have an easy time with organization, for a variety of reasons set forth by Alice Kessler-Harris (items 571–73). Moreover, Ronald Schatz has found that union leaders were usually not typical of the industry's workforce (item 610); Priscilla Long records Mother Jones's ambivalence toward women (item 306); Ricki Carole Myers Cohen uses Fannia Cohn to look at the interaction between traditional and work lives of women labor leaders (item 295); and Gary E. Endelman shows Rose Schneiderman moving toward government planning rather than self-help for women workers (item 643).

Something can be learned about working-class women from the activities of those who attempted to help them. Susan Porter Benson shows sympathetic middle- and upper-class allies active as early as the 1830s and 1840s (item 115), while David M. Kennedy's study of Margaret Sanger transcends biography to examine the entire birth control movement, including its interests in working-class women (item 274). Similarly, Henry B. Leonard has looked at the Immigrants' Protective League of Chicago (item 276), Lynn Weiner has studied the housing efforts of the Minneapolis Woman's Christian Association (item 288), and Allis Rosenberg Wolfe has investigated the National Consumers' League (item 289). Biographical studies of reformers, such as dissertations on Lillian D. Wald by Allan Edward Reznick (item 311) and Doris Groshen Daniels (item 297), should add to this facet of the literature.

Opinion is divided among historians on the success or failure of the efforts of these "allies"; and much of the debate concentrates on the Women's Trade Union League, a topic reintroduced in the 1960s by Allen F. Davis (item 637). On the one hand, James J. Kenneally argues that the WTUL stood virtually alone in producing favorable results for women workers (items 569 and 570), while others place greater emphasis on class and ideological problems. Carolyn Daniel McCreesh's study of efforts of organized garment workers between 1880 and World War I (item 578), Nancy Schrom Dye's extensive examination of the New York branch of the WTUL (items 640–42), and Robin Miller Jacoby's explorations of the American and British Leagues (items 645 and 646) concentrate on the tensions between feminism and trade unionism, showing that suffrage and protective legislation won out over self-help and organization, a conclusion in which I concurred in a general study of Progressive reformers' interaction with working-class women (item 647).

The efforts of reformers to establish protection by society produced considerable public and archival material, which has attracted many historians. Jacob Lieberman explores the hours and wages movement from 1890 to 1925 (item 697) as does Joseph L. Candela, Jr., with concentration on Illinois (item 669), and Bettina Eileen Berch compares the American experience with that of England and France (item 662). J. Stanley Lemons takes the study of "social feminism" into the postsuffrage period of the 1920s (items 695 and 696), ground also covered by Jean Elizabeth Mulligan who presses on to the 1960s (item 706). Studies of individual agencies, such as Judith A. Sealander's of the Women's Bureau of the Department of Labor (item 744), will undoubtedly enrich this avenue of exploration. But recent, "new feminist" analysis views this protection as having become a liability for employed women; what began as an attempt to help has evolved into a limitation, says Judith A. Baer in *The Chains of Protection*, which concentrates on law (item 660), and Ann Corrine Hill in her study of the courts (item 684).

Meanwhile, others are probing the relationship of personal and family lives to work lives. Elizabeth H. Pleck urges historians to discover how people reconcile the worlds of work and of family (item 51); Martha Norby Fraundorf looks at labor force participation of married women at the turn of the century (item 245); Leslie Woodcock Tentler examines the lack of opportunity for individuality and autonomy in both work and marriage for women between 1900 and 1930 (item 231); Miriam J. Cohen shows that despite differences in kinds of employment before marriage, first- and second-generation Italian women in the first half of the twentieth century entered traditional marriages (items 240 and 241).

Cataclysmic events, like economic depression and world wars, pinpoint changing realities and unchanging attitudes in women's lives. Despite the magnitude of the Great Depression, Julia Kirk Blackwelder shows that women's participation in the labor force in Atlanta, New Orleans, and San Antonio was still shaped by a complicated set of cultural attitudes, economic necessities, and personal viewpoints (item 776). Similarly, Winifred Bolin's study of the 1930s and 1940s concludes that most married women were not gainfully employed, regardless of the economic levels of their families (item 237). And Lois Scharf documents strong societal assumptions that married women belonged at home (item 789). But women as household managers still had to cope with the impact of that Depression, in ways recorded by Jeane Westin in *Making Do* (item 791).

In the same vein, war made great changes, for a time at least, in the lives of working-class and other women; but long-term adjustments were another matter. On the one hand, Maurine Weiner Greenwald argues that World War I increased the numbers of women working but added to sex-segregation of work (items 755 and 756); and Nancy E. Malan comes to a similar conclusion, showing that women held jobs previously done by men, but lost those positions to returning veterans (item 762). Analysis of World War II, however, involves some debate. Chester W. Gregory argues that the war represented a major step toward self-emancipation for women (item 992), a point of view reiterated in Karen Anderson's dissertation on the Puget Sound area (item 975). Conversely, Josephine Chandler Holcomb concludes that employed women only increased their numbers during the war; attitudes and opportunities did not change (item 994). And Eleanor Straub's examination of government policy toward civilian women shows few permanent gains; reality did not live up to the glossy image of wartime propaganda (items 1003–5). Indeed, Melva Joyce Baker sees wartime films strengthening traditional images of women (item 978) and D'Ann Campbell finds that women actually resisted media and government appeals to abandon temporarily their traditional roles for participation in war work (item 981). For working-class women in particular, however, employment remained a necessity; Paddy Quick shows those women enjoying relatively attractive wages during wartime but returning to lower-paid service or clerical jobs in peacetime (item 998).

Clearly, the richness of the emerging literature on white working-class women tantalizes more than it satisfies. Every new dissertation hints at the dozens of others which should be written. Working-class women are finding their way into collections of documents and articles such as *America's Working Women*, edited by Rosalyn Baxandall, Linda Gordon, and Susan Reverby (item 33), *Root of Bitterness*, edited by Nancy F. Cott (item 35), and *The Female Experience*, edited by Gerda Lerner (item 37). Syntheses like my own *If All We Did Was to Weep at Home* (item 22) as well as histories of working women such as Barbara M. Wertheimer's *We Were There* (item 32) and Philip S. Foner's *Women and the American Labor Movement* (item 20) testify to the emergence of the field and stand as invitations for further work.

The intention of this bibliography is to assist those who will undertake such studies. It is arranged according to two general principles to reflect both historical sequence and at the same time some definition compatible with recent work in the history of women.

Since the subject of white working-class women is only now receiving much serious attention from scholars, the section on General Works is necessarily brief and often ranges into broader themes. In a number of cases, women of the working class have been subsumed under general topics and issues dealing with women; in other instances, they have received some passing attention in studies of their class or in analyses dealing with such subjects as labor or economics or sociology. Users may find the most productive guidance in the collection of articles and essays dealing with the state of the art, which can be used to place working-class women's studies within the contexts of related fields.

The other four sections of the book have a chronological superstructure, establishing rough categories of time in American history during which some cohesive view of working-class women may be developed. As Gerda Lerner has been pointing out for more than a decade, the boundaries of time which have been used for "men's" history do not necessarily apply to "women's." But the concept of classes clearly has a great deal to do with industrialization. And from that idea has derived the eras "Pre-Industrial," "Industrializing," "Modern," and "Recent." In general, the seventeenth and eighteenth centuries can be regarded as pre-industrial, the nineteenth as industrializing, the first half of the twentieth century as modern, and the period from World War II as recent.

The subcategories, however, differ markedly from "traditional" arrangements. In recognition of the historical realities of women's lives in America, the arrangement begins closest to the person and moves outward toward the larger world. Beginning with personal lives, the categories grow to home and family, to community, to class, to employment. The distribution of available information within these groupings is highly uneven, with the smallest numbers of studies thus far available on personal considerations and the largest on the world of work outside the home. But recent scholarship in social history is doing much to redress that imbalance. Finally, each chronological section concludes with a separate listing of Historical Conditions, reflecting those events such as the American Revolution or the Great Depression which, by themselves, had significant impact upon white working-class women, in addition to the broader treatments of self or class or working condition.

In many cases, a single source properly "belongs" in several subcategories, or in a few instances in more than one large time frame. Placement has been determined by the primary applicability of a citation. Each citation appears only once in the body of annotations to avoid endless repetition. The subject index, however, is intended to help resolve the multiple applications of such items. In addition, an author index will lead readers to all of the works by any individual.

Compiling this bibliography would have been impossible without the resources of many institutions and the generous help of many librarians. In addition to Janet McNeil of the James Branch Cabell Library of Virginia Commonwealth University, I am indebted to the staffs of the Archives of Labor History and Urban Affairs of Wayne State University, the Arthur and Elizabeth Schlesinger Library on the History of Women in America at Radcliffe College, the Library of Congress, the National Archives, the National Center for Urban Ethnic Affairs, the New York State School of Industrial and Labor Relations at Cornell University, the Sophia Smith Collection at Smith College, Tamiment Library at New York University, and the Virginia State Library.

Above all others, Dorothy Ogden Estabrook has offered her usual support, both maternal and clerical. My husband, E. Craig Kennedy, Jr., best knows his role in contributing to my work. And my students, especially those in History of Women classes, have been as tolerant of the many references to "The Bibliography" as they were earlier of those to "The Book"; I thank them all. In particular, my warmest gratitude goes to a special kind of colleague, Thelma Sara Biddle, for whom the dedication of this book is only the slightest indication of my affection and acknowledgment of her years of friendship.

AMERICA'S WHITE
WORKING-CLASS WOMEN

I. GENERAL WORKS

A. BIBLIOGRAPHIES

1. Bickner, Mei Liang. *Women at Work: An Annotated Bibliography.* Los Angeles: Manpower Research Center, Institute of Industrial Relations, University of California at Los Angeles, 1974.

   Collects, annotates, and cross-catalogues articles, government documents, pamphlets, papers, and some books covering a wide range of topics related to employed females, such as earnings, occupations, special categories of women, and public policy. Working-class women are subsumed under some occupational categories but are not treated separately.

2. ———, and Marlene Shaughnessy. *Women at Work--Volume II.* Los Angeles: Institute of Industrial Relations, University of California at Los Angeles, 1977.

   Updates item 1, with more inclusion of scholarly studies.

3. Common Women Collective. *Women in U.S. History: An Annotated Bibliography.* Cambridge, Mass.: Common Women Collective, 1976. 114 pp.

   Summarizes and evaluates books, pamphlets, and articles on women throughout American history, with particular notation of authors' awareness of class, race, sex, and concepts.

4. Een, Jo Ann Delores, and Marie B. Rosenberg-Dishman. *Women and Society--Citations 3601 to 6000: An Annotated Bibliography.* Beverly Hills: Sage Publications, 1978. 275 pp.

   Continues item 12.

5. Friedman, Barbara, *et al. Women's Work and Women's Studies 1973-1974.* New York: Barnard College Women's Center, 1975. 370 pp.

Lists books, articles, papers, and bibliographies on
women in general, organized by topic, such as education,
employment, health, and resources.

6. Haber, Barbara. *Women in America: A Guide to Books,
    1963-1975.* Boston: G.K. Hall and Co., 1978. 202pp.

    Briefly digests books relating to women, by topic, in-
    cluding lifestyles, literature, religion, sexuality, and
    work.

7. Harrison, Cynthia, ed. *Women in American History.* Santa
    Barbara, Calif.: ABC-Clio, 1979. 374 pp.

    Reprints abstracts of journal articles from *America:
    History and Life* (1963-1976) on such topics as women's
    organizations, roles, status, employment, and social
    problems.

8. Jacobs, Sue-Ellen. *Women in Perspective: A Guide for
    Cross-Cultural Studies.* Urbana: University of Illinois
    Press, 1974. 299pp.

    Lists works relating to women, along topical and geo-
    graphical lines, with a section on "Economics and Employ-
    ment" but no particular concentration on classes or
    working-class women.

9. Kohen, Andrew I., et al. *Women and the Economy: A Bib-
    liography and a Review of the Literature on Sex Dif-
    ferentiation in the Labor Market.* N.p.: Center for
    Human Resource Research, Ohio State University, 1975,
    1977. 109pp.

    Lists articles and books relating to the history and
    current condition of women workers, including earnings,
    occupations, unionism, law, and sex differentiation.

10. Lynn, Naomi, Ann B. Matasar, and Marie Barovic Rosenberg.
    Research Guide in Women's Studies. Morristown, N.J.:
    General Learning Press, 1974. 194pp.

    Instructs in researching and writing a project in
    women's studies, and lists relevant general sources of
    information.

11. Oakes, Elizabeth H., and Kathleen E. Sheldon. *A Guide
    to Social Science Resources in Women's Studies.* Santa
    Barbara, Calif.: ABC-Clio, 1978. 162pp.

Summarizes contents of studies on women of all classes
and countries in anthropology, economics, history, psychology, and sociology as well as contemporary feminism.
Working-class women are subsumed under such topics as
working, unionization, family, and broader themes.

12. Rosenberg, Marie Barovic, and Len V. Bergstrom, ed.
*Women and Society: A Critical Review of the Literature
with a Selected Annotated Bibliography.* Beverly Hills:
Sage Publications, 1975. 354 pp.

Lists and briefly annotates books and articles on
women, organized by scholarly discipline including sociology, political science, and history, with sub-
groupings such as family, class and status, feminism,
manners and customs, and economic position.

13. Soltow, Martha Jane, and Mary K. Wery. *American Women
and the Labor Movement, 1825-1974: An Annotated Bibliography.* Metuchen, N.J.: The Scarecrow Press, Inc.,
1976. 247 pp.

Revises and updates item 14, with a 50 percent increase
in entries and inclusion of materials beyond the 1930s.
Entries are particularly drawn from trade union periodicals such as the *American Federationist* and *Labor Age*
as well as a sampling of such journals as the *Survey*,
the *Nation*, and the *New Republic*.

14. Soltow, Martha Jane, Carolyn Forche, and Murray Massre.
*Women in American Labor History, 1825-1935: An Anno-
tated Bibliography.* East Lansing, Mich.: School of
Labor and Industrial Relations and The Libraries,
Michigan State University, 1972. 150 pp.

Summarizes books, articles, pamphlets, government documents, and manuscript collections on topics relating to
the employment, working conditions, trade union involvement and activities of working women and their supporters.

15. Stineman, Esther. *Women's Studies: A Recommended Core
Bibliography.* Littleton, Colo.: Libraries Unlimited,
Inc., 1979. 670 pp.

Evaluates books relating to women, with heavy emphasis
on literature but including such fields as labor, history, sociology, and reference.

16. Terris, Virginia R. *Woman in America: A Guide to Information Sources*. Detroit: Gale Research Company, 1980. 520 pp.

    Surveys a wide range of literary and other sources containing information on women's role, status, image, history, education, sociology, employment, health, and the arts. Among the non-traditional sources included are microfilms, slides, and oral histories.

B. GENERAL HISTORIES

17. Cantor, Milton, and Bruce Laurie, eds. *Class, Sex, and the Woman Worker*. Westport, Conn.: Greenwood Press, 1977. 253 pp.

    Contains items 43, 87, 108, 118, 165, 187, 241, 572, 648, 654.

18. Commons, John R., *et al*. *History of Labor in the United States*. New York: The Macmillan Company, 1921-1935. 4 vols.

    Documents the history of American workers, their occupations and labor organizations, emphasizing job consciousness and trade union movements. Women are included when they participated in trade unions or when reformers or legislators examined their conditions of labor.

19. Foner, Philip S. *History of the Labor Movement in the United States*. New York: International Publishers, 1947-1965. 4 vols.

    Argues that class is an essential element in understanding labor organization and that labor organization extends beyond occupationally-oriented trade unionism. The history of American labor movements from Colonial times to World War I reveals working-class men and women making significant contributions in democratic and social struggles.

20. ————. *Women and the American Labor Movement: From Colonial Times to the Eve of World War I*. New York: The Free Press, Macmillan Publishing Co., 1979. 621 pp.

    Presents women as militant and aggressive in their own behalf from the earliest days of the factory system

despite having to face "the double obstacle of employer-
public hostility and the indifference of most male-
dominated unions." Workingwomen cannot be separated
from workingmen, however, nor from the major events of
social, economic, and political history.

21. James, Edward T., ed. *Notable American Women 1607-1950:
    A Biographical Dictionary.* Cambridge, Mass.: Belknap
    Press of Harvard University Press, 1971. 3 vols.

    Gives brief factual summaries of the lives of American
    women who achieved "distinction in their own right of
    more than local significance." Among the working-class
    women or those who worked with working-class women are
    Sarah G. Bagley, Mary Harris Jones, Lucy Larcom, Agnes
    Nestor, Leonora O'Reilly, Margaret Dreier Robins, Harriet
    H. Robinson, and Augusta Lewis Troup.

22. Kennedy, Susan Estabrook. *If All We Did Was to Weep at
    Home: A History of White Working-class Women in America.*
    Bloomington: Indiana University Press, 1979. 331 pp.

    Shows that white working-class women have been an un-
    self-conscious minority throughout American history until
    recently. Such women saw themselves more as in the proc-
    ess of becoming middle-class than they did as part of the
    working classes. Caught between poverty and economic
    security, they struggled to maintain survival for their
    families while pursuing middle-class values and norms.

23. Kessler-Harris, Alice. "Women, Work, and the Social
    Order." In *Liberating Women's History: Theoretical
    and Critical Essays,* edited by Berenice A. Carroll.
    Urbana: University of Illinois Press, 1976. Pp. 330-
    43.

    Argues that internal and external concepts of the fam-
    ily and its relationship to the community influence the
    kinds of work women have performed. Nineteenth-century
    insistence on woman's place in the home, for example,
    encouraged men to work harder to keep their women out
    of the workforce, undermined the development of class
    consciousness among premarital female industrial workers,
    and permitted employers to regard female earnings as
    merely supplemental. More recently, changing economic
    needs have opened new jobs and altered women's functions
    within families.

24. Maupin, Joyce. *Labor Heroines: Ten Women Who Led the
    Struggle.* Berkeley, Calif.: Union WAGE Educational
    Committee, 1974. 31 pp.

Gives brief biographical sketches of Sarah Bagley,
Augusta Lewis, Kate Mullaney, Leonora Barry, Hannah
O'Day, Clara Lemlich, Rose Schneiderman, Mother Jones,
Agnes Nestor, Elizabeth Gurley Flynn.

25. ————. *Working Women and their Organizations: 150 Years
of Struggle*. Berkeley, Calif.: Union WAGE Educational
Committee, 1974. 33 pp.

Surveys the history of exploitation and unionization
of women workers in America, leading up to the argument
for organization, especially in Union WAGE.

26. O'Sullivan, Judith, and Rosemary Gallick. *Workers and
Allies: Female Participation in the American Trade
Union Movement, 1824-1976*. Washington, D.C.: Smith-
sonian Institution Press, 1975. 96 pp.

Illustrates how women have participated in the American
labor movement since colonial times, first in sisterly
self-improvement societies, later in their own trade
unions, and more recently in "demanding full admission,
rights and responsibilities" in unions previously dominated by men. The Smithsonian Institution developed a
traveling bicentennial exhibition to illustrate women's
involvement in trade unionism.

27. Ryan, Mary P. *Womanhood in America: From Colonial Times
to the Present*. New York: New Viewpoints/Franklin
Watts, 1975. 496 pp.

Analyzes the changing imagery and intellectual-cultural
content of femininity, womanhood, and motherhood in
American history in order to show the deterioration of
women's status.

28. Scott, Anne Firor. *The Southern Lady: From Pedestal to
Politics, 1830-1930*. Chicago: University of Chicago
Press, 1970. 247 pp.

Argues that Southern women at all social levels actually
coped with work, family, and lifestyle problems but were
subjected to an image of "Ladyhood" which denied all such
practical activity.

29. ————, ed. *The American Woman: Who Was She?* Englewood
Cliffs, N.J.: Prentice-Hall, 1971. 182 pp.

Examines "the relationship between the changing role
of women in American society and the changes in women's

education, in their patterns of work, their participation in reform movements, and their views of family life," with selected readings as illustration.

30. Smuts, Robert W. *Women and Work in America.* New York: Columbia University Press, 1959. 176 pp.

Shows that the typical employed woman throughout much of American history was young and unmarried. The survey includes kinds of work women have done, kinds of women who have worked, demands and rewards of women's work, and values and attitudes of women and men regarding work.

31. Sochen, June. *Herstory: Woman's View of American History.* New York: Alfred Publishing Company, Inc., 1974. 423 pp.

Argues that American history must be examined from the point of view of those who were not White Anglo-Saxon Males; instead, the past is examined through the recurring theme of the commonality of victims--women, Blacks, Indians, and environment.

32. Wertheimer, Barbara M. *We Were There: The Story of Working Women in America.* New York: Random House/Pantheon Books, 1977. 427 pp.

Recounts the stories of women who have always been part of America's work force. Women were economic partners for two centuries before industrialization; slave women labored without wages; pioneer women continued the role of colonial women. With the nineteenth century came industrialization, rapid growth, and rapid multiplications of the numbers of employed women who could not afford the Victorian model of femininity and defied convention to struggle for women's rights and improved labor conditions, eventually in unions, until the watershed of 1914, after which working women entered the same unions as men but at the cost of abdicating leadership to men.

C. DOCUMENT COLLECTIONS

33. Baxandall, Rosalyn, Linda Gordon, and Susan Reverby, eds. *America's Working Women.* New York: Random House, 1976. 408 pp.

Argues that working-class women can reconstruct society
into one in which people set their own priorities; but
only with feminism can there be a movement of the whole
working class toward sexual equality and eradication of
sexual power relationships. Several documents cover the
experiences of working women throughout American history.

34. Brownlee, W. Eliot, and Mary M. Brownlee. *Women in the
    American Economy: A Documentary History, 1675 to 1929*.
    New York: Yale University Press, 1976. 350 pp.

    Shows that women's participation in the marketplace
    has been complex. Women at work receive the greatest
    attention, although there is some treatment of the con-
    sumer and the taxpayer.

35. Cott, Nancy F., ed. *Root of Bitterness: Documents of
    the Social History of American Women*. New York: E.P.
    Dutton and Co., 1972. 373 pp.

    Argues for an analysis which will "emphasize the in-
    teraction of personal lives with cultural norms," as
    shown in selected readings which include a section on
    industrialization.

36. Feldstein, Stanley, and Lawrence Costello. *The Ordeal
    of Assimilation: A Documentary History of the White
    Working Class*. Garden City, N.Y.: Anchor Press/
    Doubleday, 1974. 500 pp.

    Describes working-class experiences such as immigration,
    nativism, slums, industrialization, unionism, assimila-
    tion, and the new pluralism. Women are absorbed into a
    male-oriented view of the working class.

37. Lerner, Gerda, ed. *The Female Experience: An American
    Documentary*. Indianapolis: Bobbs-Merrill Company,
    1977. 509 pp.

    Argues that a male-oriented conceptual and historical
    framework impedes understanding of the history of women,
    and seeks "to order the female past from within its own
    consciousness." Selected readings are organized from
    the personal to the institutional, from self and family
    to group and society.

D. STATE-OF-THE-ART STUDIES

38. Almquist, Elizabeth M. "Review Essay: Women in the Labor Force." *Signs*, 2 (Summer 1977): 843-55.

    Reviews scholarship on women in the workforce which appeared since the 1960s but especially during 1974 to 1977. There has been a great increase in interest in the subject of the status of women at work but research thus far lacks either theory or analysis of policy implications and "does not predict rapid improvement in women's status in the near future."

39. Gordon, Ann D., Mari Jo Buhle, and Nancy E. Schrom. "Women in American Society: An Historical Contribution." *Radical America*, 5 (July-August 1971): 3-66.

    Argues that historians have concentrated on the powerful and, therefore, have ignored women who have received attention only in institutional, tokenist, and prescriptive history. Women's self-awareness has depended primarily on economic organization, in a changing set of views affected by labor-scarce Colonial society, industrialization, and modern Capitalism.

40. Jusenius, Carol L. "Review Essay: Economics." *Signs*, 2 (Autumn 1976): 177-89.

    Summarizes articles and papers on the status of women in the economy which appeared during 1975. Women's concentration in a few gender-segregated occupations significantly influences wages. More research is needed on the causes of this and on division of labor within the family.

41. Kahne, Hilda. "Review Essay: Economic Research on Women and Families." *Signs*, 3 (Spring 1978): 652-65.

    Shows how recent research has moved beyond the themes of labor-force participation, earnings differentiation, and occupational segregation to now include such issues as women's access to jobs, relationship of employment and family fertility and child-rearing, as well as the influence of such factors on work histories.

42. Kessler-Harris, Alice. "Women's Wage Work as Myth and History." *Labor History*, 19 (Spring 1978): 287-307.

Argues that the literature on wage-earning women should
move beyond repeated attempts to justify the economic
necessities for women seeking paid employment. Instead,
questions should address the labor force as a whole, not
as auxiliary female entry into a male bastion, and attempt "to understand women's role in the context of larger
economic and social issues."

43. Kleinberg, Susan. "The Systematic Study of Urban Women."
     Historical Methods Newsletter, 9 (December 1975): 14-
     25. Reprinted in *Class, Sex, and the Woman Worker*,
     edited by Milton Cantor and Bruce Laurie. Westport,
     Conn.: Greenwood Press, 1977. Pp. 20-42.

Asserts that women's participation in the labor force
was affected by class, marital status, age, children,
ethnic attitudes, available occupations, and economic
opportunities open to men. But the interaction of women
and industrialization awaits systematic analysis by such
methods as case studies of cities, cohort analysis of
census records, death records, records of urban agencies
such as health bureaus and public safety commissions,
oral histories, demographic and employment materials, and
examinations of social, political, and religious activities.

44. Roby, Pamela. "Sociology and Women in Working-Class
     Jobs." *Sociological Inquiry*, 45 (1974): 203-30. Re-
     printed in *Another Voice: Feminist Perspectives on
     Social Life and Social Science*, edited by Marcia
     Millman and Rosabeth Moss Kanter. Garden City, N.Y.:
     Anchor Press/Doubleday, 1975. Pp. 203-39.

Argues that research on women employed in blue-collar,
industrial, and service occupations has been minimal but
should increase significantly; it should, however, be
policy-oriented rather than research for its own sake.
Suggestions of research topics include wages and working
conditions, training and occupational mobility, living
off-the-job, women's attitudes and "consciousness," and
unionization.

45. Sicherman, Barbara. "Review Essay: American History."
     Signs, 1 (Winter 1975): 461-85.

Surveys major trends in historical scholarship relating
to women. The field as yet lacks a conceptual framework
except for that advanced by Gerda Lerner. Significant
work is being done on eighteenth-century life cycles and

family patterns and on the idea of a female sub-culture in the nineteenth century. Working-class women receive attention in work dealing with women's economic roles.

46.   ————, E. William Monter, Joan Wallach Scott, and Kathryn Kish Sklar. *Recent United States Scholarship on the History of Women: A Report Presented at the XV International Congress of Historical Sciences*. Washington, D.C.: American Historical Association, 1980. 53 pp.

Identifies conceptual themes and substantive topics in the work of American historians of women, with particular emphasis on the scholarship of the 1970s. Analysis is divided into "Women's Work," "The Private Sphere," and "The Public Sphere." The field of history of women has developed dynamically because of increasing awareness of the interdependence of the several dimensions of women's experience.

II. PRE-INDUSTRIAL AMERICA:
THE SEVENTEENTH AND EIGHTEENTH CENTURIES

A. PERSONAL, HOME, FAMILY, COMMUNITY

47. Carr, Lois Green, and Lorena S. Walsh. "The Planter's Wife: The Experience of White Women in Seventeenth-Century Maryland." *William and Mary Quarterly*, 3d Ser., 34 (1977): 542-71. Reprinted in *A Heritage of Her Own: Toward a New Social History of American Women*, edited by Nancy F. Cott and Elizabeth H. Pleck. New York: Simon and Schuster, 1979. Pp. 25-57.

    Examines the life cycle of female immigrants to Maryland in the second half of the seventeenth century. Many women came as indentured servants, spent four or five years fulfilling their contracts, and then took advantage of the favorable sex ratio to marry. Such late marriages limited the size of families, as did early deaths of husbands; but re-marriage was common.

48. Demos, John. *A Little Commonwealth: Family Life in Plymouth Colony*. New York: Oxford University Press, 1970. 201 pp.

    Suggests that there was a considerable degree of mutual responsibility and sexual equality among husbands and wives in colonial New England. Class does not appear to have been a differentiating factor in these relationships.

49. Farnam, Anne. "Olive Prescott, Weaver of Forge Village." *Essex Institute Historical Collections*, 115 (July 1979): 129-43.

    Uses material culture as a reflection of late eighteenth- and early nineteenth-century domestic production. Olive Adams Prescott, second wife and mother of eight, was a proficient and prize-winning weaver of blankets, coverlets, and other household items, who lived in a small New England community at the turn of the nineteenth century.

50. Leonard, Eugenie Andruss, Sophie Hutchinson Drinker, and
     Miriam Young Holden. *The American Woman in Colonial
     and Revolutionary Times, 1565-1800: A Syllabus with
     Bibliography.* Westport, Conn.: Greenwood Press Pub-
     lishers, 1962. 169 pp.

     Outlines topics and resources containing references to
     women's lives and activities in seventeenth- and
     eighteenth-century America, including home and community
     spheres, status and rights, religion and education. More
     than a thousand books and articles are listed, without
     identifying their specific relevance to women.

51. Pleck, Elizabeth H. "Two Worlds in One: Work and Fam-
     ily." *Journal of Social History,* 10 (Winter 1976):
     178-95.

     Shows that home and work were separated even before
     industrialization. Historians must examine how people
     reconciled the two worlds, work and family, within a
     larger whole.

52. Spruill, Julia Cherry. *Women's Life and Work in the
     Southern Colonies.* Chapel Hill: University of North
     Carolina Press, 1938. 426 pp.

     Argues that women in the colonial South lived wide-
     ranging lifestyles which included education, occupations,
     and participation in public affairs. Records tend to
     concentrate on non-working-class women, but female life-
     style and life cycles are examined.

53. Thompson, Roger. *Women in Stuart England and America:
     A Comparative Study.* Boston: Routledge and Kegan Paul,
     1974. 276 pp.

     Argues that women were better off from the beginning
     in America than if they had remained in England. England
     was patriarchal, while American women had opportunities
     to assert and advance themselves because of unbalanced
     sex ratios, the law of supply and demand, New England
     Puritanism, and the frontier society.

54. Wechsler, Louis K. *The Common People of Colonial America:
     As Glimpsed through the Dusty Windows of the Old Al-
     manacks, Chiefly of New York.* New York: Vantage, 1978.
     172 pp.

     Demonstrates that "the subject of the fair sex" was
     treated almost exclusively from a male viewpoint "as one

might expect" in New York almanacs of the eighteenth century. Women were extolled to preserve virtue, avoid the
dangers of fashion and beauty, and embrace the limited
sphere of married life.

B. EMPLOYMENT

55. Blumenthal, Walter Hart. *Brides from Bridewell: Female
    Felons Sent to Colonial America*. Rutland, Vt.: Charles
    E. Tuttle Co., Inc., 1962. 139 pp.

    Argues that a large portion of indentured servants who
    came to the British North American colonies were felons.
    Contractors systematically trafficked in prisoners with
    the cognizance of British authorities in the latter half
    of the seventeenth and most of the eighteenth centuries.
    Therefore, the claims of free-born and aristocratic an-
    cestry advanced by Americans are frequently invalid.

56. Clark, Alice. *Working Life of Women in the Seventeenth
    Century*. New York: E.P. Dutton and Co., 1919. 328 pp.

    Believes that the women who were employed in colonial
    America were primarily middle-aged business women or
    wives helping husbands in skilled trades and crafts;
    lack of skills and technical knowledge were less of a
    problem for women entering retail trades. Work is de-
    fined as non-domestic labor.

57. Manges, Frances May. "Women Shopkeepers, Tavernkeepers,
    and Artisans in Colonial Philadelphia." Ph.D. Disser-
    tation, University of Pennsylvania, 1958. 120 pp.

    Argues that women made a significant contribution to
    the colonial economy as shopkeepers, tavernkeepers, and
    craftswomen; many were widows who continued family busi-
    nesses. Female economic activity appears to have at-
    tracted no particular comment in this pre-industrial
    society.

58. Montgomery, David. "The Working Classes of the Pre-
    Industrial American City, 1780-1830." *Labor History*,
    9 (Winter 1968): 3-22.

    Shows that women, children, and charitable institutions
    constituted significant elements in the factory labor
    force in this period. The Hamiltonian argument that

manufacturing would not lure men from the farm placed
considerable emphasis on the use of females and children,
especially widows, paupers, and the abandoned.

59. Morris, Richard. *Government and Labor in Early America.*
     New York: Octagon/Farrar, Straus and Giroux, Inc.,
     1946. 557 pp.

     Includes some illustration of women workers, especially
     indentured servants, receiving harsher treatment and
     less training than males. Law and social custom in the
     American colonies was heavily influenced by the scarcity
     of labor.

60. Nash, Gary B. "The Failure of Female Factory Labor in
     Colonial Boston." *Labor History*, 20 (Spring 1979):
     165–88.

     Argues that late eighteenth-century Boston experimented
     with factory labor for women as a system of poor relief,
     not because of entrepreneurial capitalism or economic
     diversification or an attempt to emancipate women from
     domesticity. The experiment failed, however, because
     the women resisted a factory work situation where they
     could not combine maternal and household responsibilities
     with intermittent labor.

61. Smith, Abbot Emerson. *Colonists in Bondage: White Ser-
     vitude and Convict Labor in America, 1607-1776.* Chapel
     Hill: University of North Carolina Press, 1947. 435 pp.

     Claims that women servants were less harshly treated
     than were men since they were given domestic duties
     rather than work in the fields unless they were "nasty,
     beastly, and not fit" for other tasks. Moreover, women
     had greater opportunities for advancement since they
     were in demand as wives.

C. HISTORICAL CONDITIONS

AMERICAN REVOLUTION

62. Blumenthal, Walter Hart. *Women Camp Followers of the
     American Revolution.* Philadelphia: George S. MacManus
     Company, 1952. 104 pp.

Shows that significant numbers of women and children travelled with the British and American forces as wives or camp followers during the Revolution. British army practice traditionally provided for such persons, but American practice varied according to the rulings of individual officers.

63. Stickley, Julia Ward. "The Records of Deborah Sampson Gannett, Woman Soldier of the Revolution." *Prologue*, 4 (Winter 1972): 233-41.

Says that accounts of the career of Deborah Sampson Gannett are often misleading since they neglected official records, especially pension applications. Sampson served in the Revolutionary army while disguised as a man; she was "discovered" as a woman when wounded and in need of medical treatment.

III. INDUSTRIALIZING AMERICA:
THE NINETEENTH CENTURY

A. PERSONAL

64. Dodge, Grace H. *A Bundle of Letters to Busy Girls on Practical Matters.* New York: Funk and Wagnalls, 1887. 139 pp.

    Advises working girls on health, shopping, housekeeping, saving, and purity.

65. ———, ed. *Thoughts of Busy Girls.* New York: Cassell Publishing Co., 1892. 137 pp.

    Claims that clubs for working girls exert a beneficial influence. The girls wrote essays extolling ideal womanhood, purity and modesty, the family, education, good manners, art, moral reform, and the power of club life.

66. Mott, F.L. "Portrait of an American Mill Town: Demographic Response in Mid-Nineteenth Century Warren, Rhode Island." *Population Studies*, 26 (1970): 147-67.

    Argues that disproportionately large numbers of immigrant women sought the many low-skill jobs available in Warren. This imbalanced sex ratio, as well as the unwillingness to marry outside one's own ethnic group, resulted in a low percentage of married women and consequent sub-normal fertility.

B. HOME AND FAMILY

67. Foster, Colin, and G.S.L. Tucker. *Economic Opportunity and White American Fertility Ratios, 1800-1860.* New Haven: Yale University Press, 1972. 121 pp.

Argues that the declining birth rate in America in the
first half of the nineteenth century was caused by the
decrease in availability of easily accessible land.

68. Grigg, Susan. "The Dependent Poor of Newburyport, 1800–
     1830." Ph.D. dissertation, University of Wisconsin-
     Madison, 1978. 376 pp.

     Concludes that poor women were more likely to receive
     outside relief while poor men could be found in alms-
     houses. Widows were more likely than widowers to use
     the earnings of older children in order to avoid re-
     marriage. And most unmarried women had some occupation,
     with the poor probably working at unskilled tasks such
     as plain sewing or washing.

69. Kleinberg, Susan J. "Technology and Women's Work: The
     Lives of Working Class Women in Pittsburgh, 1870–1900."
     Labor History, 17 (Winter 1976): 58–72.

     Demonstrates that the economy of late nineteenth-
     century Pittsburgh offered few opportunities for women
     to work for pay outside the home. Moreover, their labor
     within the home, while significant to family income,
     continued to be difficult because working-class women
     lacked access to municipal services (paved streets, water
     supply, sewer connections) and technological improvements
     (washing machines, central heating, toilets, iceboxes).

70. Modell, John, and Tamara K. Hareven. "Urbanization and
     the Malleable Household: An Examination of Boarding
     and Lodging in American Families." *Journal of Marriage
     and the Family*, 35 (August 1973): 467–79.

     Argues that boarding or lodging houses helped the fam-
     ily cope with urban life. Women could thus earn income
     without leaving their households, and widows or older
     women could maintain households rather than live with
     their families.

71. Smith, Daniel Scott. "Family Limitation, Sexual Control,
     and Domestic Feminism in Victorian America." *Feminist
     Studies*, 1 (Winter-Spring 1973): 40–57. Reprinted in
     *A Heritage of Her Own: Toward a New Social History of
     American Women*, edited by Nancy F. Cott and Elizabeth
     H. Pleck. New York: Simon and Schuster, 1979. Pp.
     222–45.

     Concludes that the decline in marital fertility in the
     nineteenth century, largely by the wife persuading or

coercing the husband to practice birth control, illustrates the extension of the autonomy of women within the family and the gradual enlargement of the domestic sphere, although men assumed and retained control of the public sphere. Demographic figures do not distinguish among classes of women.

72. ————, and Michael S. Hindus. "Premarital Pregnancy in America 1640-1971: An Overview and Interpretation." *Journal of Interdisciplinary History*, 5 (Spring 1975): 537-70.

Shows that the record of premarital pregnancy among white Americans follows a cyclical pattern with troughs in the seventeenth century, mid-nineteenth century, and contemporary America. The decline in the early nineteenth century was influenced by the social incorporation of groups previously prone to "disorder" and the expansion of religious participation which preached sexual restraint while it provided an alternative outlet for female needs.

73. Vinovskis, Maris. "Women's Employment and Fertility Patterns." Paper, Conference on Class and Ethnicity in Women's History, SUNY at Binghamton, 21 September 1974.

Demonstrates an inverse relationship between industrialization-urbanization and the birth rate. The degree of industrialization is more important than the degree of urbanization in influencing fertility.

IMMIGRANTS

74. Abbott, Edith. *Immigration: Select Documents and Case Records*. Chicago: University of Chicago Press, 1924. 809 pp.

Sets out public and domestic problems of immigrants in a casebook for use in training social service professionals. Regulations and limitations imposed on immigrants included steerage, admission, exclusion, or expulsion. Domestic difficulties included availability and conditions of employment, industrial accidents, and protection of girls from loss of luggage or tickets or non-arrival at their destination.

75. ————. *The Immigrant and the Community*. New York: The Century Company, 1917. 303 pp.

Chapter 3 outlines the special problems of immigrant
girls, especially Eastern Europeans in Chicago. Seduction and betrayal are particular problems.

76. Baum, Charlotte, Paula Hyman, and Sonya Michel. *The
     Jewish Woman in America*. New York: The Dial Press,
     1976. 290 pp.

     Shows the amalgamation of cultural perceptions and
     practices as European Jewish women migrated to America,
     despite contrasts between German and Eastern European
     emigration experiences, which resulted from political and
     economic structures and time of migration.

77. Cohen, Rose. *Out of the Shadow*. New York: George H.
     Doran Company, 1918. Reprint. New York: Jerome S.
     Ozer, Publisher, 1971. 313 pp.

     Recounts the experiences of Rose Cohen, emigrating
     from Russia, working as a domestic servant and garment
     worker, struggling for health and education, and praising
     the opportunities of American life.

78. Dickinson, Joan Younger. "The Role of the Immigrant
     Women in the U.S. Labor Force, 1890-1910." Ph.D. dis-
     sertation, University of Pennsylvania, 1975. 234 pp.

     Concludes that a higher proportion of immigrant than
     native-born women worked for wages, but participation
     and occupational distribution varied by ethnic group.
     Immigrant women were primarily found in domestic service,
     textile work, and the needle trades.

79. Ehrlich, Richard L., ed. *Immigrants in Industrial Ame-
     rica: 1850-1920*. Charlottesville: University of Vir-
     ginia, 1977. 218 pp.

     Contains items 86, 87, and 107.

80. Ellis, Christine. "People Who Cannot be Bought." In
     *Rank and File: Personal Histories by Working-Class
     Organizers*, edited by Alice Lynd and Staughton Lynd.
     Boston: Beacon Press, 1973. Pp. 9-33.

     Recounts Ellis' experiences as an immigrant from Jugo-
     slavia in the Iowa mining region, her exposure to
     nativist-immigrant antagonisms, the awakening of class
     consciousness, and her association with the Communist
     Party.

81. Ets, Marie Hall, ed. *Rosa: The Life of an Italian Immi-
    grant.* Minneapolis: University of Minnesota Press,
    1970. 254 pp.

    Describes the experiences of Rosa Cavaleri who migrated
    from Lombardy to Missouri to Chicago, with rich details
    about culture and social customs as well as the expediency
    whereby Rosa and her family survived.

82. Fenton, Edwin. *Immigrants and Unions, A Case Study:
    Italians and American Labor, 1870-1920.* New York:
    Arno Press, 1975. 630 pp.

    Contrasts young Italian garment workers with the am-
    bitions for independence of young American and Jewish
    women. The Italian women's submissiveness made them
    "poor material for a militant trade union movement."

83. Ginger, Ray. "Labor in a Massachusetts Cotton Mill,
    1853-60." *Business Historical Society Bulletin,* 28
    (March 1954): 67-91.

    Shows that it was possible for a group of single,
    skilled immigrant women to save 25 to 50 percent of their
    wages in a prosperous period. Fifty-six women weavers
    from Scotland in the mills of Holyoke, Massachusetts, in
    the 1850s were able to pay the debts incurred for their
    passage within four months after their arrival.

84. Glanz, Rudolf. *The Jewish Women in America: Two Female
    Immigrant Generations, 1820-1929.* New York: Ktav Pub-
    lishing House, Inc. and the National Council of Jewish
    Women, 1976. 2 vols.

    Claims that the situation of Jewish immigrant women in
    America was heavily influenced by their differing cul-
    tural backgrounds. German Jewish women operated within
    a restrictive milieu which emphasized male activities.
    Eastern European Jewish women, however, frequently came
    to America as young, unmarried women and often used their
    artisan skills in the needle trades where many became
    active trade unionists.

85. Glasco, Laurence A. "The Life Cycles and Household
    Structure of American Ethnic Groups: Irish, German,
    and Native-Born Whites in Buffalo, New York, 1855."
    Journal of Urban History, 1 (May 1975): 339-64.

    Demonstrates how domestic service advanced the accul-
    turation of immigrant, adolescent females. Unlike their

brothers and unlike native-born girls, female adolescent
immigrants lived and worked with native-born families
for extended periods, thereby learning language and cultural values sooner than their male counterparts; and
they passed this learning on to their children earlier
and more effectively than the schools.

86. Golab, Caroline. "The Impact of the Industrial Experience
     on the Immigrant Family: The Huddled Masses Reconsid-
     ered." In *Immigrants in Industrial America: 1850-1920*,
     edited by Richard L. Ehrlich. Charlottesville: Uni-
     versity Press of Virginia, 1977. Pp. 1-32.

     Argues that the family lies at the heart of ethnic per-
     sistence in America. Rather than obliterating or homo-
     genizing the immigrant family in America, the industrial
     experience merely afforded new applications and adapta-
     tions of the "family as an organization of primary rela-
     tions" with values and expectations arising from that
     central fact.

87. Groneman, Carol. "'She Earns as a Child--She Pays as a
     Man': Women Workers in a Mid-Nineteenth Century New
     York City Community." In *Immigrants in Industrial
     America: 1850-1920*, edited by Richard L. Ehrlich.
     Charlottesville: University Press of Virginia, 1977.
     Pp. 33-46. Reprinted in *Class, Sex, and the Woman
     Worker*, edited by Milton Canter and Bruce Laurie.
     Westport, Conn.: Greenwood Press, 1977. Pp. 83-100.

     Shows how Irish and other immigrant women in the 6th
     Ward of New York City contributed to family income. Most
     women who worked outside the home were young and single;
     married women supplemented family income within their
     homes by taking in lodgers or laundry or needle work.

88. ————. "Working-Class Immigrant Women in Mid-Nineteenth
     Century New York: The Irish Woman's Experience." *Jour-
     nal of Urban History*, 4 (May 1978): 255-74.

     Argues that the young, unmarried Irish immigrant women
     left Ireland to avoid early and economically limited mar-
     riages but faithfully sent money to their families in
     Ireland; married women supplemented irregular and low
     male wages as well. But both categories of Irish immi-
     grant women represent the continuance rather than the
     dissolution of traditional patterns of work, leisure,
     and family ties.

89. Howe, Irving. *World of Our Fathers.* New York: Simon and
    Schuster, 1976. 714 pp.

    Describes the transition of Eastern European Jews from
    the *shtetl* to the East Side of New York, including ghetto
    life, social conflicts, labor and socialism, politics,
    Yiddish culture, and dispersion. Women appear throughout
    the narrative in home, workplace, unions, and strikes as
    well as in cultural and power conflicts.

90. Inglehart, Babbette. "Daughters of Loneliness: Anzia
    Yezierska and the Immigrant Woman Writer." *Studies in
    American Jewish Literature*, 1 (Winter 1975): 1-10.

    Shows that Yezierska produced a unique and significant
    contribution to the literature of immigration, painting
    the darker side of alienation and loneliness of the immi-
    grant woman who must leave family and traditions in order
    to become Americanized.

91. Kessler-Harris, Alice. "Wage-Earning Women." Paper,
    Third Berkshire Conference on the History of Women,
    Bryn Mawr College, 9 June 1976.

    Argues that Russian Jewish women were exposed to two
    cultures in the *shtetl*--patriarchal male dominance and
    women as an economic force. Many who came to America
    continued to work and contribute to family income but
    did not take advantage of this for themselves, and they
    left income-earning to their husbands as quickly as this
    became economically feasible.

92. Kessner, Thomas. *The Golden Door: Italian and Jewish
    Immigrant Mobility in New York City, 1880-1915.* New
    York: Oxford University Press, 1977. 224 pp.

    Claims that mobility was not restricted to a select
    few well-born individuals. Both natives and immigrants
    were mobile but the amplitude and frequency of progress
    were affected by ethnicity, with Jews doing better than
    Italians in New York.

93. Krause, Corinne Azen. "Italian, Jewish, and Slavic Grand-
    mothers in Pittsburgh: Their Economic Roles." *Fron-
    tiers*, 2 (Summer 1977): 18-28.

    Illustrates how both single and married first- and
    second-generation Italian, Jewish, and Slavic immigrant
    women had important economic functions in their families
    which were not reported in the census data. These women

earned because of economic necessity, although their
employment opportunities were limited by Pittsburgh's
heavy industry; and their worklives often overlapped
with homemaking.

94. Mattis, Mary Catherine. "The Irish Family in Buffalo,
     New York, 1855–1875: A Socio-Historical Analysis."
     Ph.D. dissertation, Washington University, 1975. 217
     pp.

     Demonstrates how the Irish in Buffalo between 1855
     and 1875 show considerable continuity with the tradi-
     tional family culture in Ireland, including marriage and
     fertility patterns, sex-role organization, and orienta-
     tion toward boundary maintenance. A relatively equali-
     tarian sex-role organization allowed Irish women to
     enter the labor force and contribute to family economy.

95. Metzger, Isaac, ed. *A Bintel Brief: Sixty Years of
     Letters from the Lower East Side to the Jewish Daily
     Forward*. Garden City, N.Y.: Doubleday and Co., Inc.,
     1971. 214 pp.

     Chronicles the concerns of New York's immigrant Jews
     including lonely mothers, grass widows, young wives
     supporting husbands, and women seeking education, union-
     ization, and personal improvement.

96. Miller, Sally M. "From Sweatshop Worker to Labor Leader:
     Theresa Malkiel, a Case Study." *American Jewish His-
     tory*, 68 (December 1978): 189-205.

     Argues that Jewish women were neither invisible nor
     passive in the emergence of the labor movement in in-
     dustries where they worked in substantial numbers.
     Theresa Serber Malkiel emigrated from Russia, worked in
     New York's sweatshops, joined a working-class organiza-
     tion, organized a union and served as its president,
     migrated with that union from the Knights of Labor to
     the Central Labor Federation, was active in the Socialist
     Labor and Socialist parties, emphasized worker solidarity
     as the key to emancipation, and supported woman suffrage.

97. Neidle, Cecyle S. *America's Immigrant Women*. Boston:
     Twayne Publishers, G.K. Hall and Co., 1975. 312 pp.

     Displays contributions of immigrant women to America,
     as evidenced in selected biographies which include a
     few trade union women and reformers.

98. Odencrantz, Louise C. *Italian Women in Industry: A Study
     of Conditions in New York City.* New York: Russell
     Sage Foundation, 1919. 345 pp.

     Records data on nativity, marital status, living con-
     ditions, occupations, earning, home work, lodgers, and
     control of income in several Italian neighborhoods in
     lower Manhattan with immigrants from northern and south-
     ern Italy, recent arrivals as well as families estab-
     lished there many years.

99. Pernicone, Carol Groneman. "The 'Bloody Ould Sixth':
     A Social Analysis of New York City Working-Class Com-
     munity in the Mid-Nineteenth Century." Ph.D. disser-
     tation, University of Rochester, 1973. 268 pp.

     Argues that the family did not disintegrate under
     pressures of uprooting of immigrants and alienation in
     a large urban center; rather, the family was important
     in terms of kinship ties and as an economic unit since
     the family was dependent on more than one income. Wo-
     men worked more than is usually assumed, and adult
     children remained at home and contributed to income.

100. The Pittsburgh Section, National Council of Jewish Wo-
     men. *By Myself, I'm a Book! An Oral History of the
     Jewish Immigrant Experience.* Waltham, Mass.: American
     Jewish Historical Society, 1972. 166 pp.

     Traces individual experiences from the *shtetl* through
     emigration to establishment of community life in Pitts-
     burgh in an integrated narrative without identifying
     interview subjects by name, age, gender, or viewpoint.

101. Rosenwaike, Ira. "Two Generations of Italians in Ame-
     rica: Their Fertility Experience." *International
     Migration Review*, 7 (Fall 1973): 271-80.

     Claims that Italians assimilated to the patterns of
     their new American environment within one generation.
     The high fertility of the first generation is compatible
     with their peasant background, but the second generation
     shows an even lower than average fertility for urban-
     dwellers.

102. Scharrenberg, Paul. "Americanizing the Immigrant: A
     Review of the Practical and Effective Americanizing
     Work in Which California Has Blazed the Way." *Life
     and Labor*, 8 (March 1918): 44-46.

Shows the work of the California Commission of Immigration and Housing in supervising labor camps and improving city housing conditions.

103.   Smith, Judith. "Work Patterns of Italian Emigrant Women in Early Twentieth Century Providence, Rhode
Island." Paper, Third Berkshire Conference on History
of Women, Bryn Mawr College, 10 June 1976.

Argues that southern Italian peasants emigrated,
earned, and owned property as families and that women
operated within this structure. Married women combined
home work with child care; daughters worked for wages
or took care of the children. The economic role of
women changed during their life cycle; they moved in
and out of the work force depending on men's income,
number of children, and other family considerations.
The system later broke down as individual income replaced the family wage and kin neighborhoods succumbed
to residential mobility and urban renewal.

104.   Steiner, Ruth Heller. "The Girls in Chicago." *American
Jewish Archives*, 26 (April 1974): 5-22.

Uses the lives of the Heller sisters to illustrate
adjustments of immigrant women and the impact of family
economic conditions. A combination of luck and nerve
sustained the sisters through careers in teaching,
nursing, and clerical and administrative work.

105.   Webster, Janice Reiff. "Domestication and Americanization: Scandinavian Women in Seattle, 1888 to 1900."
Journal of Urban History, 4 (May 1978): 275-90.

Concludes that steady jobs, economic security, and
increasing prosperity of Scandinavian husbands in Seattle
made it unnecessary for their wives to work outside or
inside the home and encouraged acculturation to American
norms and aspirations as well as the abandonment of
European patterns.

106.   Yans-McLaughlin, Virginia. *Family and Community: Italian Immigrants in Buffalo, 1880-1930*. Ithaca, N.Y.:
Cornell University Press, 1977. 286 pp.

Shows how Southern Italian immigrants in Buffalo, New
York, relied on traditional family-based values as they
adjusted to new socioeconomic situations. Men remained
dominant in the household despite their underemployment,
and married women remained within the home.

107. ———. "A Flexible Tradition: Southern Italian Immi-
      grants Confront a New Work Experience." *Journal of
      Social History*, 7 (1974): 429-45. Reprinted in *Im-
      migrants in Industrial America: 1850-1920*, edited by
      Richard L. Ehrlich. Charlottesville: University Press
      of Virginia, 1977. Pp. 67-84.

      Argues that when South Italian immigrants had to face
      new work situations in America, they sought solutions
      which would minimize family strains; migrant labor, for
      example, permitted mothers and children to work togeth-
      er and to evade legal restrictions. Despite new work
      situations, these people held to traditional cultural,
      moral, and sexual attitudes. In both home work and the
      canneries, the family continued as the basic unit of
      production and, while women were arbiters of household
      tasks, they retained positions inferior to their hus-
      bands.

108. ———. "Italian Woman and Work: Experience and Per-
      ception." In *Class, Sex, and the Woman Worker*, edited
      by Milton Cantor and Bruce Laurie. Westport, Conn.:
      Greenwood Press, 1977. Pp. 101-19.

      Demonstrates how women themselves undervalued their
      labor; Italian immigrant women regarded men's work as
      worth more than women's, and they tended to hide earn-
      ing by women. These women frequently told investigators
      that they did not work, although they kept boarding
      houses, made artificial flowers at home, were domestics,
      and earned by other means as well.

109. ———. "Like the Fingers of the Hand: The Family and
      Community Life of First-Generation Italian-Americans
      in Buffalo, New York, 1880-1930." Ph.D. dissertation,
      State University of New York at Buffalo, 1970. 579
      pp.

      Concludes that the immigrant family was affected by
      both class and ethnicity. Southern Italian immigrants
      in Buffalo brought a nuclear family structure with
      them, which they retained; they experienced little fam-
      ily disorganization under industrialization and urbani-
      zation. Women had few employment options outside the
      home.

110. ———. "Patterns of Work and Family Organization:
      Buffalo's Italians." *Journal of Interdisciplinary
      History*, 2 (Autumn 1971): 299-314.

Claims that Italian immigrants favored conservative
forms of female employment usually at home or under the
supervision of relatives because of traditions of male
superiority and paternal control. Women wage-earners
did not necessarily gain bargaining power in their families since male authority did not depend entirely on
fulfillment of economic obligations. But families
tended to send male children rather than adult women
into the work force to compensate for low wages or
seasonal unemployment of husbands.

C. COMMUNITY

111.   Cumbler, John Taylor. *Working-Class Community in In-
       dustrial America: Work, Leisure, and Struggle in Two
       Industrial Cities, 1880-1930.* Westport, Conn.: Green-
       wood Press, 1979. 283 pp.

       Argues that although women shoe workers participated
       with men in unionism and labor militancy, their lives
       were circumscribed by family necessities. Women worked
       to supplement the low wages of the family's central
       wage-earner and families tried to control daughters'
       lives, especially regarding marriage, in order to re-
       tain that income.

112.   Dawley, Alan. *Class and Community: The Industrial Re-
       volution in Lynn.* Cambridge, Mass.: Harvard Univer-
       sity Press, 1976. 301 pp.

       Includes brief treatment of women workers, their di-
       vision of tasks by marital status, the impact of mech-
       anization on their employment, and their significant
       participation in labor protest especially the Great
       Strike of 1860.

113.   Walkowitz, Daniel J. *Worker City, Company Town: Iron
       and Cotton-Worker Protest in Troy and Cohoes, New
       York, 1855-84.* Urbana: University of Illinois Press,
       1978. 292 pp.

       Analyzes how the changing relationship of class and
       ethnicity as well as the introduction of new technology
       affected workers' ability to organize socially and pol-
       itically. Workers struggled to maintain their achieve-
       ments and union power against management encroachment

in the nineteenth century, although upward mobility eventually lured many into an ethnic middle class with ties to urban commercial interests.

114. ————. "Working-class Women in Gilded Age: Factory, Community and Family Life among Cohoes, New York Cotton Workers." *Journal of Social History*, 5 (Summer 1972): 464-90.

Argues that "industrial capitalism divested the worker of control over work conditions and threatened the family's quest for social and economic security," but in Cohoes "by 1880 both the factory and the community had come to sustain the cotton worker family, and especially the female-headed household." Moreover, the working class experienced embourgeoisement which gave them middle-class values of status, security, property, and family which were out of line with their fragile economic existence.

D. CLASS

115. Benson, Susan Porter. "Business Heads and Sympathizing Hearts: The Women of the Providence Employment Society, 1837-1858." *Journal of Social History*, 12 (Winter 1978): 303-12.

Shows how the women of the Providence Employment Service tried to operate as mediators between rich and poor, to improve the situation of seamstresses. But their ties to class and gender left them uncomfortable both with their male relatives and class peers and with the working-class women they sought to aid.

116. Buell, Charles Chauncey. "The Workers of Worcester: Social Mobility and Ethnicity in a New England City, 1850-1880." Ph.D. dissertation, New York University, 1974. 204 pp.

Concludes that industrialization and the addition of Irish to the Yankees in Worcester led to the fall of old social controls and the rise of moral and ethnic antagonisms. The Irish came to dominate unskilled trades while Yankees advanced out of semi-skilled levels more rapidly.

117. Faler, Paul. "Cultural Aspects of the Industrial Revo-
      lution: Lynn, Massachusetts, Shoemakers and Industrial
      Morality, 1826-1860." *Labor History*, 15 (Summer 1974):
      367-94. Reprinted in *American Workingclass Culture:
      Explorations in American Labor and Social History*,
      edited by Milton Cantor. Westport, Conn.: Greenwood
      Press, 1979. Pp. 121-48.

      Argues that shoemakers divided into traditionalists
      and those who accepted new and more restricted cultural
      and moral norms of education, pleasure, and recreation.
      These divisions impeded the formation of class-conscious-
      ness.

118. Jameson, Elizabeth. "Imperfect Unions: Class and Gender
      in Cripple Creek, 1894-1904." *Frontiers*, 1 (Spring
      1976): 89-117. Reprinted in *Class, Sex, and the Woman
      Worker*, edited by Milton Cantor and Bruce Laurie.
      Westport, Conn.: Greenwood Press, 1977. Pp. 166-202.

      Examines women in western mining towns who were iso-
      lated in the home, and working women who remained sub-
      ordinate within unions. Class and gender were never
      successfully merged and, hence, provided no concerted
      effective attack on corporate capitalism.

119. Srebnick, Amy. "The Middle Class Creates the Working
      Girl, New York City, 1840-1860." Paper, Fourth
      Berkshire Conference on History of Women, Mt. Holyoke
      College, 24 August 1978.

      Argues that bourgeois novelists of the nineteenth cen-
      tury used gender conflict to mask class conflict. Sen-
      timental accounts of working-class women denied class
      stratification and asserted universal femininity. By
      holding men responsible for women's poverty, they evaded
      discussion of emerging capitalism.

                            E. EMPLOYMENT

GENERAL

120. Abbott, Edith. "Harriet Martineau and the Employment
      of Women in 1836." *Journal of Political Economy*, 14
      (December 1906): 614-26.

      Shows that Harriet Martineau underestimated the num-
      bers and range of occupations available to women in

1836, since in fact more than a hundred trades were open to women, with sewing work the dominant occupation. But low wages prevented women from becoming self-sufficient.

121. Aurand, Harold W. "Diversifying the Economy of the Anthracite Regions, 1880-1900." *Pennsylvania Magazine of History and Biography*, 94 (1970): 54-61.

Argues that the sporadic employment pattern for men in the mining industry led to attempts to provide employment opportunities for women. Women's earnings were intended to supplement family income.

122. Baker, Ross K. "Entry of Women into Federal Job World-- At a Price." *Smithsonian*, 8 (July 1977): 82-91.

Explains that women entered federal service in the Civil War era, but throughout their work history they have encountered differential rates of pay, male resentment and harassment, and relegation to low-level positions. Sex-discrimination is still a problem.

123. Barnhart, Jacqueline Baker. "Working Women: Prostitution in San Francisco from the Gold Rush to 1900." Ph.D. dissertation, University of California at Santa Cruz, 1976. 294 pp.

Demonstrates that prostitution was an area of employment open to women. "Like those involved in any business or profession they were successful because they supplied a service that was in demand." When San Francisco became an "instant city" in 1849, social mores were suspended and prostitutes maintained a "unique position of respectability" which deteriorated later in the century as the city adopted a modified version of eastern middle-class Victorian social values.

124. Bernard, Richard, and Maris Vinovskis. "The Female School Teacher in Ante-Bellum Massachusetts." *Journal of Social History*, 10 (March 1977): 332-45.

Asserts that so many white women (one out of five) in pre-Civil War Massachusetts endured the low pay and low status of school teaching in order to gain a sense of independence. Since there was little chance for advancement, many women sought alternative occupations in industry.

125. Blicksilver, Jack. *Cotton Manufacturing in the Southeast: An Historical Analysis.* Atlanta: Bureau of

Business and Economic Research, Georgia State College
of Business Administration, 1959. 176 pp.

Examines the heavy reliance of southern cotton textile
mills on women and children as workers in the 1880s and
1890s. By 1900, however, female labor had declined to
only a third of the total employees.

126.   Campbell, Helen. *Prisoners of Poverty: Women Wage-*
       Workers, Their Trades and Their Lives. Boston: Robert
       Brothers, 1887. 257 pp.

Pleads for modern enlightenment to bring about social
solutions to the problems documented in case studies of
women garment workers in New York. Factual summaries
are juxtaposed with descriptions of individual women.

127.   ————. *Women Wage-Earners: Their Past, Their Present,*
       and Their Future. Boston: Robert Brothers, 1893.
       313 pp.

Analyzes the evolution of work and wages for women
from the invention of the cotton gin, through the ex-
perimental stage and perfection of the spinning system,
to the introduction of power machinery and growth of
the modern factory system of the 1890s.

128.   ————. "The Working-Women of Today." *Arena,* 4 (August
       1891): 329-39.

Argues that factory labor changed from opportunity to
oppression for working women. The earliest female employees of the New England mills considered industrial
work a means of obtaining independence. By the 1890s,
however, their situation had deteriorated to low wages,
long hours, and inadequate working conditions.

129.   Deutrick, Bernice M. "Propriety and Pay." *Prologue,*
       3 (Fall 1971): 67-72.

Concludes that employment of women by the federal
government during the 1860s was a result of need and
economy rather than of any commitment to equal opportunities for females. Women copyists entered the Patent
Office in the 1850s, and the Treasury Department hired
women during the Civil War to trim currency because
they would accept low wages and were presumed to have
superior manual dexterity.

130. Long, Clarence D. *Wages and Earnings in the United States: 1860-1890.* Princeton: Princeton University Press, 1960. 169 pp.

    Collects and analyzes statistical data on daily wages and annual earnings, both of which rose by 50 percent between 1860 and 1890. A brief treatment of wages by sex, based on admittedly inadequate evidence, shows women generally earning less than men except in cotton goods, woolen goods, and books and newspapers where males and females did the same kind of job.

131. McGraw, Judith A. "'A Good Place to Work.' Industrial Workers and Occupational Choice: The Case of Berkshire Women." *Journal of Interdisciplinary History*, 10 (Autumn 1979): 227-48.

    Argues that some nineteenth-century women industrial workers were active shapers rather than passive victims of their world. They had employment alternatives among several industries and occupations; the ability to move and the availability of different kinds of mills gave women a measure of choice, autonomy, and security, especially for those whose family needs and expectations did not impose additional limitations.

132. Nelson, Daniel. *Managers and Workers: Origins of the New Factory System in the United States, 1880-1920.* Madison: University of Wisconsin Press, 1975. 234 pp.

    Charges that employers seldom used special methods to recruit women workers, who were most likely to enter the labor market if male relatives had factory jobs, frequently in the same plant. In 1880, 1900, and 1920 "a high wage and the social and familial ties of the workers were the principal means of attracting unskilled and semi-skilled workers." Although some employers established special training rooms to familiarize women workers with factory operations, most women received their training on the job, as did men. Women who took factory jobs after 1915 usually became semi-skilled machine tenders.

133. O'Donnell, Edward. "Women as Bread Winners." *American Federationist*, 4 (October 1897): 186-87.

    Asserts that the employment of women takes jobs from men and undermines men's wages. Moreover, female em-

ployment threatens the social order by defeminizing
women.

134. Penny, Virginia. *The Employment of Women: A Cyclopaedia
      of Woman's Work*. Boston: Walker, Wise and Company,
      1863. 500 pp.

      Notes that women have found employment in more than
      five hundred occupations, a remarkable increase from
      listings of "women's work" at the beginning of the nine-
      teenth century.

135. Riegel, Robert E. *American Women: A Story of Social
      Change*. Rutherford, N.J.: Fairleigh Dickinson Uni-
      versity Press, 1970. 376 pp.

      Assumes that the largest group of women workers in
      the nineteenth century were filling time between school
      and marriage. Women went into occupations which were
      "natural" for them, such as domestic service.

136. Summer, Helen. *History of Women in Industry in the
      United States*. Vol. 9 of *Report on Conditions of
      Woman and Child Wage-Earners in the United States*.
      Washington, D.C.: Government Printing Office, 1910.
      277 pp.

      Documents women's historical presence in the work
      force and as a factor in the total economy of society.
      The nineteenth century saw a transformation from unpaid
      to paid labor and home to factory or workshop which in-
      creased the range of possible employment for women while
      it destroyed their monopoly on traditional occupations,
      replaced the individuality of their work with a stan-
      dardized product, and subjected them to deteriorating
      conditions of labor, as shown by the historical experi-
      ences of women workers in textiles, sewing, domestic
      service, other manufacturing, and trade and transporta-
      tion. Despite some successes of trade unions, only
      legislation "has improved the working conditions of any
      large number of women wage-earners."

137. Wright, Carroll D. *The Working Girls of Boston*. Boston:
      Wright and Potter Printing Co., 1889.

      Describes the occupations, hours, working conditons,
      wages and earnings as well as social and moral condi-
      tions of employed women in Boston in the 1880s as argu-
      ments in favor of reform. Honest labor should be re-

spected; training should be offered to improve efficiency and earnings; hours of labor should be limited; and
homes should be established for working girls.

INDUSTRIALIZATION

138. Boulding, Elise Marie Niorn-Hansen. "The Effects of
    Industrialization on the Participation of Women in
    Society." Ph.D. dissertation, University of Michigan,
    1969. 418 pp.

    Argues that traditional religious institutions have
    had a strong effect on active participation of women
    (in 124 countries with a population over one million)
    in both traditionalized and modern labor forces and to
    a lesser extent on participation of women in educational
    institutions of society.

139. Chafe, William H. *Women and Equality: Changing Patterns
    in American Culture.* New York: Oxford University
    Press, 1977. 207 pp.

    Includes the argument that industrialization not only
    separated the home from the workplace, but introduced
    an occupational double standard. Black and immigrant
    women could be employed; middle-class women should not
    be. Thus, working-class women served as marginal, un-
    derpaid, and exploited workers while middle-class women
    were denied the opportunity for employment.

140. Clark, Christopher. "The Household Economy, Market
    Exchange and the Rise of Capitalism in the Connecticut
    Valley, 1800-1860." *Journal of Social History*, 13
    (Winter 1979): 169-89.

    Concludes that the sale of surplus products and then
    the movement of production out of the rural household
    was a slow process and embraced the Connecticut fam-
    ilies in order to subsist rather than in pursuit of
    grandiose profits. Local exchange networks facilitated
    this interaction between the market, capitalist pro-
    duction, and life in the rural household. The resultant
    decline of household manufacture meant that "most women
    engaged in production had to find work with outside
    employers."

141. Davis, Rebecca Harding. *Life in the Iron Mills; or the
    Korl Woman.* New York: The Feminist Press, 1972. (Re-

printed from the 1861 edition in *Atlantic Monthly*.)
174 pp.

Exposes an unromantic vignette of life in the iron
mills, contrasting the degradation of a real woman with
the abstract strength and beauty of a statue, and dra-
matizing the power of money to combat drudgery.

142. Davis, Stephen Robert. "From Plowshares to Spindles:
      Dedham, Massachusetts, 1790-1840." Ph.D. dissertation,
      University of Wisconsin, 1973. 457 pp.

      Argues that urbanization brought about a transition
      in power from agrarians to the village group after con-
      flicts over adaptation of local institutions to the new
      influx of population. These local changes, such as in-
      creased occupational specialization and breakdown of the
      Congregational Church, have a parallel in national pol-
      itics with the transition from Republican to Federalist
      to Whig, with the Jacksonians gaining strength. Women
      are not treated specifically.

143. Dunnigan, Kate, Helen Kebabian, Laura B. Roberts, and
      Maureen Taylor. "Working Women at Work in Rhode Is-
      land, 1880-1925." *Rhode Island History*, 38 (February
      1979): 3-23.

      Argues that development of a broader market economy
      and of industrialization gradually transformed home and
      family. More women entered the work force, but values
      continued to glorify home and motherhood.

144. Easton, Barbara. "Industrialization and Femininity: A
      Case Study of Nineteenth Century New England." *Social
      Problems*, 23 (April 1976): 389-401.

      Speculates that female domesticity is not an inevitable
      consequence of industrial capitalism, although it came
      about with the move from farming village to industrial-
      izing town. Children could have been cared for communal-
      ly or by fathers while women worked outside the house-
      hold. But male power enforced women's domesticity and
      men benefitted from it.

145. Gordon, Ann D., and Mari Jo Buhle. "Sex and Class in
      Colonial and Nineteenth-Century America." In *Liberat-
      ing Women's History: Theoretical and Critical Essays*,
      edited by Berenice A. Carroll. Urbana: University of
      Illinois Press, 1976. Pp. 278-300.

Shows that the development of market economy by the
end of the eighteenth century transformed women's essential role in the family. Middle-class women assumed
the status of their husbands, exchanging integral economic functions for idleness, passivity, and femininity.
But working-class women shared with men the opportunities
to earn money, and those who joined men in the ranks of
organized labor "rejected notions of feminine frailty,
of weakness, of social purity and moral superiority,
and passivity."

146. Gutman, Herbert G. *Work, Culture, and Society in Industrializing America: Essays in American Working-
Class and Social History.* New York: Alfred A. Knopf,
1973. 343 pp.

Argues, like E.P. Thompson, that a continuing repetition of the transition from preindustrial to industrial
society is central to the history of American workers,
but incorporates anthropologist Clifford Geertz's dis-
tinction between culture and society.

147. Haines, Michael R. "Fertility, Marriage and Occupation
in Pennsylvania Anthracite Region, 1850-1880." *Journal of Family History*, 2 (Spring 1977): 28-55.

Concludes that miners' wives in the anthracite region
in the mid- and later nineteenth century showed a high
level of marital fertility because the region urbanized
gradually, there was little female labor participation
outside the household, and young adult males had dif-
ferentially more favorable opportunities in mining.
Residence, ethnicity, literacy, and husband's occupation all influenced fertility.

148. Hamilton, Alexander. "Report on the Subject of Manu-
factures." *The Papers of Alexander Hamilton*, vol.
10, edited by Harold C. Syrett. New York: Columbia
University Press, 1966. Pp. 1-340.

Includes the argument that the development of industry
will not undermine the agricultural labor supply, since
factories can employ women and children. Farmers will
not only lose their sons to manufacturing, but they
will reap extra income from the paid labor of their
daughters and wives.

149. Hirsch, Susan E. *Roots of the American Working Class:
The Industrialization of Crafts in Newark, 1800-1860.*

Philadelphia: University of Pennsylvania Press, 1978.
170 pp.

Shows how industrialization changed craft work significantly but not cataclysmicly. Craft workers accepted mechanization but also formed trade unions in an
effort to maintain a measure of control over their work.
Women provided cheap, unskilled labor with the introduction of machinery, but the female work force was
young and unmarried, because craftsmen shared "Victorian
family norms of male dominance and the non-working wife
and child" even at the sacrifice of added family income.

150. Kleinberg, Susan J. "Technology's Stepdaughters, the
      Impact of Industrialization upon Working Class Women,
      Pittsburgh, 1865-1890." Ph.D. dissertation, Univer-
      sity of Pittsburgh, 1973. 302 pp.

      Claims that working-class women, their families, and
      their communities suffered as a result of industrializa-
      tion and emphasis on heavy industry. The nature of
      Pittsburgh's economy prevented movement of working-class
      women from their homes into the marketplace and rein-
      forced traditional economic and social roles. Social
      services became more institutional, professional, and
      cosmopolitan so that working-class women received aid
      from middle-class intruders rather than people they
      knew.

151. Laurie, Bruce Gordon. "The Working People of Philadel-
      phia, 1827-1853." Ph.D. dissertation, University of
      Pittsburgh, 1971. 293 pp.

      Concludes that workers in Philadelphia in the 1820s
      to 1850s were not more wage-conscious than class-
      conscious, since they were divided into a variety of
      ethnic and occupational groups differing in status,
      life-styles, and values. Unions were organized along
      lines of skill; hence, native-born artisans with higher
      skills were unsympathetic to unskilled and semi-skilled
      foreign-born workers.

152. Lerner, Gerda. "The Lady and the Mill Girl: Changes in
      the Status of Women in the Age of Jackson." *Midcon-
      tinent American Studies Journal*, 10 (Spring 1969):
      5-14. Reprinted in *A Heritage of Her Own: Toward a
      New Social History of American Women*, edited by Nancy
      F. Cott and Elizabeth H. Pleck. New York: Simon and
      Schuster, 1979. Pp. 182-96.

Argues that the shortage of women and the importance
of their economic function gave females an advantage in
the English colonies but this status had deteriorated
by the second half of the nineteenth century as women's
economic and social functions narrowed. Moreover, industrialization accentuated and increased dissimilarities
among women of different classes, opening opportunities
for the "mill girl" but precluding paid labor for the
"lady" who now had much leisure and little meaningful
work. Both ladies and mill girls, however, were isolated from decision-making and were acted upon by a
male-oriented society beyond their control.

153. McMahon, Theresa Schmidt. "Women and Economic Evolu-
tion, or The Effects of Industrial Changes upon the
Status of Women." Ph.D. dissertation, University of
Wisconsin, 1909. 131 pp.

Asserts that women more than men have profited in
increased leisure and gratification of wants by the
greater productivity which comes from industrialization.

154. Shorter, Edward. "Women's Work: What Difference Did
Capitalism Make?" Paper, Conference on Class and Eth-
nicity in Women's History, SUNY at Binghamton, 21
September 1974.

Argues that capitalism improved the status of lower-
class women since the market economy linked job and
status, women's wages became a weapon of power especially through threats to withdraw work or income, and work
outside the home enabled women to avoid the supervision
and pressure of neighbors. Evidence for eighteenth-
and nineteenth-century France and Germany probably holds
for other areas as well. The reverse impact of capitalism is true for middle-class women.

155. Srebnick, Amy Gilman. "True Womanhood and Hard Times:
Women and Early New York Industrialization, 1840-
1860." Ph.D. dissertation, State University of New
York at Stony Brook, 1979. 283 pp.

Describes 1840-1860 as a crucial period in the development of women's work, wages, and occupational sex
roles. The discrepancy between the real lives of these
working-class women and contemporary ideals of domesticity sparked a formative period in social welfare ideas
and policies, including industrial training, the work
house, and home visitation. These "significant policies

of poor relief" date from the mid-nineteenth century
rather than the Progressive reform era.

156. Ware, Norman. *The Industrial Worker, 1840-1860: The
     Reaction of American Industrial Society to the Advance
     of the Industrial Revolution.* Boston: Houghton
     Mifflin Company, 1924. 249 pp.

     Argues that the state of the nation and of the worker
     gave rise to worker discontent, organization, and pro-
     test including demands for land reform and the ten-hour
     movement. The labor movement appeared defensive in the
     1840s and aggressive in the 1950s. Women workers do not
     receive separate analysis.

157. Zimmerman, Libby. "Women in the Economy: A Case Study
     of Lynn, Massachusetts, 1760-1974." Ph.D. disserta-
     tion, Brandeis University, 1977. 149 pp.

     Concludes that women in Lynn occupied an economically
     inferior position because of the hierarchical division
     of labor which carried over from early domestic produc-
     tion to industrialization as well as the profit struc-
     ture of employers. Moreover, sexual division of labor
     "mitigates against men and women uniting to change wo-
     men's status."

WALTHAM SYSTEM

158. Adickes, Sandra. "Mind Among the Spindles: An Examina-
     tion of Some of the Journals, Newspapers, and Memoirs
     of the Lowell Female Operatives." *Women's Studies*,
     1 (1973): 279-87.

     Claims that women textile workers in New England in
     the 1830s found both dignity and sisterhood in their
     mill experience. They regarded their industrial careers
     as temporary, but also thought of them as character-
     building and as opportunities for self-improvement. By
     the end of the 1840s, however, conditions had deterio-
     rated and the labor force changed to immigrants.

159. Appleton, Nathan. *Introduction of the Power Loom, and
     Origin of Lowell.* Lowell: B.H. Penhallow, 1858.
     36 pp.

     Argues that New England women provided a fund of well-
     educated and virtuous labor for cotton factories as
     machinery spelled the end of household manufacture.

Daughters of respectable farmers were induced to enter
the mills temporarily by the attention given to their
boarding-house and religious life.

160. Bartlett, Elisha. *A Vindication of the Character and
Condition of the Females Employed in the Lowell Mills
Against the Charges Contained in The Boston Times and
the Boston Quarterly Review.* Lowell, Mass.: Leonard
Huntress, Printer, 1841. 24 pp.

Asserts that mills girls are properly lodged, fed, and
supervised in boarding houses, that they are the health-
iest portion of the population of Lowell, and that they
exhibit high intellectual and moral character.

161. "A Citizen of Lowell." *Corporations and Operatives:
Being an Exposition of the Condition of Factory Oper-
atives, and a Review of the "Vindication" by Elisha
Bartlett, M.D.* Lowell, Mass.: Samuel J. Varney,
Printer, 1843. 72 pp.

Argues that the corporations in Lowell force their
operatives to work for excessive lengths of time for
declining wages and to live in crowded conditions which
undermine their health. The testimony of mill girls in
the *Lowell Offering* must be seen in light of owner spon-
sorship and control of the journal.

162. Dublin, Thomas. *Women at Work: The Transformation of
Work and Community in Lowell, Massachusetts, 1826-
1869.* New York: Columbia University Press, 1979.
312 pp.

Shows how the community of women in Lowell who worked
together in the factories and lived together in the
boarding houses developed a strong sense of cohesiveness
which sustained workers during the labor protests of the
1830s and 1840s. But the community declined until, in
the 1850s, immigrant families replaced the Yankee women
in the mills.

163. ————. "Women, Work, and the Family: Female Operatives
in the Lowell Mills, 1830-1860." *Feminist Studies*, 3
(Fall 1975): 30-39.

Examines the original workers of Lowell--young, single,
native-born females who lived in a highly-cohesive community in the 1930s. This close-knit living and working
situation contributed to collective labor protest in the

1840s. But after 1845, an immigrant family work force
undermined the Yankee community and its labor movement.

164.   ————. "Women Workers and the Study of Social Mobil-
       ity." *Journal of Interdisciplinary History*, 9 (Spring
       1979): 648-65.

       Argues that women workers in the early Lowell mills
       had real opportunities for, and interest in, occupa-
       tional mobility and wage gains. Moreover, these oppor-
       tunities did not undermine the growth of their collec-
       tive protest. Historians have erred in dismissing women
       from mobility studies.

165.   ————. "Women, Work, and Protest in the Early Lowell
       Mills: 'The Oppressing Hand of Avarice Would Enslave
       Us.'" *Labor History*, 16 (Winter 1974): 99-116. Re-
       printed in *Class, Sex, and the Woman Worker*, edited
       by Milton Cantor and Bruce Laurie. Westport, Conn.:
       Greenwood Press, 1977. Pp. 43-63. Also in *American
       Workingclass Culture: Explorations in American Labor
       and Social History*, edited by Milton Cantor. Westport,
       Conn.: Greenwood Press, 1979. Pp. 167-87.

       Demonstrates how a homogeneous work force and strong
       sense of community in working and living arrangements
       contributed to the ability of women factory workers to
       engage in protests against deteriorating conditions in
       the Lowell mills of the 1830s and 1840s.

166.   Dubnoff, Steven Jan. "The Family and Absence from Work:
       Irish Workers in a Lowell, Massachusetts Cotton Mill,
       1860." Ph.D. dissertation, Brandeis University, 1976.
       151 pp.

       Argues that "the nature of working-class family life
       is strongly determined by the father's ability to bring
       sufficient and significant resources into the internal
       economy of the family." Families in Lowell tended to
       use children rather than mothers in the mills to sup-
       plement the father's wages or in the cases of households
       headed by mothers.

167.   ————. "Mill Women of Lowell, Massachusetts in the
       1860s." Paper, Third Berkshire Conference on the
       History of Women, Bryn Mawr College, 11 June 1976.

       Examines the family as the unit of economic and social
       life. In Ireland the father controlled the labor of the

entire family and received all their wages, which gave
him great authority; but his position was eroded in
Lowell by the payment of separate wages, thereby break-
ing down the old balance of power within the family.

168. Eisler, Benita, ed. *The Lowell Offering: Writings by
New England Mill Women (1840-1845)*. Philadelphia:
J.B. Lippincott Company, 1977. 223 pp.

Reprints selections from the writings of the seventy
women who contributed to the *Lowell Offering*, "our most
valuable record of a moment caught between reality and
myth, seized by the women who lived it." They described
mill and boarding-house life, intellectual activities,
motivations for working, contemporary New England, and
responses to reform efforts.

169. Foner, Philip S., ed. *The Factory Girls*. Urbana: University of Illinois Press, 1977. 360 pp.

Collects the writings of female operatives under the
Waltham System in the 1840s, with emphasis on their
militant labor activities, particularly the Female Labor
Reform Associations and the agitation for the ten-hour
workday.

170. Gitelman, H.M. "The Waltham System and the Coming of
the Irish." *Labor History*, 8 (Fall 1967): 227-53.

Analyzes the original Waltham system in terms of new
technology, a new scale of manufacturing enterprises,
entrepreneurs concerned with social implications, and a
largely transient labor force drawn from the intelligent
native-born. When conditions deteriorated in the 1840s,
the decline was more relative than real, but workers
saw enlarged work assignments and reduction of the piece
rates as arbitrary and unwarranted. Eventually the
native-born withdrew from the mills, giving place to
Irish immigrants whose family labor meant a fundamental
adjustment in the factory population.

171. Horowitz, Richard P. "Architecture and Culture: The
Meaning of the Lowell Boarding House." *American
Quarterly*, 25 (March 1973): 64-82.

Claims that boarding houses attempted to imitate rural
cottages because the population identified the rural
home with the virtues of permanence, comfort, and kinship. Claims for the boarding houses' attractiveness
and advantages were exaggerated, however.

172. Josephson, Hannah. *The Golden Threads: New England's
      Mill Girls and Magnates*. New York: Duell, Sloan and
      Pearce, 1949. 325 pp.

      Argues that owners recruited women workers for the
      textile mills in the early nineteenth century to avoid
      intractable male labor and overcome male concerns about
      the loss of agricultural workers. Working and living
      conditions of those women workers were entirely con-
      trolled by the capitalist manufacturers.

173. Larcom, Lucy. "Among Lowell Mill-Girls: A Reminiscence."
      Atlantic Monthly, 48 (November 1881): 593-612.

      Asserts that work is superior to idleness, that it
      was the natural expectation of young people in the nine-
      teenth century, and that the years Larcom and her con-
      temporaries spent in the mills were "full of stimulus."
      Mill girls were not particularly concerned with concepts
      of "rich" or "poor," showed great tolerance for one
      another's attitudes, did not adjust their evaluations
      because of literary or other pursuits, and for them
      "life never seemed contracted."

174. ————. *A New England Girlhood*. New York: Houghton
      Mifflin, 1889. 274 pp.

      Recounts the educational and social opportunities
      offered to factory girls under the Waltham System but
      warns of the dangers of drudgery in such a life.

175. Little, Frances. *Early American Textiles*. New York:
      Century Company, 1931. 267 pp.

      Describes fabrics and laws relevant to the early
      mills, without particular attention to the role of women
      in those factories.

176. *Lowell Offering*. Series 1, Nos. 1-4, 1840-41; Series
      2, Nos. 1-5, 1841-45.

      Contains prose, fiction, poetry, and vignettes, all
      written by the factory workers of the Waltham System
      mills.

177. Mailloux, Kenneth Frank. "The Boston Manufacturing
      Company of Waltham, Massachusetts, 1813-1848: The
      First Modern Factory in America." Ph.D. dissertation,
      Boston University, 1957. 239 pp.

Argues that the Boston Manufacturing Company built a
system which served as a laboratory and nursery for the
American textile industry. Waltham pioneered in training men who were used in other factories, and in providing comparatively good wages and hours for girls
from the surrounding countryside, over whom the company
assumed moral and physical guardianship.

178. Miles, Henry A. *Lowell, As It Was, and As It Is.*
      Lowell: N.L. Dayton, 1846. 234 pp.

      Celebrates Lowell as a unique success story in urban-
      ization, business stability, employment, and intellec-
      tual and moral superiority.

179. Nisonoff, Laurie. "Bread and Roses: The Proletarian-
      isation of Women Workers in New England Textile Mills,
      1827-1848." Paper, Conference on Class and Ethnicity
      in Women's History, SUNY at Binghamton, 21 September
      1976.

      Argues that the merchant capitalists who established
      the Waltham-Lowell mills recruited petit-bourgeois
      women workers from the farms in order to avoid labor
      problems they had observed abroad; but by the 1840s
      capitalism had reached the stage of increasing surplus
      value and the model system had changed into something
      fit only for immigrant women. The speed of operation
      and the number of looms each woman tended increased
      more rapidly than their wages.

180. Porter, Rev. James. *The Operative's Friend, and De-
      fence: or, Hints to Young Ladies, Who Are Dependent
      on Their Own Exertions.* Boston: Charles H. Pierce,
      1850. 229 pp.

      Asserts that vocation is not a criterion of respec-
      tability, that the factory business is an honorable
      one, and that it is unjust to suspect the character of
      factory operatives. Mill girls in Lowell live in super-
      vised boarding houses and support the churches. But
      workers are advised to behave circumspectly, selecting
      the best companions, for example.

181. Robinson, Harriet H. *Early Factory Life in New England.*
      Boston: Wright and Potter Printing Company, 1883.
      26 pp.

Describes the Yankee girls who worked in the Lowell mills between 1832 and 1848 as "simple folk" who earned their own living and frequently that of others, tried to educate and improve themselves, held high moral and religious standards, and "were wholly untroubled by conventionalities or thoughts of class distinctions.

182. ———. *Loom and Spindle: or, Life Among the Early Mill Girls*. New York: Thomas Y. Crowell and Company, 1898. 128 pp.

Argues that girls and young women were recruited as factory workers in New England textile mills because they would be a reliable work force. But a boarding-house living system was necessary to provide them with residences, and strict regulations governed their spiritual and moral welfare. These conditions also gave the mill girls opportunities for a more stimulating intellectual environment than they might have had in rural villages or on farms, and a number of them exhibited their intellectuality by writing for the *Lowell Offering*.

183. Scoresby, Rev. William. *American Factories and Their Female Operatives*. Boston: William D. Tichnor, 1845. 136 pp.

Claims that the mill girls of Lowell enjoy a superior moral and intellectual climate to English factory workers. The Lowell workers are products of the yeoman farmer class, working for spare money, rather than from the urban lower class, brought up as children in the factories.

184. Shlakman, Vera. "Economic History of a Factory Town: A Study of Chicopee, Massachusetts." Ph.D. dissertation, Columbia University, 1938. 264 pp.

Describes the experience of Chicopee as parallel to that of Lowell with the use of Yankee girls in factories, the boarding-house system, and the transition to Irish labor in the 1850s.

185. Stearns, Bertha Monica. "Early Factory Magazines in New England: *The Lowell Offering* and Its Contemporaries." *Journal of Economic and Business History*, 2 (August 1930): 685-705.

Claims that the *Lowell Offering* and similar periodicals were intended to show the cultural superiority of the factory girls. The *Offering* was not a vehicle for labor or class interests against those of the factory owners and remained neutral during the worker reform activities of the 1840s.

186. Thompson, Agnes L. "New England Mill Girls." *New England Galaxy*, 16 (1974): 43-49.

Argues that farm girls sought employment in the mills of Lowell in order to have a period of economic independence before marriage. However, they received close supervision in both workplace and boarding house, suffered long hours and low wages, and had only limited social and educational opportunities. In the 1850s they withdrew in the face of Irish and French Canadian competition.

187. Vogel, Lise. "Hearts to Feel and Tongues to Speak: New England Mill Women in the Early Nineteenth Century." In *Class, Sex, and the Woman Worker*, edited by Milton Cantor and Bruce Laurie. Westport, Conn.: Greenwood Press, 1977. Pp. 64-82.

Examines the testimony of "ordinary" women working in the New England mills, as well as their better-publicized leaders, who spoke of discontent and resistance in the mills, but said that labor reform activists could not maintain their organizations in opposition to the corporations.

188. ————. "Humorous Incidents and Sound Common Sense: More on the New England Mill Women." *Labor History*, 19 (Spring 1978): 280-86.

Analyzes the experiences of mill women who went back and forth between factory town and rural community, showing them to be aware of the complexity of limitations and opportunities of their situation. They saw factory life as an opportunity for liberty, but at the same time their writings should be viewed as part of their struggle with the manufacturers.

189. ————. "Their Own Work: Two Documents from the Nineteenth-Century Labor Movement." *Signs*, 1 (Spring 1976): 787-802.

Demonstrates how organizers of women factory workers in the 1840s appealed to contemporary themes such as the contrast between nature and the mill, the ideology of liberty and equality in America, fears of Old World

working conditions, and the comparison of Northern mill
work with Southern slavery.

190. Ware, Caroline F. *The Early New England Cotton Manu-
      facture: A Study in Industrial Beginnings.* Boston:
      Houghton Mifflin, 1934. 349 pp.

      Portrays women as forming much of the labor base for
      the early textile mills. Although conditions of work
      appeared relatively favorable in the beginning, by the
      1840s feelings of exploitation led to demands for reform.

191. Wright, Helena. "The Uncommon Mill Girls of Lowell."
      History Today, 33 (January 1973): 10-19.

      Argues that, unlike the British and Rhode Island fac-
      tory systems, the Waltham experiment drew its female
      workers from the rural middle class of New England.
      These women did not become part of the permanent working
      classes but gained financial independence and engaged
      in literary and cultural activities during their years
      in the mills. Conditions deteriorated, however, and by
      1850 half the workers in the Waltham System factories
      were Irish immigrants.

TECHNOLOGY

192. Baker, Elizabeth Faulkner. *Technology and Woman's Work.*
      New York: Columbia University Press, 1964. 460 pp.

      Argues that technological advances made possible the
      acceptance of women into the labor market and the use
      of their unskilled and cheap labor to reduce costs after
      technology took away the traditional work which women
      had done.

193. Long, Clarence D. *The Labor Force under Changing Income
      and Employment.* Princeton: Princeton University Press,
      1958. 439 pp.

      Concludes that female labor force participation in-
      creased because technology released women from home
      housework and child care, women received relatively more
      education, and reduction of the normal workweek enabled
      women workers to be employed but "still have time to
      shop, cook, and do a minimum of house cleaning, rest a
      bit, provide husbands with some companionship, and par-
      take of some occasional amusements."

194. MacLean, Annie Marion. *Women Workers and Society*. Chicago: A.C. McClurg and Co., 1916. 135 pp.

    Surveys changes in the industrial system which was established based on men's work with that of women supplementary; but adjustments of machinery and development of the factory system made women competitors. Since employers did not know how to cope with this situation, they established the fiction that women were working for pin money and need not be paid as much as men.

195. Webb, S. "The Alleged Differences in the Wages Paid to Men and to Women for Similar Work." *Economic Journal*, (December 1891): 635-62.

    Claims that women receive low wages because they do unskilled, manual, inferior work. Their wages are the results of lack of skill and job mobility.

TRADE UNIONS AND WORKER PROTEST

196. Andrews, John B., and W.D.P. Bliss. *History of Women in Trade Unions*. Vol. 10 of *Report on Conditions of Woman and Child Wage-Earners in the United States*. Washington, D.C.: Government Printing Office, 1911. 236 pp.

    Documents the history of women in labor organizations from 1825 to the A.F. of L., examining women as cheap labor, early organizations and strikes, and reserved or negative male attitudes in established unions.

197. Blewett, Mary H. "The Union of Sex and Craft in the Haverhill Shoe Strike of 1895." *Labor History*, 20 (Summer 1979): 352-75.

    Argues that not all young women workers in the late nineteenth century were passive and powerless. A linkage between sex and craft, in some cases, such as shoe stitchers in Haverhill, provided a base for union and strike activity. These women were skilled, native-born, unmarried, living independently of their families, and conscious of their class.

198. Delzell, Ruth. *The Early History of Women Trade Unionists in America*. Chicago: National Women's Trade Union League of America, 1919. 15 pp.

Reprints items 199-203, articles and charts from five
issues of *Life and Labor*, drawn from John B. Andrews'
and W.D.P. Bliss' *History of Women in Trade Unions* (item
196).

199.   ————. "1847--First Ten-hour Law for Women in America."
        Life and Labor, 2 (June 1912): 184-85.

        Summarizes the ten-hour agitation of the 1840s, and
        the first success in New Hampshire in 1847, with heavy
        quotation from *History of Women in Trade Unions* by John
        B. Andrews and W.D.P. Bliss (item 196).

200.   ————. "1869--The Daughters of St. Crispin: The First
        National Women's Trade Union in the United States."
        Life and Labor, 2 (October 1912): 303.

        Describes local and national organization of the women
        shoe binders, especially in the 1860s, following the
        account in *History of Women in Trade Unions* by John B.
        Andrews and W.D.P. Bliss (item 196).

201.   ————. "1866--Laundry Workers' Union, Troy, N.Y."
        Life and Labor, 2 (November 1912): 333.

        Outlines efforts of women collar laundresses of Troy
        to form first a union and then a cooperative in the
        1860s, as presented in *History of Women in Trade Unions*
        by John B. Andrews and W.D.P. Bliss (item 196).

202.   ————. "1828--First Woman's Strike in America: Be-
        ginning of Organization Among Cotton Mill Operators."
        Life and Labor, 2 (March 1912): 82-84.

        Describes activities of cotton operatives on strike
        in Dover, New Hampshire, in 1828, in adaptation of ac-
        count in *History of Women in Trade Unions* by John B.
        Andrews and W.D.P. Bliss (item 196).

203.   ————. "1825-1851--Organization of Tailoresses and
        Seamstresses." *Life and Labor*, 2 (August 1912): 242-
        44.

        Looks at attempts at trade organization, establishment
        of price scales, and cooperatives by sewing women, es-
        pecially in New York, Philadelphia, and Baltimore; drawn
        from *History of Women in Trade Unions* by John B. Andrews
        and W.D.P. Bliss (item 196).

204.   Foster, E.P. "Women's Work in the Labor Movement."
        American Federationist, 2 (July 1894): 86-87.

Argues that trade unionism will not be effective until
women become equal members. But women need education
in industrial and political awareness before they can
join the men who currently dominate organization.

205. Garlock, Jonathan Ezra. "A Structural Analysis of the
Knights of Labor: A Prologomenon to the History of the
Producing Classes." Ph.D. dissertation, University
of Rochester, 1974. 464 pp.

Concludes that the Knights of Labor were larger,
earlier, and more important than has been recognized.
Based on a computerized study of twelve thousand As-
semblies in 1,500 counties of the United States, Canada,
and abroad.

206. Janiewski, Dolores. "Making Common Cause: The Needlewomen of New York, 1831-1869." *Signs*, 1 (Spring 1976):
777-86.

Examines the New York needlewomen in the 1830s, 1840s,
1850s, and 1860s and finds them among the most militant
and articulate workers of their class and sex. They
formed a number of organizations which attempted to deal
with subsistence-level wages, exploitative homework,
piecework, competition, and chronic unemployment. These
groups either concentrated on an analysis of class and
sex oppression or attempted to obtain favorable publicity to attract the broadest possible public support.

207. Kelley, M.E.J. "Women and the Labor Movement." *North
American Review*, 166 (March 1898): 408-17.

Claims that women factory workers have long been dissatisfied with their working situation and have shown
increasing militancy in their trade union and strike
activities. Women have become part of the labor movement despite lack of encouragement from the American
Federation of Labor.

208. Levine, Sue. "'Strive for Your Rights, Oh Sisters
Dear': The Carpet Weavers' Strike and the Knights of
Labor, 1885." Paper, Third Berkshire Conference on
History of Women, Bryn Mawr College, 11 June 1976.

Demonstrates the ambivalence of the Knights of Labor
toward "Lady Knights," encouraging women to press for
unionization, wages, and strikes but believing that women's proper sphere was in the home and that the objective of the union should be to alter American industrial
society so that they could return there.

209. Melder, Keith. "Women in the Shoe Industry: The Evidence
     from Lynn." *Essex Institute Historical Collections*,
     115 (October 1979): 270-87.

     Argues that an accurate and analytical assessment of
     women shoe workers is hampered by spotty and inacces-
     sible evidence. But there is some material for a fuller
     description of their work in a sex-segregated industry
     subject to mechanical and technological changes, and
     their involvement in the labor movement.

210. O'Neill, Elizabeth. "Rebel Girls and Union Maids."
     Lithopinion, 6 (Spring 1971): 56-63.

     Portrays women as participants in struggles for labor,
     civil, and human rights throughout American history.
     While women may be disappointed with the male record of
     support for their causes, they do not view men as ene-
     mies but as fellow victims.

211. Rhine, Alice Hyman. "Women in Industry." In *Woman's
     Work in America*, edited by Annie Nathan Meyer. New
     York: H. Holt and Co., 1891. Pp. 276-322.

     Claims that labor organizations and industrial schools
     were more successful than philanthropy in aiding women,
     but the real solution requires "Nationalism," socialis-
     tic nationalization of the means of production.

212. Scharnau, Ralph. "Elizabeth Morgan, Crusader for Labor
     Reform." *Labor History*, 14 (Summer 1973): 340-51.

     Shows how Elizabeth Morgan worked to organize employed
     women and then to produce protection of women and chil-
     dren in Illinois. She pioneered in exposing conditions
     of labor and in organizing the Ladies' Federal Labor
     Union and the Illinois Women's Alliance to agitate for
     remedial legislation.

213. Stevens, George A. *New York Typographical Union No. 6:
     A Study of a Modern Trade Union and Its Predecessors*.
     Albany: J.B. Lyon Company, 1913. Chapter 21, pp. 421-
     40.

     Recounts how women printers in New York formed local
     No. 1 and were admitted to the typographers' union.

F. HISTORICAL CONDITIONS

FEMINISM AND SUFFRAGE

214. Flexner, Eleanor. *Century of Struggle: The Women's Rights Movement in the United States.* Cambridge, Mass.: Harvard University Press, 1959. 384 pp.

Includes accounts of women's organizations and trade union activities in the course of tracing the development of the suffrage movement.

215. Kugler, Israel. "The Trade Union Career of Susan B. Anthony." *Labor History*, 2 (Winter 1961): 90–100.

Argues that Anthony's disappointment with the Republican Party by 1868 led her to consider merger with other reform elements into a new party; therefore, she explored the young National Labor Union which at first shared her sympathy for woman suffrage, equal pay for equal work, and the organization of women into trade unions. She and other women delegates participated in the 1868 N.L.U. Convention, and Anthony sponsored the Workingwomen's Association and the Woman's Typographical Union. But she was ousted as a delegate to the 1869 convention on the grounds that she encouraged the training of replacements during a printers' strike.

216. ————. "The Woman's Rights Movement and the National Labor Union (1866–1872): What Was the Nature of the Relationship between the National Labor Union and the Woman's Rights Movement and What May Serve to Explain Periods of Cooperation and Subsequent Divergence?" Ph.D. dissertation, New York University, 1954. 570 pp.

Concludes that despite a brief period of cooperation between the N.L.U. and the Woman's Rights Movement, women's groups became radicalized over the suffrage issue and in 1869 abandoned their labor orientation in favor of general women's rights agitation such as advising women to act as strike breakers in order to learn a trade. Skilled trade unionists, therefore, refused suffragists' representation in the N.L.U. convention.

217. White, Mary Ogden. "Susan B. Anthony, Labor Leader." *Life and Labor*, 9 (April 1919): 89–90.

Celebrates the golden jubilee of the National American Woman Suffrage Association. Attempts to tie the suffrage movement to the labor movement by citing Anthony's activities, including cooperation in establishment of the Workingwomen's Association.

IV. MODERN AMERICA:
THE EARLY TWENTIETH CENTURY

A. PERSONAL

218. Clark, Sue Ainslie, and Edith Wyatt. *Making Both Ends
Meet: The Income and Outlay of New York Working Girls*.
New York: The Macmillan Company, 1911. 270 pp.

Exhibits the economic difficulties of self-supporting
women living away from home, especially problems of
unskilled and seasonal factory workers who suffer monotony and fatigue in addition to low and irregular wages.
Scientific management would bring improvement.

219. Fisher, Juliet. *The Nonworking Time of Industrial Wo-
men Workers: Study by Students of the Hudson Shore
Labor School*. U.S. Department of Labor, Women's
Bureau. Bulletin No. 181. 1940. 10 pp.

Argues that non-working-time activities deserve serious study since the shorter work week and two-day week-
end provide opportunity for recreation, education,
trade-union and other workers' organizations, and roles
in a democratic society.

220. Ginzberg, Eli, and Hyman Berman. *The American Worker
in the Twentieth Century: A History through Autobiographies*. New York: The Free Press, 1963. 368 pp.

Collects self-portraits of workers including women
such as Rose Schneiderman and middle-class observers
who temporarily entered working-class situations.

221. "The Girls' Own Stories." *Life and Labor*, 1 (February
1911): 51-52.

Describes poor working and living conditions of Chicago
garment workers by presenting the personal case histories of young women.

222. "Girls' Stories." *Life and Labor*, 4 (August 1914): 243-
      44.

      Exposes working conditions and personal experiences of
      young women workers in the needle trades strikes.

223. Goldberg, Jacob A., and Rosamund W. Goldberg. *Girls
      on City Streets: A Study of 1400 Cases of Rape*. New
      York: American Social Hygiene Association, 1935.
      384 pp.

      Argues that girls who are the victims of sexual vio-
      lation are often the products of economically and emo-
      tionally deprived homes, or they are assaulted by the
      male products of such environments. Runaways and those
      who frequent public dance halls, beaches, and other
      resorts, unchaperoned and uncontrolled, are likely sub-
      jects of sex delinquency and violation.

224. Hatcher, Orie Latham. *Rural Girls in the City for Work:
      A Study Made for the Southern Woman's Educational
      Alliance*. Richmond, Va.: Garrett and Massie, Inc.,
      Publishers, 1930. 154 pp.

      Surveys the types of work, ages, and living conditions
      of 255 girls in Richmond, Virginia, and Durham, North
      Carolina, in the spring of 1927.

225. Hourwich, Andria Taylor, and Gladys L. Palmer, eds.
      I Am a Woman Worker: A Scrapbook of Autobiographies.
      New York: The Affiliated Schools for Workers, Inc.,
      1936. 152 pp.

      Collects brief personal statements on getting a job,
      life in the factory, open shops and company unions,
      trade unions and organized shops, strikes, and other
      observations by women attending summer schools for work-
      er education.

226. Laughlin, Clara E. *The Work-a-Day Girl: A Study of
      Some Present-Day Conditions*. New York: Fleming H.
      Revell Company, 1913. 320 pp.

      Asserts that inadequate wages lead to moral degrada-
      tion; therefore, young women should be cautious, and
      both society and legislatures should demonstrate con-
      cern, especially with the minimum wage.

227. A New New Yorker. "Stories Too Pleasant." *Life and
      Labor*, 1 (December 1911): 384.

Requests more realistic fiction and less romanticism and escapism in the journal distributed by the Woman's Trade Union League. Factory workers are too tired at the end of the day to "do much thinking" and, therefore, "need inspirational stories."

228. Palmer, Gladys L. *The Industrial Experience of Women Workers at the Summer Schools, 1928 to 1930.* U.S. Department of Labor, Women's Bureau. Bulletin No. 89. 1931. 60 pp.

Describes the characteristics, background, job history, and working and living conditions reported by women who attended summer school sessions at Bryn Mawr, Barnard, Wisconsin, and the Southern School in North Carolina.

229. Richardson, Dorothy. *The Long Day: The Story of a New York Working Girl.* New York: The Century Company, 1905. 303 pp.

Exposes the lifestyle of working-class young women from the perspective of a middle-class observer, with frequent recitations of dramatic event and moralizations.

230. Richmond, Mary E., and Fred S. Hull. *A Study of Nine Hundred and Eighty-Five Widows Known to Certain Charity Organization Societies in 1910.* New York: Charity Organization Department of the Russell Sage Foundation, 1913. 83 pp.

Highlights women heads of households and summarizes their work participation, income, earnings, hours, occupations, and morality with special attention to the problem of taking lodgers.

231. Tentler, Leslie Woodcock. *Wage-Earning Women: Industrial Work and Family Life in the U.S. 1900-1930.* New York: Oxford University Press, 1979. 288 pp.

Argues that employment did not mean emancipation for adolescent working-class women who joined the industrial work force in increasing numbers between 1900 and 1930. Although they found some satisfaction in "a relatively unrestricted social environment" among their co-workers, these women lacked opportunity to achieve individuality and autonomy. They left the industrial work force for traditionally subordinate roles in marriage and maternity.

232. VanVorst, Mrs. John, and Marie VanVorst. *The Woman
      Who Toils: Being the Experiences of Two Gentlewomen
      as Factory Girls.* New York: Doubleday, Page and Com-
      pany, 1903. 303 pp.

      Pleads for attention to the damage done to the souls
      of working-class women by the dirt and ugliness with
      which they are surrounded. Middle-class sisters-in-law
      took factory jobs in Pittsburgh; Chicago; Perry, New
      York; Lynn, Massachusetts; and Columbia, South Carolina,
      to discern and articulate the problems of women workers.

233. Whitney, Frances R. *What Girls Live On--And How: A
      Study of the Expenditures of a Sample Group of Girls
      Employed in Cincinnati in 1929.* Cincinnati: Consumers'
      League, 1930. 52 pp.

      Documents the requirements for a minimum standard of
      health and self-respect for a self-supporting girl. It
      would take $17.50 per week to achieve these in 1929, but
      59 percent of girls interviewed earned less. Girls who
      live at home, and, therefore, need less income, lower
      the wages of self-supporting girls.

234. Woods, Robert A., and Albert J. Kennedy, eds. *Young
      Working Girls: A Summary of Evidence from Two Thou-
      sand Social Workers.* Boston: National Federation of
      Settlements, Houghton Mifflin, 1913. 185 pp.

      Concludes that parents do not prepare children for
      industrial careers, public education is irrelevant, and
      young girls appear frivolous in their attitudes toward
      continuing employment and selfish in their desires for
      amusement and clothing.

                          B. HOME AND FAMILY

235. Abbott, Edith. *The Tenements of Chicago, 1908-1935.*
      Chicago: University of Chicago Press, 1936. 505 pp.

      Argues that neither private enterprise nor local gov-
      ernment is equipped to handle or solve the problems of
      tenement life among diverse ethnic groups; the federal
      government should intervene.

236. Anthony, Katherine. *Mothers Who Must Earn.* New York:
      Russell Sage Foundation, Survey Associates, 1914.
      223 pp.

Demonstrates how the condition of a family depends on
the condition of the principal breadwinner, who is often
a woman among the German, Irish, English, and Scottish
families on the West Side of New York. Many women con-
ceal their families when they seek employment because
of employer prejudice. Ambitious families seek the
middle-class status of married women who do not go out
of the household to work.

237. Bolin, Winifred Dorothy Wandersee. "Past Ideals and
Present Pleasures: Women, Work and the Family, 1920-
1940." Ph.D. dissertation, University of Minnesota,
1978. 501 pp.

Claims that the great majority of American women in
the 1920s and 1930s were committed to traditional domestic roles within the family. Most married women
were not gainfully employed despite high social expectations and low economic levels of many American families.

238. Brown, Emily C. *A Study of Two Groups of Denver Mar-*
ried Women Applying for Jobs. U.S. Department of Labor, Women's Bureau. Bulletin 77. 1929. 10 pp.

Concludes that married women seek employment because
of economic necessity, most having no support from husbands, and many with young children.

239. Byington, Margaret. *Homestead: The Households of a*
Mill Town. New York: Russell Sage Foundation, 1910.
292 pp.

Examines household life which was subordinated to mill
life in Homestead. An irregular succession of men's
long working hours interfered with orderly routine,
housekeeping, and child-rearing. The mill wage required additional sources of family income, but women
rarely worked outside the home; instead, they earned by
taking in lodgers.

240. Cohen, Miriam J. "From Workshop to Office: Italian Women and Family Strategies in New York City, 1900-
1950." Ph.D. dissertation, University of Michigan,
1978. 360 pp.

Argues that the lives of first-generation Italian
women and their daughters in New York, in the first decades of the twentieth century, were dominated by home
and domestic duties as well as supplementary earning.

Toward the end of the 1930s, however, Italian women began to remain in school and by 1950 were better educated
than their male counterparts. The earlier group earned
at home or in the garment industry; the more recent
group were white-collar workers before marriage, after
which they, like their mothers and older sisters, assumed traditional female responsibilities as wives and
mothers.

241.   ———. "Italian-American Women in New York City, 1900-
        1950: Work and School." In *Class, Sex, and the Woman
        Worker*, edited by Milton Cantor and Bruce Laurie.
        Westport, Conn.: Greenwood Press, 1977. Pp. 120-43.

Argues that working-class Italian families were more
likely to keep their female children in school as the
twentieth-century progressed, not as part of the embourgeoisement of American ethnics but as part of a
shift in New York's employment patterns and Italian-
American family strategies in response to the opening
of white-collar jobs to women.

242.   *The Commercialization of the Home through Industrial
        Home Work*. U.S. Department of Labor, Women's Bureau.
        Bulletin No. 135. 1935. 49 pp.

Attacks full-time production in the home for commercial enterprises as undermining family life as well as
the standards of factory working conditions. Unemployment of wage-earners increases the number and willingness of other family members to accept low rates of pay
for home work.

243.   *The Family Status of Breadwinning Women: A Study of
        Material in the Census Schedules of a Selected Local-
        ity*. U.S. Department of Labor, Women's Bureau. Bul-
        letin No. 23. 1922. 43 pp.

Examines census data for Passaic, New Jersey, to show
that it can reveal important information about the personal and family responsibilities of women breadwinners.
Census schedules document ethnicity, marital status, age,
family responsibilities, home tenure, industries, and
occupations. An additional personal survey can add information about the lifestyles of working mothers.

244.   *Family Status of Breadwinning Women in Four Selected
        Cities*. U.S. Department of Labor, Women's Bureau.
        Bulletin No. 41, Revision and Extension of Bulletin
        No. 23. 1925. 145 pp.

Concludes that a high proportion of women are breadwinners, that they are not transients in the work force,
that marriage and maternity do not necessarily mean the
end of breadwinning, and that many of the problems con-
nected with breadwinning wives and mothers would be dis-
sipated if husbands and fathers received adequate wages.

245. Fraundorf, Martha Norby. "The Labor Force Participation
      of Turn-of-the-Century Married Women." *Journal of
      Economic History*, 39 (June 1979): 401-18.

Argues that married women's participation in the paid
labor force was negatively related to the number of
older children who might be sent out to earn in place
of their mothers. Working, for these women, was affected more by the availability of jobs than by high
wages. Labor force participation was also influenced
by other family income, male unemployment, and literacy.

246. Gannett, Alice. "Bohemian Women in New York: Investiga-
      tion of Working Mothers." *Life and Labor*, 3 (February
      1913): 49-52.

Argues that conditions under which these women work
forces the neglect of their children.

247. Hagood, Margaret Jarman. *Mothers of the South: Por-
      traiture of the White Tenant Farm Women*. Chapel Hill:
      University of North Carolina Press, 1939. 252 pp.

Explores the struggle of tenant farm mothers of the
Piedmont against "almost every imaginable adverse external condition" to function in the triple role of
mother, housekeeper, and field laborer. In particular,
"involuntary and overfrequent" childbearing has an especially devastating effect upon these women and their
children.

248. Hareven, Tamara K. "Family Time and Industrial Time:
      Family and Work in a Planned Corporation Town, 1900-
      1924." *Journal of Urban History*, 1 (May 1975): 365-
      89. Revised as "Family and Work Patterns of Immigrant
      Laborers in a Planned Industrial Town, 1900-1930."
      In *Immigrants in Industrial America: 1850-1920*, edited
      by Richard L. Ehrlich. Charlottesville: University
      Press of Virginia, 1977. Pp. 47-66.

Claims that migration did not break down kinship ties,
but, rather, the kin group directed, organized, and assisted chain migration. Individuals and families relied

on relatives or former townsmen as sources of support,
sociability, and employment contacts as they moved to
the city.

249.   ————. "The Laborers of Manchester, New Hampshire,
        1912-1922: The Role of Family and Ethnicity in Adjust-
        ment to Industrial Life." *Labor History*, 16 (Spring
        1975): 249-65.

        Argues that the family was not breaking down in the
        face of new industrial conditions among textile workers
        in Manchester. The family played a key role in recruit-
        ing workers; entire families often worked in the same
        place, or young women remained in the same factory as
        proxies for the re-introduction of male relatives who
        had migrated among the textile cities where other rela-
        tives provided temporary housing, job information, and
        job placement.

250.   ————, and Randolph Langenbach. *Amoskeag: Life and
        Work in an American Factory-City.* New York: Pantheon
        Books, 1978. 395 pp.

        Describes industrial work, lifestyle, and labor pro-
        test in Manchester, New Hampshire, through selected
        oral-history interviews with former employees of the
        Amoskeag which dominated life there. "Most of these
        people had a highly developed sense of place and formed
        tightly knit societies around their kin and ethnic as-
        sociates."

251.   Hareven, Tamara K., and Maris A. Vinovskis. "Marital
        Fertility, Ethnicity, and Occupation in Urban Families:
        An Analysis of South Boston and South End in 1880."
        Journal of Social History, 8 (Spring 1975): 69-93.

        Shows fertility as a major variable in family behavior
        in nineteenth-century American urban populations. Fer-
        tility was affected by ethnicity, occupation, and loca-
        tion within the city. Additional study of fertility
        should add to understanding of women's work, education,
        religion, and income.

252.   Hewes, Amy, ed. *Women Workers and Family Support: A
        Study Made by Students in the Economics Course at the
        Bryn Mawr Summer School.* U.S. Department of Labor,
        Women's Bureau. Bulletin No. 49. 1925. 10 pp.

        Argues that women's contributions to family support
        were less obvious, but no less real, than men's. Tes-

timony of 101 students at the Bryn Mawr Summer School
in 1924 indicates significant contributions to family
support whether or not the women lived in the family
household.

253. *Home Environment and Employment Opportunities of Women
   in Coal-Mine Workers' Families*. U.S. Department of
   Labor, Women's Bureau. Bulletin No. 45. 1925. 61 pp.

   Examines women's contributions to the coal-mining industry as homemakers and supplementary breadwinners.
   But such women face limited employment opportunities
   because of the location of the mines, especially in the
   bituminous regions. Wives and families keep miners in
   the mining region, and if wives cannot earn in other
   ways, they take in lodgers; but in this, they are seriously handicapped by lack of facilities such as water,
   sanitation, and lighting. Miners themselves fail to
   improve their environment because they feel insecure
   about home tenure since they live in company-owned
   houses.

254. Hughes, Elizabeth A. *Living Conditions for Small-Wage
   Earners in Chicago*. Chicago: Department of Public
   Welfare, 1925. 62 pp.

   Pleads for the city housing plans, transportation
   system, and programs for industrial development to consider small-wage industrial families. Houses unfit for
   continued occupancy should be gradually replaced. Also
   includes descriptive and statistical data on living conditions, earnings, and occupations.

255. Hughes, Gwendolyn Salisbury. *Mothers in Industry: Wage-
   Earning by Mothers in Philadelphia*. New York: New
   Republic, Inc., 1925. 265 pp.

   Concludes that the consequences of 728 mothers working
   in Philadelphia are highly negative for women and for
   their families.

256. Jones, Thomas Jesse. *The Sociology of a New York City
   Block*. New York: Columbia University Press, 1904.
   136 pp.

   Favors systematic investigation of "the prevailing
   traits of mind and of character" as an additional tool
   to effect acculturation since "every possible agency
   should be used to change the numerous foreign types into
   the Anglo-Saxon ideal." Women are subsumed in the general conclusions.

257. Kiser, Clyde Vernon. *Group Differences in Urban Fer-
      tility: A Study Derived from the National Health Sur-
      vey.* Baltimore: Williams and Wilkins, 1942. 284 pp.

      Asserts that levels of reproduction are low in cities
      but the lower classes are more fertile than the middle
      and upper classes.

258. Krause, Corrine Azen. "Urbanization without Breakdown:
      Italian, Jewish, and Slavic Immigrant Women in Pitts-
      burgh, 1900 to 1945." *Journal of Urban History*, 4
      (May 1978): 291-306.

      Shows how Italian, Jewish, and Slavic women in Pitts-
      burgh in the first half of the twentieth century main-
      tained their cultural pluralism while adjusting to
      variations of an "American" model. Informal networks
      of relatives, neighbors, and children facilitated ad-
      justment for these women. They became "at home" in
      Pittsburgh and achieved "urbanization without breakdown."

259. Litoff, Judy Barrett. "Forgotten Women: American Mid-
      wives at the Turn of the Twentieth Century." *His-
      torian*, 40 (Fall 1978): 235-51.

      Claims that only very rich and very poor women de-
      livered their children in hospitals; all other women
      used midwives. These women lacked formal training, es-
      pecially in obstetrics, and usually had a clientele of
      friends and relatives, who paid them less than half what
      a physician would demand. But by 1910 high rates of
      maternal and infant mortality called the use of mid-
      wives into question, and the role was virtually defunct
      by 1930.

260. Lobsenz, Johanna. *The Older Woman in Industry.* New
      York: Charles Scribner's Sons, 1929. 281 pp.

      Summarizes data from the Fourteenth Census regarding
      the numbers and distribution of middle-aged and older
      women working in the New York City area.

261. Peterson, Agnes L. "What the Wage-Earning Woman Con-
      tributes to Family Support." *Annals of the American
      Academy of Political and Social Science*, 143 (May
      1929): 74-93. Reprinted as U.S. Department of Labor,
      Women's Bureau. Bulletin No. 75. 1929. 20 pp.

      Argues that women work in industry because male wages
      fail to meet the cost of living, yet women suffer from

misguided and ill-informed social attitudes about their employment opportunities and wages.

262. Pidgeon, Mary Elizabeth. *The Employed Woman Homemaker in the United States: Her Responsibility for Family Support.* U.S. Department of Labor, Women's Bureau. Bulletin No. 148. 1936. 22 pp.

Concludes that more than a third of all gainfully employed women in the United States are also responsible for the homemaking for their families, that they work because of economic necessity, that nearly a third of them have no male head of the household, and that an eighth of them are the only wage-earners in their families.

263. ————, and Margaret Thompson Mettert. *Employed Women and Family Support.* U.S. Department of Labor, Women's Bureau. Bulletin No. 168. 1939. 57 pp.

Documents the conditions of women working to support themselves and others or at least to contribute heavily to family needs. Such women tend to work in manufacturing or domestic service; they are mature but younger than the rest of the female population. At least a sixth are in families with no male wage-earner and a third combine the responsibilities of breadwinner and homemaker.

264. Rhyne, Jennings J. *Some Southern Cotton Mill Workers and Their Villages.* Chapel Hill: University of North Carolina Press, 1930. 214 pp.

Shows how the mill dominates housing, educational facilities, health of working women and children, and relations of individuals and families to the community in the cotton mill town, company town, suburban mill village, and rural mill village.

265. *The Share of Wage-Earning Women in Family Support.* U.S. Department of Labor, Women's Bureau. Bulletin No. 30. 1923. 170 pp.

Examines women wage-earners who support themselves and meet definite responsibilities in the support of others or in maintaining higher standards of living in their families. Men tend to support younger dependents; women assist older people.

266.   Simkovitch, Mary Kingsbury. *The City Worker's World in
       America*. New York: The Macmillan Co., 1917. 235 pp.

       Examines problems of immigration and democratization
       of city life, including standard of living, dwellings,
       education, and work.

267.   Winslow, Mary N. *Married Women in Industry*. U.S.
       Department of Labor, Women's Bureau. Bulletin No.
       38. 1924. 8 pp.

       Argues that "if we are going to keep on raising the
       family income through the earnings of married women,"
       they deserve fair treatment which recognizes the needs
       of industry, the family, and the individual.

                            C. COMMUNITY

REFORMS

268.   Brettell, Mamie. "Woman's Union Label League." *American
       Federationist*, 12 (May 1905): 276.

       Asks that the purchasing power of women be used to
       support the labor movement by demanding the union label.

269.   Chambers, Clarke A. *Seedtime of Reform: American Social
       Service and Social Action, 1918-1933*. Minneapolis:
       University of Minnesota Press, 1963. 326 pp.

       Places the Women's Trade Union League, the Women's
       Bureau, Women's Industrial Conference, and the workers'
       education movement within the general development of
       reform and social work.

270.   Curry, Margery. "The Labor Party for Women." *Life and
       Labor*, 9 (March 1919): 64-66.

       Urges women to use their votes to rectify social pro-
       blems.

271.   Gompers, Samuel. "Trade Unionism and Woman Suffrage."
       Life and Labor, 5 (July 1915): 122-23.

       Advocates suffrage as common justice to which trade
       unionism is dedicated. Asserts that women will need
       unions for protection, maintenance, and promotion of
       workers' rights and interests even after they obtain
       the vote.

272. Harrison, Dennis Irven. "The Consumers' League of Ohio:
      Women and Reform, 1909-1937." Ph.D. dissertation,
      Case Western Reserve University, 1975. 367 pp.

      Claims that the League attempted "to improve the
      working conditions of women and children by urging con-
      sumers to shop selectively, purchasing only goods known
      to be made under proper working conditions." But after
      1909 the League shifted to protective legislation such
      as minimum wage, the eight-hour day, and unemployment
      insurance.

273. Hinchey, Margaret. "Thirty Days." Life and Labor, 3
      (September 1913): 264-65.

      Pleads for women's participation in civic affairs, and
      speculates that unjust conviction of a woman striker
      and cruel treatment of women in jail might be different
      if women had a hand in electing judges and policemen
      and in making laws.

274. Kennedy, David M. Birth Control in America: The Career
      of Margaret Sanger. New Haven: Yale University Press,
      1970. 320 pp.

      Examines the birth control movement, including Sanger's
      early hopes that birth control would be a tool for bet-
      terment of the working classes and the later shift in
      view to regard it as a means of social control.

275. Kennedy, Susan Estabrook. "Poverty, Respectability, and
      Ability to Work." International Journal of Women's
      Studies, 2 (September/October 1979): 401-14.

      Argues that Progressive reformers faced an essential
      dilemma between offering protection and self-protection
      to working-class women. As attempts to organize working-
      class women met with slim success, and cross-class co-
      operation deteriorated, reformers turned to regulatory
      legislation to solve practical problems of living and
      working for working-class women.

276. Leonard, Henry B. "The Immigrants' Protective League
      of Chicago, 1908-1921." Journal of the Illinois State
      Historical Society, 66 (1973): 271-84.

      Examines the Immigrants' Protective League offer of
      humane and enlightened guidance to southern and eastern
      European immigrants who were regarded as racially in-
      ferior by earlier immigrants. The IPL helped immigrants

to adjust to American urban-industrial life and sought
government protection for them in employment, education,
and the legal system.

277. Morley, Herbert. "The Union Label." *Life and Labor*,
      1 (July 1911): 203.

      Urges buyers to look for the label testifying to manu-
      facture by trade union members because "the purchaser
      is the ultimate employer."

278. Nathan, Maud. *The Story of an Epoch-Making Movement*.
      Garden City, N.Y.: Doubleday, Page and Co., 1926.
      245 pp.

      Uses the story of the National Consumers' League to
      advocate investigation, reform, and middle-class concern
      for societal improvement.

279. Nienburg, Bertha M. *A Policy Insuring Value to the
      Woman Buyer and a Livelihood to Apparel Makers*. U.S.
      Department of Labor, Women's Bureau. Bulletin No.
      146. 1936. 22 pp.

      Asks women buyers to insist upon a consumer-protection
      label in garments, specifying manufacture under fair
      labor standards, to insure that buyers receive fair
      value for money expended and workers receive equitable
      treatment.

280. O'Brien, Agnes. "Suffrage and the Women in Industry."
      Life and Labor, 5 (August 1915): 132-33.

      Links suffrage and organization and praises such groups
      as the Women's Trade Union League and the National Con-
      sumers' Union for their accomplishments through organi-
      zation.

281. Peck, Mary Gray. "Some American Suffragists." *Life
      and Labor*, 1 (December 1911): 368-73.

      Argues that suffrage is one aspect of the fundamental
      economic question relating to women, not an independent
      issue. Suffrage is tied to trade unionism with union-
      ism taking priority.

282. "Report on Industrial Relations Commission." *Life and
      Labor*, 5 (September 1915): 142-45.

      Summarizes results of a two-year investigation of in-
      dustrial unrest including the Manly report on unjust

distribution of wealth, unemployment, denial of justice, and denial of the right and opportunity to form effective organizations, and the Commons report on the breakdown in administration of labor laws.

283. Robins, Margaret Dreier. "Women in American Industry." *Life and Labor*, 1 (November 1911): 324-25.

Reports conclusions of four years of investigation of women and children wage-earners and appearance of a nineteen-volume federal government statement of facts (item 284). The investigating period should end and action should begin to abolish the intolerable conditions dramatized by the great strikes of the past year.

284. United States Bureau of Labor. *Report on Conditions of Women and Child Wage Earners in the United States.* 19 vols. Washington, D.C.: Government Printing Office, 1910-1913.

Contains items 136 and 196.

285. van Kleeck, Mary. *Industrial Investigations of the Russell Sage Foundation.* New York: Russell Sage Foundation, Committee on Women's Work, 1915.

Demonstrates the value of industrial investigation in court decisions. The Russell Sage Foundation seeks to improve social and living conditions in the United States. Its publications on industrial problems are listed.

286. ————. *What Industry Means to Women Workers.* U.S. Department of Labor, Women's Bureau. Bulletin No. 31. 1923. 10 pp.

Argues that the great number and variety of problems of women in industry must be addressed by the gathering and analysis of factual evidence and the reconstruction of industry, in which voluntary organizations of women should have a part in the responsibility.

287. Walker, John H. "The Need for and the Advantages to the Workers of the Co-operative Movement." *Life and Labor*, 6 (August 1916): 121-24.

Asserts that workers are robbed both in the price they receive for their labor and the price they pay for what they buy.

288. Weiner, Lynn. "'Our Sisters Keepers': The Minneapolis
      Woman's Christian Association and Housing for Working
      Women." *Minnesota History*, 46 (Spring 1979): 189-200.

      Examines the boarding club movement which existed to
      accommodate the increasing numbers of women who were
      leaving their homes to seek employment in cities. Most
      such women earned "desperately low wages" and, therefore,
      needed lodgings which were cheap as well as respectable.

289. Wolfe, Allis Rosenberg. "Women, Consumerism, and the
      National Consumers' League in the Progressive Era,
      1900-1923." *Labor History*, 16 (Summer 1975): 378-92.

      Studies the National Consumers' League as an effort
      of middle- and upper-class women to use their latent
      power as purchasers of products to better American so-
      ciety. The League's objectives included reform of
      working conditions for women and children. But their
      efforts failed in the face of internal difficulties,
      conflicts with organized labor, divisions over feminist
      priorities and techniques, and an unsympathetic business
      and public climate in the 1920s.

REFORMERS

290. Anderson, James Russell. "The New Deal Career of Frances
      Perkins, Secretary of Labor, 1933-1939." Ph.D. dis-
      sertation, Case Western Reserve University, 1963.
      374 pp.

      Concludes that Perkins' experience in the Social Gos-
      pel and Progressivism movements led her to believe that
      collective action of the majority could lessen the bad
      aspects of unrestrained capitalism; thus, she was more
      concerned with collective bargaining than with unioni-
      zation, and she opposed both socialism and the pater-
      nalistic state, hoping to preserve the free enterprise
      system by reform.

291. Anderson, Mary, and Mary N. Winslow. *Woman at Work.*
      Minneapolis: University of Minnesota Press, 1951.
      266 pp.

      Describes the life of Anderson from her immigration
      from Scandinavia through early work in Chicago, trade
      unionism, the Women's Trade Union League, the garment
      strikes in Chicago, organizing women into unions, and
      activities on behalf of equal pay, protection, and

worker education through the Women-in-Industry Service
and the Women's Bureau of the Department of Labor.

292. Bruere, Martha Bensley. "Frances Kellor, Chief Investi-
gator." *Life and Labor*, 1 (February 1911): 44-46.

Gives an inspirational portrait of head of six-week-
old Bureau of Industries and Immigration, who had been
part of the College Settlement and worked against white
slavery in New York.

293. Carlton, Frank T. "Crusade to Improve Working Conditions." *Life and Labor*, 4 (April 1914): 108-9.

Presents an historical overview of efforts to improve
the lot of women workers, from Matthew Carey through
Leonora Barry.

294. *Carola Woerishoffer: Her Life and Work.* Bryn Mawr, Pa.:
Class of 1907, Bryn Mawr College, 1912. 137 pp.

Eulogizes Woerishoffer as a reformer, idealist, and
representative of Bryn Mawr objectives.

295. Cohen, Ricki Carole Myers. "Fannia Cohn and the International Ladies' Garment Workers' Union." Ph.D. dissertation, University of Southern California, 1976.

Uses Cohn's biography to illuminate "the interaction
between women, work, and the American labor movement."
Cohn deliberately elected a life of work rather than
marriage, suffering psychological dislocations from
this as well as from the empty power of her token position as the garment workers' first female vice-president.
But she pressed for worker education, preparing the way
for others to win praise when that movement came into
its own in the 1930s.

296. Daly, Sister John Marie. "Mary Anderson, Pioneer Labor
Leader." Ph.D. dissertation, Georgetown University,
1963. 284 pp.

Explores the career of Anderson as Swedish immigrant,
menial laborer, union member, boot and shoe worker,
canvasser for the Union Labor League, worker for the
Chicago Federation of Labor, member of the Chicago Women's Trade Union League, union organizer especially
among garment workers, assistant to the chief of the
Women-in-Industry Service, and director of the Women's
Bureau from 1920 to 1944.

297. Daniels, Doris Groshen. "Lillian D. Wald: The Progres-
      sive Woman and Feminism." Ph.D. dissertation, City
      University of New York, 1977. 345 pp.

      Includes among Wald's feminist activities her attempt
      to interpret the working class and middle class to each
      other in the trade union and suffrage movements.

298. Dreier, Mary E. *Margaret Dreier Robins: Her Life, Let-
      ters, and Work*. New York: Island Press Cooperative,
      Inc., 1950. 278 pp.

      Eulogizes the social feminist reformer who served as
      president of the Women's Trade Union League.

299. Fetherling, Dale. *Mother Jones, the Miners' Angel: A
      Portrait*. Carbondale and Edwardsville: Southern Il-
      linois University Press, 1974. 263 pp.

      Displays Mother Jones as a "personality" especially
      in her efforts to organize men who worked in mines.

300. Flynn, Elizabeth Gurley. *I Speak My Own Piece: Auto-
      biography of "The Rebel Girl."* New York: Masses and
      Mainstream, 1955. 326 pp. Reissued as *The Rebel
      Girl, An Autobiography: My First Life (1906-1926)*.
      New York: International Publishers, 1973. 351 pp.

      Recounts Gurley Flynn's experiences from 1890 to 1926
      in class conflict with emphasis on her work as a Social-
      ist and I.W.W. agitator as well as her activities on
      behalf of civil liberties and labor's rights during and
      after World War I. A Socialist America will be "an
      America free from poverty, exploitation, greed and in-
      justice," she argues.

301. Goldmark, Josephine C. *Impatient Crusader: Florence
      Kelley's Life Story*. Urbana: University of Illinois
      Press, 1953. 217 pp.

      Narrates Kelley's life and reform career including
      establishment of the National Consumers' League and the
      United States Children's Bureau.

302. Hill, Caroline M. *Mary McDowell and Municipal House-
      keeping: A Symposium*. Chicago: Millar Publishing Com-
      pany, n.d. 132 pp.

      Eulogizes McDowell for her work in the settlements,
      urban reform, and labor organizations, and praises her
      as the "Angel of the Stockyards."

303. Howe, Frances Hovey. "Leonora O'Reilly, Socialist and Reformer, 1870-1927." Honors thesis, Radcliffe College, 1952. 86 pp.

    Outlines O'Reilly's life with emphasis on her commitment to training and apprenticeship for women workers.

304. Jones, Mary. *Autobiography of Mother Jones*. Chicago: Charles H. Kerr and Co., 1925. 242 pp.

    Presents Jones' version of her activities as a labor organizer and socialist, especially among mine workers, with brief mention of her tactics in using women for the betterment of her "boys."

305. "Katherine Coman, Educator." *Life and Labor*, 1 (March 1911): 71-73.

    Summarizes Coman's life as the daughter of a lawyer-abolitionist, whose consciousness was raised to the cause of working women. Coman's work included the tailoresses' Thursday Evening Club, the 1891 Massachusetts Anti-Sweat Shop Law, and the Chicago Garment Workers' Strike.

306. Long, Priscilla. *Mother Jones, Woman Organizer*. Cambridge, Mass.: Red Sun Press, 1976. 40 pp.

    Argues that Jones held conservative views on women's roles which affected her attitudes toward all women. Class consciousness was of such exclusive importance to her that she would not risk her unique position in the male labor movement by raising women's rights questions. Her actual behavior toward women was frequently suspicious, hostile, or exploitative.

307. Marot, Helen. "Carola Woerishoffer." *Life and Labor*, 1 (December 1911): 358-61.

    Applauds the work of middle-class "allies" in the Women's Trade Union League through the obituary of Woerishoffer who did clerical work for W.T.U.L., canvassed for the union label, supported strikers with bail money, and was killed in a car accident while on duty as an inspector for the New York Immigration Bureau.

308. Nathan, Maud. *Once Upon a Time and Today*. New York: G.P. Putnam's Sons, 1933. 327 pp.

    Demonstrates how private privilege can be used to serve public life, as Nathan did in the white list campaign, suffrage movement, and National Consumers' League.

309. Nestor, Agnes. *Woman's Labor Leader: An Autobiography.*
     Rockford, Ill.: Bellevue Books, 1954.   307 pp.

     Records Nestor's life as a glove worker and trade
     union activist from factory work in Chicago, through
     strikes and unionization, the Women's Trade Union League,
     the struggle to obtain a Women's Bureau in the Depart-
     ment of Labor, and the fight for glove manufacture codes
     under NRA.

310. Pesotta, Rose. *Bread Upon the Waters,* edited by John
     Nicholas Beffel. New York: Dodd, Mead and Co., 1944.
     435 pp.

     Recounts Pesotta's life and career from her emigration
     to America through her work in the garment trades and
     organizing for the I.L.G.W.U., especially organizing
     strike activities on the West Coast in the 1930s.

311. Reznick, Allan Edward. "Lillian D. Wald: The Years at
     Henry Street." Ph.D. dissertation, University of
     Wisconsin, 1973.   470 pp.

     Argues that although Wald recognized the need to in-
     teract with immigrants on a basis of mutual respect,
     she felt compelled to dispense charity which impeded
     equality. Her inclination toward feminism and trade
     unionism was modified by the need to obtain financial
     aid from the German-Jewish banking elite. She did,
     however, foster the careers of nurses and trade union-
     ists through the Henry Street Settlement.

312. Sanger, Margaret. *Margaret Sanger: An Autobiography.*
     New York: W.W. Norton and Co., 1938.   504 pp.

     Records Sanger's personal convictions and public ac-
     tivities in the birth control movement, with evidence
     from Sanger's nursing career among working-class women.

313. Schneiderman, Rose, with Lucy Goldthwaite. *All for
     One.* New York: Paul S. Erikson, Inc., 1967.   264 pp.

     Shows Schneiderman's early economic and personal in-
     securities, sense of group loyalty, and career as worker,
     trade unionist, reformer, and government official.

314. Scholten, Pat Creech. "The Old Mother and Her Army:
     The Agitative Strategies of Mary Harris Jones." *West
     Virginia History,* 40 (Summer 1979): 365-74.

Says that Mary Harris Jones "never doubted her role as rebel leader of the poor and fighter for freedom." She adopted the working class as her children and both symbolized and articulated their hopes and dreams.

315. Sharp, Kathleen Ann. "Rose Pastor Stokes: Radical Champion of the American Working Class, 1879-1933." Ph.D. dissertation, Duke University, 1979. 225 pp.

Argues that Stokes' own immigrant origins contributed to her commitment to the working class; her marriage gave her means and prominence to pursue her aims, which were shaped by her experience with the Socialist Party before 1910, progressive reform between 1910 and 1916, and the Communist Party after World War I. Stokes' inconsistencies indicate the complexity of American radicalism.

316. Wechsler, Eva. "Frances Perkins, State Industrial Commissioner." *Life and Labor*, 9 (April 1919): 76-78.

Offers Perkins' career as the inspirational success story of a woman reformer; Perkins is labelled a "radical."

317. Werstein, Irving. *Labor's Defiant Lady: The Story of Mother Jones*. New York: Thomas Y. Crowell Company, 1969. 146 pp.

Recounts Jones' career as a union organizer for the Knights of Labor and United Mine Workers, including her use of miners' wives "as shock troops in a strike" to confront strike-breakers and company guards.

EDUCATION

318. Brameld, Theodore, ed. *Workers' Education in the United States*. New York and London: Harper and Brothers Publishers, 1941. 338 pp.

Examines the involvement of public education in workers' education because of the intimate relationship between workers' education and the ideals of American democracy.

319. Brody, Doris Cohen. "American Labor Education Service, 1927-1962: An Organization in Workers' Education." Ph.D. dissertation, Cornell University, 1973. 264 pp.

Documents the evolution of the American Labor Education Service out of the workers' summer school movement
of the 1920s which grew out of workers' education, progressive education, and the women's movement; traces the
major projects of the ALES until its closure in 1962.

320. Carter, Jean, and Hilda W. Smith. *Education and the
      Worker-Student: A Book about Workers Education Based
      upon the Experience of Teachers and Students.* New
      York: Affiliated Schools for Workers, Inc., 1934.
      72 pp.

      Expresses the hope that workers' classes will offer
      what the students want and presents a handbook for
      teachers advising on how to adjust to the teaching situ-
      ation and to develop a curriculum including current so-
      cial and economic problems, social health, and recrea-
      tion.

321. Cohn, Fannia M. "Educational and Social Activities."
      American Federationist, 36 (December 1929): 1446-52.

      Claims that educational departments in unions aid the
      labor movement by awakening workers' awareness to the
      possibilities of a better life and by developing leader-
      ship from within the rank and file.

322. ————. "Facing the Future." *American Federationist*,
      42 (November 1935): 1203-8.

      Asserts that young women who have joined the Inter-
      national Ladies Garment Workers Union understand the
      harsh realities of industrial life and appreciate the
      union as their sole opportunity for betterment. But
      they also enjoy the social and cultural offerings of the
      I.L.G.W.U.'s Educational Department.

323. Frederickson, Mary. "The Southern Summer School for
      Women Workers in Industry: A Female Strategy for Col-
      lective Action in the South, 1920-1940." Paper, Fourth
      Berkshire Conference on History of Women, Mt. Holyoke
      College, 24 August 1978.

      Examines the Southern Summer School as a cross-class
      alliance which created opportunities for young women
      industrial workers to develop knowledge, solidarity,
      confidence, and strategies for social action. The ses-
      sions provided social space, presented the faculty as
      non-passive role models, and offered an ideological vi-
      sion of a social order with genuine democracy and worker
      ownership.

324. Howlett, Charles F. "Brookwood Labor College and Worker Commitment to Social Reform." *Mid-America*, 61 (January 1979): 47-66.

Surveys Brookwood Labor College's commitment to peace and to organization of unskilled industrial workers, arising out of its concern for heightening the social consciousness of the worker and challenging "the status quo policies of traditional trade unionism by encouraging the development of a social system responsive to the needs of all workers."

325. Lape, Esther. "Americanizing Our New Women Citizens." *Life and Labor*, 8 (May 1918): 96-98, 104.

Urges that immigrant women learn the English language and American institutions, and records some common misconceptions by these women such as the belief that the mayor determines the price of the food they buy.

326. Robins, Margaret Dreier. "Educational Plans of the National Women's Trade Union League." *Life and Labor*, 4 (June 1914): 164-67.

Surveys worker education, especially in cooperation with universities so that workers may learn about economics, labor problems, and current social and industrial issues, as well as acquire a knowledge of their rights and the values of their labor power.

327. Schneider, Florence H. *Patterns of Worker Education: The Story of the Bryn Mawr Summer School*. Washington, D.C.: American Council on Public Affairs, 1941. 158 pp.

Examines the establishment and mechanics of union and non-union summer school programs for workers in industry from Bryn Mawr to Hudson Shore.

328. Seller, Maxine. "The Education of the Immigrant Women: 1900-1935." *Journal of Urban History*, 4 (May 1978): 307-30.

Argues that immigrant women often established more effective educational programs through their own organizations than were available through public facilities which were biased by the belief that women needed training only in practical tasks related to their domestic role. Immigrant women frequently dropped out of programs which did not meet their needs and gravitated toward

bilingual programs in cultural groups, ethnic parishes,
labor organizations, and women's clubs; they also educated themselves by reading.

329. Smith, Hilda W. "Bryn Mawr Summer School of 1927."
      "... 1928," "... 1929." *American Federationist*, 34
      (October 1927): 1217-23; 35 (October 1928): 1498-
      1500; 36 (September 1929): 1107-10.

      Reviews the summer programs offered for trade-union
      women at Bryn Mawr and other colleges but emphasizes
      the unstable nature of employment which led to difficult
      recruiting and withdrawal of many applicants.

330. van Kleeck, Mary. *Working Girls in Evening Schools: A
      Statistical Study*. New York: Russell Sage Foundation,
      Survey Associates, Inc., 1914. 252 pp.

      Surveys the reasons why female industrial workers are
      attending night school, such as vocational improvement.

331. Ware, Caroline F. *Labor Education in Universities: A
      Study of University Programs*. New York: American Labor
      Education Service, Inc., 1946. 138 pp.

      Says that universities have cooperated and should
      continue to cooperate in programs for the education of
      workers in industry. The study sets out organizations,
      administration, control, recruitment of students, fac-
      ulty, and relation to other university activities.

332. Ware, Edward J. "Open the Schools." *Life and Labor*,
      1 (August 1911): 238-40.

      Appeals for use of public school facilities in the
      evening so that workers may educate themselves for civic
      and social responsibility.

VICE

333. Addams, Jane. *A New Conscience and an Ancient Evil*.
      New York: The Macmillan Company, 1913. 219 pp.

      Argues that prostitution is a particular danger to
      young factory and department store girls because, for
      the first time in history, many women are working without
      the direct stimulus of family interest and affection and
      are unable to apportion their hours of work and intervals
      of rest according to their strength. Illicit trade seems
      attractive when compared with long hours, small wages,
      and monotonous work.

334. Barrett, Kate Waller. *Some Practical Suggestions on the Conduct of a Rescue Home.* Washington, D.C.: National Florence Crittenton Mission, 1903. 115 pp.

Preaches moral uplift and rehabilitation of unwed mothers by strict regulation in the operation of rescue homes.

335. "Emilie L. Glorieux: The Minneapolis Policewomen." *Life and Labor*, 2 (March 1912): 87-88.

Moralizes about the evils of dance halls.

336. Feldman, Egal. "Prostitution, the Alien Woman, and the Progressive Imagination, 1910-1915." *American Quarterly*, 19 (Summer 1967): 192-206.

Argues that social reformers had a dual objective in their crusade against prostitution. Not only did they want to eliminate vice, they also sought to rescue the reputation of immigrant women who were indiscriminately condemned by agrarian nativists. Therefore, reformers simultaneously worked for the end of prostitution, changes in immigration procedures, and protective associations for young women.

337. Henry, Alice. "The Latest Word on the Social Evil." *Life and Labor*, 7 (February 1917): 28-29.

Warns against vice and calls for social remedies to eliminate the causes of the problem.

338. Mason, Ethel, and S.M. Franklin. "Low Wages and Vice-- Are They Related?" *Life and Labor*, 3 (April 1913): 108-11.

Charges that women turn to prostitution because they cannot earn enough in other occupations, and counters testimony of merchants that there is no connection between wages and vice.

339. Sanger, William W. *The History of Prostitution: Its Extent, Causes, and Effects throughout the World.* New York: Harper and Brothers, Publishers, 1859. 685 pp. Reprint. New York: Arno Press, 1972.

Concludes that women interviewed in New York claimed that they turned to prostitution primarily "to gratify their sexual passions" or avoid starvation. If genuine opportunities for respectable and remunerative employment were available to women, "the daughters of shame would be happy and virtuous members of the community."

340. Waterman, Willoughby Cyrus. *Prostitution and Its Re-*
      pression in New York City, 1900-1931. New York:
      Columbia University Press, 1932. 164 pp. Reprint.
      New York: AMS Press, Inc., 1968.

      Shows how law and police enforcement have altered the
      methods of conducting prostitution since 1900, virtually
      eliminating street solicitation and open houses of pros-
      titution, but leading to private dance studios, speak-
      easys, closed dance halls, and tenement "call flats."
      Efforts should now be directed against the initial luring
      of young women into the profession and toward making
      prostitutes so expensive and difficult to find that men
      will be discouraged from hunting them.

                              D. CLASS

341. Barkey, Frederick Allan. "The Socialist Party in West
      Virginia from 1898 to 1920 as a Study in Working Class
      Radicalism." Ph.D. dissertation, University of
      Pittsburgh, 1971. 274 pp.

      Argues that the Socialist Party attracted mostly na-
      tive American workers, skilled or semi-skilled members
      of both craft and industrial unions, the better edu-
      cated, and those socially sensitive to the undermining
      effect of employer-employee relations and technological
      innovations. The Party worked through existing union
      organizations until 1914 when it changed to a direct
      industrial union, but it lost the labor vote by stres-
      sing larger-than-local issues.

342. Bloor, Ella R. *We Are Many: An Autobiography.* New
      York: International Publishers, 1940. 319 pp.

      Pleads for awareness, organization, and militancy of
      workers through the story of a woman from a wealthy
      family who became a socialist and an organizer. Strikes
      and massacres of laborers receive prominent attention.

343. Buhle, Mari Jo. "Feminism and Socialism in the United
      States, 1820-1920." Ph.D. dissertation, University
      of Wisconsin, 1974. 415 pp.

      Argues that the appearance of Marxism in the United
      States solidified the ideological rejection of feminism
      by socialists. The Socialist Party of America between

1901 and 1919 provided an amorphous and localistic political movement in which women might attain status, but
males objected to threats to socialist values which they
saw in women's self-emancipation and sexual self-identity.
After 1912 both the socialist movement and women's role
in it declined.

344. ————. "Socialist Women and Class Organization, 1900-
1920." Paper, Conference on Class and Ethnicity in
Women's History, SUNY at Binghamton, 22 September 1974.

Demonstrates how socialist women were caught in the
struggle for economics and politics. They were welcomed
when they joined socialist ranks but were not recruited,
proved effective in educating women but felt inadequate
to assume leadership, and generally had more success
in rural than in major urban settings. In the long
run, socialist women encountered ideological conflicts
such as the condemnation of suffragists as threats to
the class struggle.

345. ————. "Socialist Women and the 'Girl Strikers,'
Chicago, 1910." *Signs*, 1 (Summer 1976): 1039-51.

Shows that socialist women in Chicago responded to
the 1910 walkout by garment workers from Hart, Schaffner
and Marx by publicizing the implications of the struggle
for workers as well as for socialists. These women were
committed to supporting the strikers in time of emergency
and "to education as the ongoing responsibility of all
Socialist activists." Their message combined the ideas
of "women's oppression through wage-labor" and "their
capacity for self-liberation."

346. Corcoran, Theresa. "Vida Scudder and the Lawrence Textile Strike." *Essex Institute Historical Collections*,
115 (July 1979): 183-95.

Examines how Vida Scudder tried unsuccessfully to
obtain support from settlement workers and others in
Wellesley and Boston for the Lawrence strikers; but her
socialism was too radical not only for the settlement
but for most of the labor leaders with whom she worked.

347. Dancis, Bruce. "Socialism and Women in the United
States, 1900-1917." *Socialist Revolution*, 6 (January-
March 1976): 81-144.

Explores issues such as equality of women as workers,
role of housewives, marriage, and monogamy discussed by

the New Left and others in the 1960s, but already debated within the American Socialist movement early in the twentieth century, although socialists held varied, and often contradictory, views. This fragmentary treatment of isolated issues as well as lack of sympathy from socialist men stood in the way of a synthesis of socialism and feminism.

348. Dixler, Elsa Jane. "The Woman Question: Women and the American Communist Party, 1929-1941." Ph.D. dissertation, Yale University, 1974. 296 pp.

Claims that "communists appealed to women in their role as wives, housekeepers, and mothers, rather than as people in their own right." Women within the Party held token positions, rose significantly less rapidly than blacks, and were not actively recruited into the Party.

349. Nowicki, Stella. "Back of the Yards." In *Rank and File: Personal Histories by Working-class Organizers*. Boston: Beacon Press, 1973. Pp. 67-88.

Recounts Nowicki's experiences as a meat-packer, socialist, member of the Young Communists' League, and union activist. Women in unions were not taken seriously by men in the 1930s and 1940s.

350. Silverman, Myra. "Class, Kinship, and Ethnicity: Patterns of Jewish Upward Mobility in Pittsburgh, Pennsylvania." *Urban Anthropology*, 7 (Spring 1978): 25-44.

Argues that closely knit kin networks and ethnic behavior and identification have been useful to lower-class families in attaining and maintaining middle-class status. These traits may then change, but they are not necessarily lost.

E. EMPLOYMENT

GENERAL

351. Abbott, Edith. "The History of Industrial Employment of Women in the United States: An Introductory Study." *Journal of Political Economy*, 14 (October 1906): 461-501; 15 (December 1907): 619-24.

Claims that women have worked in order to support themselves. Moreover, women do not compete with men workers and thus erode wage levels.

352. ———. *Women in Industry: A Study in American Economic History.* New York: D. Appleton and Co., 1910. 408 pp.

Argues that women do not drive men out of industrial tasks. The employment of women has changed from agriculture through domestic services and early training in spinning and weaving to the modern factory system.

353. ———, and Sophonisba P. Breckenridge. "Employment of Women in Industries: Twelfth Census Statistics." *Journal of Political Economy*, 14 (January 1906): 14-40.

Uses the Twelfth Census to show women monopolizing certain occupations due to their greater facility and willingness to accept low wages. Women rarely compete with men since women perform peripheral work while men dominate highly skilled occupations.

354. American Association of University Women, comp. *Summaries of Studies on the Economic Status of Women.* U.S. Department of Labor, Women's Bureau. Bulletin No. 134. 1935. 20 pp.

Lists books, articles, and pamphlets of the 1930s on the economic condition of college, business and professional, and industrial women as well as materials divided by occupation, earnings, education, age, marriage, children, dependents, discrimination, unemployment, and turnover.

355. Benson, Marguerite B. "Labor Turnover of Working Women." *Annals of the American Academy of Political and Social Science*, 143 (May 1929): 109-19.

Argues that labor turnover is more a function of task, age, urban or rural location, management policy, and business cycles than it is of sex.

356. Best, Ethel L. *A Study of a Change from One Shift of 9 Hours to Two Shifts of 6 Hours Each.* U.S. Department of Labor, Women's Bureau. Bulletin No. 116. 1934. 14 pp.

Asserts that women work to earn a living rather than for pin money; therefore, they prefer working arrangements

which permit adequate income. Consequently, most prefer
the nine-hour to the six-hour shift when the hourly rate
of pay remains the same.

357. ————. *Technological Changes in Relations to Women's
      Employment.* U.S. Department of Labor, Women's Bureau.
      Bulletin No. 107. 1935. 39 pp.

      Concludes that mechanization jeopardizes prosperity
      since fewer workers can machine-produce more goods than
      consumers, who are also wage-earners, can absorb.
      Automation leads to lay-offs or quits and declining
      earnings.

358. Carpenter, Elizabeth. "More Truth about Women in In-
      dustry." *North American Review*, 179 (1904): 215-25.

      Argues that employment of women does not necessarily
      hurt men's wages, nor does it harm the family or threaten
      women's reproductive functions.

359. Dempsey, Mary V. *The Occupational Progress of Women,
      1910 to 1930.* U.S. Department of Labor, Women's Bu-
      reau. Bulletin No. 104. 1933. 87 pp.

      Shows that the number of working women increased be-
      tween 1910 and 1920 because of the development and spe-
      cialization of industry and of the World War, while the
      numbers rose unexpectedly between 1920 and 1930 because
      male war casualties and influenza victims left permanent
      gaps in the labor force, restriction of immigration
      shut off the continuous supply of young adult men, and
      the war succeeded in breaking down imaginary barriers
      to the employment of women in many occupations.

360. *Effects of Applied Research upon the Employment Oppor-
      tunities of American Women.* U.S. Department of Labor,
      Women's Bureau. Bulletin No. 50. 1926. 54 pp.

      Applauds scientific research for contributing to the
      new or more efficient use of methods and materials of
      manufacture, thereby opening employment opportunities
      to women such as development of new raw materials for
      the perfume industry. Occupations from which women were
      barred by physical demands have been opened by mechanical
      invention.

361. Ethelburt, Stewart. "Trend of Employment of Men and
      Women in Specified Industries." *Monthly Labor Review*,
      20 (April 1925): 739-50.

Says that the percentage of employed women increased
more rapidly than that for men in the 1890s, but in industries other than manufacturing. In industries which
traditionally employed women, the proportion of women
relative to men decreased, as did women's wages.

362. *Fact Finding with the Women's Bureau.* U.S. Department
of Labor, Women's Bureau. Bulletin No. 84. 1931.
35 pp.

Argues that women form a significant and growing seg-
ment of the paid labor force, and that their presence
and conditions require the systematic investigation of
the circumstances under which they work, with the objective of establishing adequate standards of wages,
hours, and working conditions which will both serve the
needs of industry and recognize the needs and responsibilities of working women.

363. *Facts about Working Women: A Graphic Presentation Based
on Census Statistics and Studies of the Women's Bureau.*
U.S. Department of Labor, Women's Bureau. Bulletin
No. 46. 1925. 64 pp.

Summarizes information from the 1910 and 1920 censuses
in tables and charts which include proportions, distri-
butions, age, nativity, and marital condition as well as
occupations, hours, and earnings of employed women.

364. Hewes, Amy, ed. *Changing Jobs: A Study Made by Students
in the Economics Course at the Bryn Mawr Summer School.*
U.S. Department of Labor, Women's Bureau. Bulletin
No. 54. 1926. 12 pp.

Concludes that "short-time jobs have become so numerous as to suggest the replacement of the old-time steady
worker by one who is in the process of becoming a pure
casual." Workers tend to leave jobs because of seasonal
trade, the character of management, and monotony and
routine of work itself. These conditions require study
and may spell the need for different industrial tactics
and employment management.

365. Hill, Joseph A. *Women in Gainful Occupations, 1870-
1920: A Study of the Trend of Recent Changes in the
Numbers, Occupational Distribution, and Family Relationship of Women Reported in the Census as Following
a Gainful Occupation.* Washington, D.C.: Government
Printing Office, 1929. 416 pp.

Compiles data from the federal censuses into tables
and statements of factual information.

366. Klaczynska, Barbara. "Why Women Work: A Comparison of
      Various Groups in Philadelphia, 1910-1930." *Labor
      History*, 17 (Winter 1976): 73-87.

      Argues that ethnicity had a major impact on whether
      women sought paid employment, both in terms of the
      ethnic group's attitudes and expectations and the way
      in which the dominant society regarded the ethnic groups.
      Italian women were least likely to work outside the home,
      black women most likely. But each group tended to with-
      draw its women from paid labor as it reached the middle
      class.

367. ————. "Working Women in Philadelphia: 1900-1930."
      Ph.D. dissertation, Temple University, 1975. 301 pp.

      Concludes that ethnic groups and neighborhoods were
      the most important influences on whether working-class
      women sought employment and what kinds of occupations
      they entered. Ethnicity had greatest influence before
      1920, neighborhood after. Working conditions and the
      social welfare system prevented women from organizing
      with men or with other women to improve their conditions.

368. Manning, Caroline. *The Immigrant Woman and Her Job*.
      U.S. Department of Labor, Women's Bureau. Bulletin
      No. 74. 1930. 179 pp.

      Demonstrates that immigrant women face particular
      problems in not learning the language and customs of
      America and that they choose places of residence and
      occupations in order to be near friends. Therefore,
      "all work is alike to them, merely a means of earning a
      livelihood."

369. Nelson, Eleanor. *Women at Work: A Century of Industrial
      Change*. U.S. Department of Labor, Women's Bureau.
      Bulletin No. 115. 1934. 60 pp.

      Traces the involvement of women as paid laborers in
      the American economy, with emphasis on their struggle
      against low wages and poor conditions, adding preliminary
      observations on the NRA codes.

370. Nienburg, Bertha M. *Potential Earning Power of Southern
      Mountaineer Handicraft*. U.S. Department of Labor,
      Women's Bureau. Bulletin No. 128. 1935. 56 pp.

Claims that handicraft must supplement family cash
earnings of most southern mountaineer craftsfolk, but
current systems of production and control make inadequate use of handicraft women and return them inadequate
income. Therefore, the work should be reorganized to
open a market at better prices, yield better weekly
wages, and insure more healthful working conditions.

371. Pidgeon, Mary Elizabeth. *Differences in the Earnings
of Women and Men*. U.S. Department of Labor, Women's
Bureau. Bulletin No. 152. 1938. 57 pp.

Says that women's wages are lower than men's in spite
of locality, type of industry, period of time, method
of pay, or changes in the general wage level, business
conditions, or source of labor supply, even under NRA
codes.

372. ————. *Women in the Economy of the United States of
America: A Summary Report*. U.S. Department of Labor,
Women's Bureau. Bulletin No. 155. 1937. 137 pp.

Shows that large and increasing numbers of women are
employed outside the home as well as making economic
contributions as homemakers, that women earn less than
men, although they work out of necessity to support
themselves and dependents, and that both the NRA and
state minimum wage laws have helped the wages of large
numbers of women.

373. *Radio Talks on Women in Industry*. U.S. Department of
Labor, Women's Bureau. Bulletin No. 26. 1924.
34 pp.

Collects brief popular articles broadcast weekly during the winter of 1922-23, including discussion of the
Women's Bureau, women's work in industry, wages, budgets, hours, health, hygiene, and myths about women in
industry.

374. *Short Talks about Working Women*. U.S. Department of
Labor, Women's Bureau. Bulletin No. 59. 127. 24 pp.

Shows that the kinds of occupations women hold are
changing with a movement away from domestic service and
agriculture and toward clerical and professional jobs as
well as some manufacturing and mechanical industries.
Since women, like men, work because of necessity, they
seek more pleasant and better-paid occupations and should
have the protection of government-backed standards of
hours, wages, working-conditions, and safety.

375. Synder, Eleanor M. *Job Histories of Women Workers at
      the Summer Schools, 1931-34 and 1938.* U.S. Department
      of Labor, Women's Bureau. Bulletin No. 174. 1939.
      25 pp.

      Portrays a hypothetical "average" student at the sum-
      mer schools for women workers; she is 24 years old,
      native-born, single, employed for approximately eight
      years but irregularly, which produces fluctuating annual
      earnings. She differs from the general group of women
      workers in her affiliation with the local Y.W.C.A. and
      membership in a trade union.

376. Thompson, F.M. "The Truth About Women in Industry."
      North American Review, 178 (May 1904): 751-60.

      Claims that the employment of women reduces the wages
      of men and disrupts the natural order in which women
      function as wives and mothers.

377. Toporoff, Ralph. "Generating Role Types Concerning the
      Occupational Participation of Women in the Twentieth
      Century." Ph.D. dissertation, Washington State Uni-
      versity, 1972. 264 pp.

      Concludes that census data for 1900-1960 shows women
      responding to circumstances in seeking employment rather
      than taking an active position in expanding employment
      opportunities. Trends seem to foretell declining employ-
      ment of working-class women as their husbands' income
      rises but increasing employment of middle-class women,
      independent of supplementing family income.

378. *Variations in Employment Trends of Women and Men.* U.S.
      Department of Labor, Women's Bureau. Bulletin No. 73.
      1930. 141 pp.

      Asks that employment figures be gathered and analyzed
      separately for women and for men, since the current sys-
      tem prohibits accurate assessment of the effect of
      changes in economic conditions such as war, depression,
      or strikes as well as industrial changes such as mech-
      anization and new technology.

379. *Women Street Car Conductors and Ticket Agents.* U.S.
      Department of Labor, Women's Bureau. Bulletin No. 11.
      1921. 90 pp.

      Claims that, while conditions of work as street car
      conductors and ticket agents are not ideal, they are not

unfit for women; some women are employed in such jobs
under conditions better than those prescribed by law.
But street car companies frequently resist hiring women,
and unions oppose their employment as well.

380. *Women Workers in Flint, Mich.* U.S. Department of Labor,
      Women's Bureau. Bulletin No. 67. 1929. 79 pp.

      Shows how the physical life of working women in Flint,
      as well as their standards of living and sense of values,
      are circumscribed because although Flint has grown mark-
      edly in the last 30 years because of the expansion of
      the auto industry, the community is almost wholly de-
      pendent on this single industry controlled by a single
      corporation; therefore, employment fluctuates from year
      to year and within the year, affecting the lives of auto
      workers' families. Moreover, women have only limited
      employment opportunities in the auto industry.

381. *Women Workers in Their Family Environment.* U.S. Depart-
      ment of Labor, Women's Bureau. Bulletin No. 183.
      1941. 82 pp.

      Argues that the wages of working women are essential
      to family income. Women workers frequently belong to
      broken families; and the unmarried daughter is the most
      important woman earner in both normal and broken homes.
      Married women work because their husbands have low in-
      comes or irregular employment or because relatives need
      financial assistance.

OCCUPATIONS: DOMESTIC AND SERVICE

382. Abbott, Mabel. "The Waitresses of Seattle." *Life and
      Labor*, 4 (February 1914): 48-49.

      Offers the inspiration of accomplishment and the ben-
      efits of organization by presenting the example of the
      only waitresses' recreation home in the United States.

383. Byrne, Harriet A. *Employment in Hotels and Restaurants.*
      U.S. Department of Labor, Women's Bureau. Bulletin
      No. 123. 1936. 105 pp.

      Describes the numbers, hours and days, wages and
      earnings, tips, and uniforms of women working as cooks,
      waitresses, and other servants in restaurants and hotels
      across the country. This material can be used in the
      rehearing of the NRA codes and in pressing for the State
      minimum wage legislation.

384. Corell, Marie. *Standards of Placement Agencies for
      Household Employees.* U.S. Department of Labor, Women's
      Bureau. Bulletin No. 112. 1934. 68 pp.

      Claims that placement agencies can contribute to the
      regulation of household labor in the absence of legal
      restrictions. Existing standards used by placement
      agencies tend to provide minimums for wages but do not
      specify hours of work, although most specify time off.
      Household employees need legislative regulation, par-
      ticularly of the length of the working day and week.

385. Donovan, Frances. *The Woman Who Waits.* Boston: Richard
      G. Bader, The Gorham Press, 1920. 228 pp.

      Argues that waitresses "represent the advance guard
      of working women," that this occupation is one of the
      most readily available to daughters who have left the
      farm or the second generation of stockyards and factory
      workers. Describes the experiences of waitresses in a
      hierarchy of establishments, based on nine months as a
      participant-observer in Chicago.

386. Erickson, Ethel. *Employment Conditions in Beauty Shops:
      A Study of Four Cities.* U.S. Department of Labor,
      Women's Bureau. Bulletin No. 133. 1935. 46 pp.

      Describes women employed in beauty shops in Philadel-
      phia, New Orleans, and Columbus as young, working long
      hours, and experiencing significant contrasts in earn-
      ings, with high proportions receiving low wages and
      virtually all receiving lower wages than men. Women
      were trained in beauty schools, thus paying for their
      training, unlike men who learned as shop apprentices.

387. Johnson, B. Eleanor. *Household Employment in Chicago.*
      U.S. Department of Labor, Women's Bureau. Bulletin
      No. 106. 1933. 62 pp.

      Asserts that domestic service could be improved with
      greater study of the characteristics and needs of em-
      ployers and employees. Household employment is unstan-
      dardized, inefficient, feudal, and suffers from a social
      stigma. Moreover, conditions have not changed appreciably
      in forty years.

388. Katzman, David M. *Seven Days a Week: Women and Domestic
      Service in Industrializing America.* New York: Oxford
      University Press, 1978. 374 pp.

Argues that domestic service failed to be affected by
modernization and industrialization despite the efforts
of reformers.   "The presence of servants permitted tra-
ditionalism to dominate in the organization of the household."   And, while domestic servants were probably as
well off economically and in working conditions as women
employed in factories, they were looked down upon by
working-class and other women, a view which the servants
themselves frequently shared.

389. *Reading List of References on Household Employment.* U.S.
      Department of Labor, Women's Bureau. Bulletins No.
      138 and 154. 1936, 1938. 15, 17 pp.

      Lists books, articles, and pamphlets published between
      1925 and 1935 and earlier on standards, training, place-
      ment, legal status, and views of employers and employees
      in domestic service (updated in 1938).

390. Robinson, Mary V. *Domestic Workers and Their Employment
      Relations: A Study Based on the Records of the Domestic
      Efficiency Association of Baltimore, Maryland.* U.S.
      Department of Labor, Women's Bureau. Bulletin No. 39.
      1924. 87 pp.

      Shows that both servants and housekeepers need train-
      ing, that the household needs organization to increase
      the efficiency of domestic service, and that women who
      have organized in clubs and societies can also organize
      for the improvement of domestic work.

391. Salmon, Lucy Maynard. *Domestic Service.* New York: The
      Macmillan Company, 1897. 307 pp. Reprint. New York:
      Arno Press, 1972.

      Wants domestic service recognized "as part of the
      great industrial questions of the day" and therefore
      subject to economic analysis. Social stigma should be
      removed from domestic service. Such work should be
      taken out of the house of the employer to simplify house-
      hold management and provide greater flexibility in house-
      hold employments. And domestic work should be put on a
      business basis.

392. Scribner, Grace. "Those Who Serve--How Long Is Their
      Day?" *Life and Labor,* 9 (April 1919): 88.

      Documents extremely long working hours of servants.
      Argues that there is no hope of improvement except

through aroused Christian consciousness which will in-
dignantly demand change.

393. Strasser, Susan M. "Never Done: The Ideology and Tech-
      nology of Household Work, 1850-1930." Ph.D. disser-
      tation, State University of New York at Stony Brook,
      1977. 438 pp.

      Argues that capitalist economic development fundamen-
      tally altered the nature of household work "by raising
      the standard of living and creating new economic roles
      for married women." Reformers' attacks on boarding and
      resident domestic service, two pre-capitalist household
      practices, "contributed to the development of a new
      ideology for the household under advanced capitalism."

394. Watson, Amy E. *Household Employment in Philadelphia.*
      U.S. Department of Labor, Women's Bureau. Bulletin
      No. 93. 1932. 85 pp.

      Concludes that conditions of work in households need
      improvement, particularly in the reduction of hours of
      work and frequency of time off. Lack of freedom and
      privacy is a major consideration for live-in employees.
      And employers of household help should become aware of
      the benefits of efficiency and scientific management.

OCCUPATIONS: INDUSTRIAL

395. Abbott, Edith. "Employment of Women in Industries:
      Cigar-making, Its History and Present Tendencies."
      Journal of Political Economy, 15 (January 1907): 1-25.

      Argues that low wages for women cigar-makers are not
      driving men from the industry. Women dominated the
      early industry, with a temporary use of skilled male
      workers in the mid-nineteenth century. Recent employ-
      ment of women is a factor of machine manufacture rather
      than lower wages; men are being displaced by machines
      rather than by women.

396. ————. "Women in Industry: The Manufacture of Boots
      and Shoes." *American Journal of Sociology*, 15 (Novem-
      ber 1909): 335-60.

      Shows how women obtained employment opportunities in
      the boot and shoe industry when the introduction of
      machinery and the division of labor permitted the use
      of unskilled labor. Machines, rather than women, have

replaced skilled male laborers outside of New England,
but New England women have expanded their skills and
taken their jobs from home to factory.

397. ————, and Sophonisba P. Breckenridge. "Women in Industry: The Chicago Stockyards." *Journal of Political
Economy*, 19 (October 1911): 632-54.

Examines the increase in numbers of women working in
the meat-packing industry since 1870 but not in tasks
directly competitive with men. Women work in unskilled
occupations where wages are low and employment irregular.
Unionization of women workers has been retarded by employers and by unsympathetic union men.

398. Anderson, Mary. "Women Workers in Textiles." *American
Federationist*, 36 (June 1929): 696-99.

Argues that solutions to workers' problems will also
benefit employers and the nation. Cooperative action
by workers and business should result in improvement of
wages, hours, night work, and unemployment.

399. Baine, C.L. "Women in the Shoe Industry." *Life and
Labor*, 3 (June 1913): 164-67.

Exhibits the equal treatment of women with men in shoe
manufacture and the early prominence of those few women
who became unionized.

400. Best, Ethel L., and Ethel Erickson. *A Survey of Laundries and Their Women Workers in 23 Cities.* U.S. Department of Labor, Women's Bureau. Bulletin No. 78.
1930. 164 pp.

Claims that the laundry industry is rapidly becoming
one of the major woman-employing industries; therefore,
the Women's Bureau collected information on wages, hours,
and working conditions in laundries as well as data
descriptive of the women in the trade.

401. Bryner, Edna. *Dressmaking and Millinery.* Cleveland:
The Survey Committee of the Cleveland Foundation,
1916. 133 pp.

Argues that since so many young women seek employment
in the sewing trades, they should receive training in a
trade school for one year or courses over two years to
prepare them for that employment. Collects statistical
and personal data on wages, regularity of employment,

and conditions of working and living for dressmakers and milliners in Cleveland.

402. "Buttons--Pearl Buttons." *Life and Labor*, 1 (May 1911): 143-45.

Describes conditions in button-making including putrid water and blood poisoning from cuts, and reports that plants were closed when workers began to unionize.

403. "The Candy Workers of Boston." *Life and Labor*, 3 (September 1913): 261-63.

Reports the successful strike of candy workers with union backing.

404. "The Day's Work in a Cannery." *Life and Labor*, 2 (November 1912): 326-28.

Describes in diary-style the experiences of a reporter who posed as a cannery worker to obtain information, with emphasis on fatigue, lack of privacy in toilets, and cut fingers of workers. (*Life and Labor* printed similar articles on other occupations in later issues, particularly those by "The Pilgrim" on packing houses, laundries, telephone exchanges, cigar-making, department stores, and others.)

405. Filley, Jane, and Theresa Mitchell. *Consider the Laundry Workers*. New York: League of Women Shoppers, Inc., 1937. 63 pp.

Exposes conditions of working and living among employees in steam and hand laundries.

406. Katzor, Clara. "Shoemaker's Story." *American Federationist*, 36 (August 1929): 978-79.

Claims that more women found employment in the shoe industry because of mechanization and the resultant division of labor. The industry was finally unionized.

407. Manning, Caroline, and Harriet A. Byrne. *The Effects on Women of Changing Conditions in the Cigar and Cigarette Industries*. U.S. Department of Labor, Women's Bureau. Bulletin No. 100. 1932. 184 pp.

Compiles information on the characteristics and conditions of women workers in cigar and cigarette manufacture, with emphasis on unemployment and displacement caused by plant removal, automation, and industrial conditions.

408. Nestor, Agnes. "A Day's Work Making Gloves." *Life and Labor*, 2 (May 1912): 137-39.

    Describes hours, penalties, and division of labor in the glove trade, with emphasis on piecework. Praises the impact of the union which held out for solidarity rather than money and obtained employer agreement to let one person do all the closing work on a single glove.

409. Oates, Mary J. *The Role of the Cotton Textile Industry in the Economic Development of the American Southeast: 1900-1940*. New York: Arno Press, 1975. 221 pp.

    Questions the role of the dominant textile manufacturing industry as a genuine transforming agent, since the Piedmont remained the most underdeveloped region in the nation in 1940.

410. Perry, Lorinda. *The Millinery Trade in Boston and Philadelphia: A Study of Women in Industry*. Binghamton, N.Y.: The Vail-Ballow Co., 1916. 122 pp.

    Urges society to regulate the employment of women because of the social consequences of women's work. Women do not compete with men for wages.

411. Pidgeon, Mary Elizabeth. *The Employment of Women in Slaughtering and Meat Packing*. U.S. Department of Labor, Women's Bureau. Bulletin No. 88. 1932. 208 pp.

    Compiles information on characteristics of women workers in various parts of the meat industry as well as their hours, wages, and conditions of labor.

412. Robinson, Mary V. *Primer of Problems in the Millinery Industry*. U.S. Department of Labor, Women's Bureau. Bulletin NO. 179. 1941. 47 pp.

    Popularizes the portion of Bulletin No. 169 (item 591) which describes conditions of employment.

413. van Kleeck, Mary. *Artificial Flower Makers*. New York: Russell Sage Foundation, Survey Associates, Inc., 1913. 261 pp.

    Gathers statistical and interview data on women who made artificial flowers, including numbers of manufacturers and employees, the industrialization process, ages, percentages, attitudes, irregularity of work, and wages.

414.   ———. "Changes in Women's Work in Binderies." *The*
       Economic Position of Women: Proceedings of the Amer-
       ican Academy of Political Science, 1 (1910): 27-30.

       Argues that the introduction of machinery was the main
       cause of unstable employment after the turn of the cen-
       tury. Mechanization at first opened a male-dominated
       trade to women who were then themselves replaced by
       machines.

415.   ———. *A Seasonal Industry: A Study of the Millinery*
       Trade in New York. New York: Russell Sage Foundation,
       1917. 276 pp.

       Argues that irregularity of employment and inadequate
       wages keep workers who make women's hats constantly on
       the verge of debt or of obtaining assistance from others.

416.   ———. *Women in the Bookbinding Trade*. New York:
       Russell Sage Foundation, Survey Associates, Inc.,
       1913. 270 pp.

       Clarifies information on wages and conditions of work
       in bookbinding by adding consideration of the irregular-
       ity of work in this occupation.

417.   West, Jackie. "The Factory Slaves." *New Society*, 39
       (24 February 1977): 384-85.

       Claims that women in a tobacco assembling and packing
       plant endure noise, smells, tedium, and machine pressure
       because wages and facilities are good and jobs are hard
       to find. Women's attitudes are shaped by the knowledge
       of choices available.

OCCUPATIONS: WHITE COLLAR

418.   Best, Ethel L. *The Change from Manual to Dial Operation*
       in the Telephone Industry. U.S. Department of Labor,
       Women's Bureau. Bulletin No. 110. 1933. 15 pp.

       Praises the telephone industry for planning the tech-
       nological changes from manual to dial operation so far
       in advance and so well that few operators lost their
       jobs and those who did were temporary workers engaged
       for only the last few months prior to the adjustment.

419.   Butler, Elizabeth Beardsley. *Saleswomen in Mercantile*
       Stores, 1909. New York: Russell Sage Foundation,
       Survey Associates, Inc., 1912. 217 pp.

Surveys training, working conditions, and beneficiary societies among saleswomen in a study conducted for the Consumers' League of Maryland.

420. Byrne, Harriet A. *Women Office Workers in Philadelphia.* U.S. Department of Labor, Women's Bureau. Bulletin No. 96. 1932. 14 pp.

Compiles data on the age, schooling, and occupational histories of women employed in offices in Philadelphia, as well as their hours, wages, and compensation in addition to wages.

421. ————. *Women Who Work in Offices.* U.S. Department of Labor, Women's Bureau. Bulletin No. 132. 1935. 27 pp.

Describes the personal characteristics as well as hours and wages of women employed in offices and seeking such employment.

422. Crawford, Caroline. "The Hello Girls of Boston." *Life and Labor,* 2 (September 1912): 260–64.

Exposes the long hours and nervous strain on telephone operators who organized and threatened to strike, and attempts to rally public opinion in their favor.

423. Davies, Margery. "Woman's Place Is at the Typewriter: The Feminization of the Clerical Labor Force." *Radical America,* 8 (July–August 1974): 1–25.

Argues that the rapid growth and consolidation of American corporations at the end of the nineteenth century required expansion of the clerical labor force. Employers hired educated women who took office jobs because they paid better than other work for which women would be hired, although women filled low-level dead-end jobs while men passed through a clerical period en route to management.

424. ————. "Woman's Place Is at the Typewriter: The Feminization of Clerical Workers and Changes in Clerical Work in the United States: 1870–1930." Ph.D. dissertation, Brandeis University, 1979. 530 pp.

Concludes that between 1880 and 1930 the clerical labor force became divided into low-level workers performing routine tasks under increasing employer control and higher-level private secretaries who were encouraged to exercise independence and initiative; at the same

time, the clerical labor force changed from predominantly
male to predominantly female. Feminization reinforced
patriarchy, with both clerks and secretaries subordinate
to their employers.

425. Donovan, Frances R. *The Saleslady*. Chicago: University
      of Chicago Press, 1929. 267 pp. Reprint. New York:
      Arno Press, 1974.

      Sees the department store as a community much like a
      small town, with similar mechanisms to restrain and con-
      trol its members. The life of the female department
      store employee is described from the perspective of a
      participant-observer during a summer in New York.

426. Erickson, Ethel. *The Employment of Women in Offices*.
      U.S. Department of Labor, Women's Bureau. Bulletin
      No. 120. 1934. 126 pp.

      Claims that employment of women in clerical and other
      office jobs has expanded more rapidly and is viewed by
      women as more desirable than domestic, industrial, and
      commercial job opportunities. Most such women are
      young and single, work 7 or 7½ hours per day and 39 to
      42 hours per week, with salaries affected by task, type
      of employer, and geographic area.

427. Maher, Amy G. *Bookkeepers, Stenographers and Office
      Clerks in Ohio, 1914 to 1929*. U.S. Department of
      Labor, Women's Bureau. Bulletin No. 95. 1932. 31 pp.

      Shows that the number of clerical workers has almost
      doubled in fifteen years and that the proportion of
      women among clerical workers has increased by almost a
      quarter in the same time, but women clerks continue to
      earn less than men and have received a lower percentage
      of increased earnings than men.

428. Nienburg, Bertha. *The Status of Women in the Government
      Service in 1925*. U.S. Department of Labor, Women's
      Bureau. Bulletin No. 53. 1926. 103 pp.

      Notes that women constitute almost half the employees
      in federal agencies investigated but are clustered in
      low-income positions.

429. ————. *Women in Government Service*. U.S. Department
      of Labor, Women's Bureau. Bulletin No. 8. 1920.
      37 pp.

Argues that women have suffered serious discrimination
in access to positions as well as appointment and entrance salaries as compared to men who work for government. But the Civil Service Commission opened all examinations to both women and men subsequent to receiving
the part of the report on access.

430. Nyswander, Rachel Fester, and Janet M. Hooks. *Employ-
ment of Women in the Federal Government, 1923 to 1939.*
U.S. Department of Labor, Women's Bureau. Bulletin
No. 182. 1941. 60 pp.

Finds the increasing numbers of female employees of
the federal government primarily in clerical rather than
technical or policy-making functions. Specialized training and proficiency, however, are as important in government as in private employment.

431. *Office Work and Office Workers in 1940: Houston, Los
Angeles, Kansas City, Richmond, Philadelphia.* U.S.
Department of Labor, Women's Bureau. Bulletin Nos.
188-1 to 5. 1940-41. 4, 58, 64, 74, 61, 102 pp.

Argues that the number of office workers has risen
more rapidly than any other large occupational group,
therefore requiring concrete information on salaries,
opportunities for advancement, types of offices and
tasks, education and experience, and personnel policies,
which are compiled for the five cities.

432. O'Leary, Iris Prouty. *Department Store Occupations.*
Cleveland: The Survey Committee of the Cleveland Foundation, 1916. 127 pp.

Describes the range of tasks and conditions of work
available in retail sales in department stores.

433. Pidgeon, Mary Elizabeth. *Women in 5-and-10 Cent Stores
and Limited-Price Chain Department Stores.* U.S. Department of Labor, Women's Bureau. Bulletin No. 76.
1930. 56 pp.

Compiles descriptive information on women workers and
their hours and earnings in the rapidly-expanding occupation of salesperson in low-price chain stores.

434. Rotella, Elyce J. "Women's Labor Force Participation
and the Growth of Clerical Employment in the United

States, 1870–1930." Ph.D. dissertation, University
of Pennsylvania, 1977. 348 pp.

Concludes that the dramatic increase in women's share
of clerical employment resulted from increases in the
supply of educated young women and technological changes
in office production.

435. *Women in the Federal Service, 1923–1947: Trends in Em-*
      ployment. U.S. Department of Labor, Women's Bureau.
      Bulletin No. 230-1. 1949. 79 pp.

Shows that increase in federal employment was pro-
portionately greater for women than for men, although
higher proportions of wartime women workers lost their
jobs at the end of the war. Civil service examinations
are open to women and equal pay is established by law,
but women generally do exacting and routine jobs at low
levels.

WAGES, HOURS, AND WORKING CONDITIONS

436. *Activities of the Women's Bureau of the United States.*
      U.S. Department of Labor, Women's Bureau. Bulletin
      No. 86. 1931. 13 pp.

Notes that the Women's Bureau enforces no law but en-
gages in research and dissemination of information regarding employed women, including analysis of their
hours and wages, health and safety, and relevant laws,
as well as studies of particular occupations and industrial topics.

437. Anderson, Mary. "Hours of Work." *American Federation-*
      ist, 32 (September 1925): 769–72.

Argues that excessive hours of labor produce fatigue
and monotony which decrease efficiency. The eight-hour
day not only improves productivity of women workers but
also responds to their great responsibilities off the
job.

438. ————. "Wages of Woman Workers." *Annals of the Amer-*
      ican Academy of Political and Social Science, 81
      (January 1919): 123–29.

Argues that better wages will improve employee productivity and decrease turnover. Wage disputes can be
handled best by collective bargaining and arbitration.

439. ———. "The Women Workers." *American Federationist*,
      32 (November 1925): 1073-76.

      Asserts that women work because of economic necessity;
      a wife's income is a significant portion of total family
      income. Working women earn enough only for current
      necessities, with no opportunity to save or plan for
      future emergencies.

440. ———. "Working Conditions." *American Federationist*,
      32 (October 1925): 946-49.

      Pleads for good working conditions to increase em-
      ployee efficiency. Therefore, where possible, wages,
      hours, and working conditions for women should be im-
      proved for the good of business as well as workers.
      Where hazardous conditions have greater effect on women
      than on men, however, such as in lead poisoning, women
      should not be allowed to work at such occupations.

441. Andrews, Irene Osgood. "Relation of Irregular Employment
      to the Living Wage for Women." *American Labor Legis-
      lation Review*, 5 (June 1914): 287-418.

      Shows that rate of pay is not the same as actual earn-
      ings for women workers because of the irregularity of
      their employment, which is worse than that of men. More-
      over, employers do not think of women as permanent em-
      ployees because so many spend only a few years in the
      labor market.

442. Best, Ethel L. *The Employment of Women in Vitreous
      Enameling*. U.S. Department of Labor, Women's Bureau.
      Bulletin No. 101. 1932. 61 pp.

      Claims that women are vulnerable to lead poisoning,
      which can damage them and their children, because of the
      content of enamel used on stoves; a third of women work-
      ers who apply such enamel show symptoms of lead poison-
      ing.

443. ———. *Hours, Earning, and Employment in Cotton Mills*.
      U.S. Department of Labor, Women's Bureau. Bulletin
      No. 111. 1933. 78 pp.

      Examines female workers in textile mills in South
      Carolina, Maine, and Texas showing them working almost
      ten hours per day and fifty-five hours per week for
      wages well below the recommended levels, and experienc-
      ing irregular demand for their labor with mills closing

or laying off workers for part of the year but running
extra night shifts at other times.

444. ———. *Piecework in the Silk-Dress Industry: Earnings,
Hours, and Production.* U.S. Department of Labor,
Women's Bureau. Bulletin No. 141. 1936. 68 pp.

Argues that minimum wages increase the weekly earning
of pieceworkers, while uniform and reduced hours of labor do not hurt productivity.

445. ———. *A Study of Change from 8 to 6 Hours of Work.*
U.S. Department of Labor, Women's Bureau. Bulletin
No. 105. 1933. 14 pp.

Claims that both management and women workers prefer
a work arrangement of four six-hour shifts to three
eight-hour shifts because of less fatigue, greater efficiency, and more time for family needs, recreation,
rest, and self-improvement.

446. ———, and Arthur T. Sutherland. *Women's Hours and
Wages in the District of Columbia in 1937.* U.S. Department of Labor, Women's Bureau. Bulletin No. 153.
1937. 44 pp.

Summarizes the hourly and weekly earnings of women
employed in laundries, dry cleaners, manufacturing,
beauty shops, retail stores, hotels, restaurants, offices, and telephone services.

447. Bowen, Louise de Koven. *The Department Store Girl,
Based on Interviews with 200 Girls.* Chicago: Juvenile
Protection Association, 1911. 15 pp.

Argues that long hours lead to physical and moral
breakdown, that most girls earn too little to live on
their own, and that conditions force girls to choose
between substandard living conditions and vice.

448. Brissenden, Paul. *Earnings of Factory Workers, 1899-
1927: An Analysis of Pay-Roll Statistics.* Washington,
D.C.: Government Printing Office, 1929. 424 pp.

Shows how increases in earnings before World War I
were cancelled out by increases in cost of living, but
between 1914 and 1927 wage-earners experienced unprecedented gains of nearly 4 percent per year. Elaborate
compilations of tables, charts, and diagrams document
wages and earnings from 1899 to 1927.

449. Brooks, Tom. "The Terrible Triangle Fire." *American Heritage*, 8 (August 1957): 54-57, 110-11.

     Recounts the story of the fire at the Triangle Shirt-waist Company on 25 March 1911 which "burned away a curtain covering the appalling state of affairs existing in the factory district of New York City and elsewhere."

450. Brown, Emily C. *Industrial Accidents to Men and Women*. U.S. Department of Labor, Women's Bureau. Bulletin No. 81. 1930. 46 pp.

     Concludes that women workers had fewer accidents than men, fewer fatalities, more permanent partial disabil-ities, and about the same proportion of permanent total disabilities.

451. Bruere, Martha Bensley. "The Triangle Fire." *Life and Labor*, 1 (May 1911): 137-41.

     Dramatizes the disaster of the Triangle Fire from per-sonal observations. The 1909 garment workers' strike did not produce improvement in conditions of labor, and the new Triangle shop was also not fireproof. Labor is skeptical of promises of reform by civic leaders.

452. Butler, Elizabeth Beardsley. *Women and the Trades: Pittsburgh, 1907-1908*. New York: Charities Publication Committee, 1909. 440 pp.

     Collects statistical and personal data about occupa-tions, wages, hours, health, costs of living, and con-ditions among employed women in Pittsburgh.

453. Byrne, Harriet A. *The Health and Safety of Women in Industry*. U.S. Department of Labor, Women's Bureau. Bulletin No. 136. 1935. 23 pp.

     Argues that sickness is a prominent cause of destitu-tion and dependency because of loss of earning power and cost of medical care. Attention to industrial standards of safety and health would reduce risk for the one in fifty workers incapacitated by illness.

454. ————, and Bertha Blair. *Industrial Home Work in Rhode Island, with Special Reference to the Lace Industry*. U.S. Department of Labor, Women's Bureau. Bulletin No. 131. 1935. 27 pp.

     Concludes that home work makes a significant, if small, contribution to family income; that wages are low; and that most households have more than one home worker.

455.   Coman, Katharine. "A Sweated Industry." *Life and Labor*,
       1 (January 1911): 13-15.

       Exposes conditions which led to the uprising of the
       Chicago garment workers, including seasonal work, un-
       organized trade, competition by recent immigrants, sweat-
       shops, lack of legal protection such as the minimum wage,
       unjust fines, differing piece rates, and petty tyrannies
       of foremen, in an appeal for citizen support of striking
       workers.

456.   Correll, Marie. *Industrial Injuries to Women in 1928
       and 1929, Compared with Injuries to Men*. U.S. Depart-
       ment of Labor, Women's Bureau. Bulletin No. 102.
       1933. 33 pp.

       Summarizes accident data and concludes that women suf-
       fer fewer injuries than men, in both absolute and rela-
       tive terms: the severity of injuries is generally similar
       regardless of sex. Women are more likely to be injured
       by machinery or falls.

457.   —————. *Sanitary Drinking Facilities with Special Ref-
       erence to Drinking Fountains*. U.S. Department of
       Labor, Women's Bureau. Bulletin No. 87. 1931. 26 pp.

       Says that most drinking fountains currently in use do
       not meet essential sanitation standards, and most State
       laws and regulations do little more than prohibit use
       of a common cup.

458.   Davis, Philip. "Women in the Cloak Trade." *American
       Federationist*, 12 (October 1905): 745-47.

       Claims that women in the cloak trade are better off
       working in shops than at home, but both groups suffer
       from irregular employment, unjust fines, contractors
       who abscond with funds, unstable rates for piece work,
       mistreatment of "green" girls, and the belief that they
       are working for "pin money."

459.   Dorr, Rheta Childe. "Bullying the Woman Worker."
       Harper's Weekly, 51 (30 March 1907): 458-59.

       Exhibits ruthless oppression of women working in shops
       and factories and violation of the law by employers.

460.   *Earnings in the Woman's and Children's Apparel Industry
       in the Spring of 1939*. U.S. Department of Labor, Wo-
       men's Bureau. Bulletin No. 175. 1940. 91 pp.

Compiles information on hours and earnings of union and non-union women employed in making dresses, blouses, children's outerwear, corsets and similar garments, underwear, and nightwear.

461. *The Employment of Women in the Sewing Trades of Connecticut: Preliminary Report.* U.S. Department of Labor, Women's Bureau. Bulletin No. 97. 1932. 13 pp.

Summarizes information on the characteristics and conditions of women employed in garment manufacture in Connecticut, including their hours, earnings, migration from factory to factory, experience with contract shops, and payment of piece work or time work.

462. Hamilton, Alice. *Women Workers and Industrial Poisons.* U.S. Department of Labor, Women's Bureau. Bulletin No. 37. 1926. 5 pp.

Claims that women are more susceptible to poisoning than men and that lead poisoning in mothers frequently leads to miscarriage or early death of children.

463. Henry, Alice. "The Fire Hazard: Report, Factory Investigating Commission, N.Y. State." *Life and Labor*, 3 (January 1913): 6-8.

Popularizes results of the state inquiry into dangerous working conditions (item 484).

464. ————. "Mrs. Winifred O'Reilly." *Life and Labor*, 1 (May 1911): 132-36.

Uses O'Reilly as an example of raised consciousness about sweating system and need for women to have the vote.

465. ————. "The Way Out." *Life and Labor*, 2 (April 1912): 120-21.

Appeals to a traditional sense of morality to condemn unsafe shop conditions and "murder by the remorseless pursuit of profits." The solution is industrial and political organization.

466. Herstein, Lillian. "Women Discuss Wages." *American Federationist*, 36 (August 1929): 949-59.

Demonstrates how women's earnings lag significantly behind men's despite increases in average hourly earnings

and the cost of living, largely because of irregularity
of women's employment. Seasonal workers such as teachers undermine regular employment for food workers. And
trade unions have failed to organize women for their own
protection.

467.   *Home Work in Bridgeport, Connecticut.* U.S. Department
       of Labor, Women's Bureau. Bulletin No. 9. 1920.
       35 pp.

       Argues that home work should be abolished, workers
       should not be obliged to bear overhead expenses of manu-
       facture, and the system includes many problems such as
       unsanitary conditions and mistakes by unsupervised work-
       ers. The community should prohibit such work or regulate
       it strictly regarding wages and working conditions.

468.   *Hours and Conditions of Work for Women in Industry in
       Virginia.* U.S. Department of Labor, Women's Bureau.
       Bulletin No. 10. 1920. 32 pp.

       Examines Virginia industries, showing that women there
       work more than eight hours a day or more than half a
       day on Saturday, are not allowed at least thirty minutes
       for a meal, and are employed between midnight and 6 a.m.
       Virginia industries also lack adequate toilet facilities,
       washing facilities, drinking water, cloakrooms, seats,
       and protection from exposure to dust and fumes.

469.   *Industrial Accidents to Women in New Jersey, Ohio, and
       Wisconsin.* U.S. Department of Labor, Women's Bureau.
       Bulletin No. 60. 1927. 316 pp.

       Compiles statistics and interview material on female
       victims of industrial accidents by cause of accident,
       frequency, severity, injury, disability, and effects on
       victims and dependents.

470.   *Iowa Women in Industry.* U.S. Department of Labor, Wo-
       men's Bureau. Bulletin No. 19. 1922. 73 pp.

       Collects data regarding daily and weekly hours of
       work, rest days and periods, piecework, working condi-
       tions, occupational opportunities, and training by the
       industries and by the state. Evidence presented should
       encourage the people of Iowa to correct unsatisfactory
       conditions since voluntary compliance with the Women's
       Bureau's standards by some employers shows their prac-
       ticality.

471. Kingsbury, Susan M., and Mabelle Moses. *Licensed Workers in Industrial Home Work in Massachusetts*. Commonwealth of Massachusetts, State Board of Labor and Industry, Industrial Bulletin, No. 4. Boston: Wright and Potter, 1915. 153 pp.

Examines industries, conditions, places of work, nativity of workers, family circumstances, and earnings of women in home work.

472. *Labor Standards and Competitive Market Conditions in the Canned Goods Industry*. U.S. Department of Labor, Women's Bureau. Bulletin No. 87. 1941. 34 pp.

Argues that regions which pay high wages to workers in canneries can compete with medium- or low-wage regions only on the basis of quality of goods; expansion of the canning industry in low-wage regions leads to its curtailment where wages are high.

473. *Lost Time and Labor Turnover in Cotton Mills: A Study of Cause and Effect*. U.S. Department of Labor, Women's Bureau. Bulletin No. 52. 1926. 203 pp.

Concludes that personal illness was the greatest single cause of time lost from work by women, that women in their thirties lost the most time, and that married women lost almost twice as much time as single women. Most such women lived in families with two wage-earners. More than half the workers changed jobs, especially in large communities, primarily for personal reasons, particularly home duties and illness.

474. MacLean, Annie Marion. *Wage-Earning Women*. New York: The Macmillan Company, 1910. 202 pp.

Uses factual and statistical information on employed women by geographic region and occupation to show significant disadvantages for such women, particularly low wages and dangers to health. While young women could improve their situation by acquiring skills, many lack interest because they see themselves as temporary workers. Betterment bodies should press for improved and uniform state legislation and employer cooperation to improve working and living conditions.

475. Manning, Caroline. *Fluctuation of Employment in the Radio Industry*. U.S. Department of Labor, Women's Bureau. Bulletin No. 83. 1913. 63 pp.

Demonstrates that employment in the radio industry is
seasonal, resulting in lowered average income and high
rates of employee turnover.

476. ————. *Hours and Earnings in Tobacco Stemmeries*. U.S.
Department of Labor, Women's Bureau. Bulletin No.
127. 1934. 29 pp.

Describes variations in hours and earnings in the
several kinds of tobacco-stemming plants to provide
material for a code of fair competition in the industry.

477. ————, and Harriet A. Byrne. *The Employment of Women
in the Sewing Trades of Connecticut: Hours and Earnings, Employment Fluctuation, Home Work*. U.S. Department of Labor, Women's Bureau. Bulletin No. 109.
1935. 45 pp.

Compiles information on weekly and annual wages, hours
scheduled and worked, conditions of labor, especially
lighting, and personal characteristics of women employed
in the garment trades in Connecticut, both those in
factories and those who work at home.

478. Mettert, Margaret T. *Industrial Injuries to Women and
Men, 1932 to 1934*. U.S. Department of Labor, Women's
Bureau. Bulletin No. 160. 1938. 37 pp.

Concludes that injuries for women increased although
men continued to suffer the most serious injuries. In-
jured women received lower wages and compensation than
men.

479. ————. *Industrial Injuries to Women in 1930 and 1931
Compared with Injuries to Men*. U.S. Department of
Labor, Women's Bureau. Bulletin No. 129. 1935. 57
pp.

Claims that women's injuries decreased less than men's
because men suffered unemployment in dangerous jobs, but
women still had absolutely and relatively fewer injuries
than men. Since women received lower wages than men,
even for comparable disabilities women recieved much
less compensation than men.

480. ————. *Injuries to Women in Personal Service Occupations in Ohio*. U.S. Department of Labor, Women's Bureau. Bulletin No. 151. 1937. 23 pp.

Describes numbers, nature, severity, cause, and victims of injuries to workers in laundries, dry cleaners, hotels, restaurants, barber and beauty shops, and households.

481. ————. *The Occurrence and Prevention of Occupational Diseases Among Women.* U.S. Department of Labor, Women's Bureau. Bulletin No. 184. 1941. 46 pp.

Shows that state compensation laws have doubled between 1935 and 1949, and more than half the States have established industrial-hygiene divisions.

482. Naden, Corrine J. *The Triangle Shirtwaist Fire, March 25, 1911: The Blaze that Changed an Industry.* New York: Franklin Watts, 1971. 58 pp.

Argues that the Triangle Fire galvanized garment workers, unionists, and reformers to action. Factual detail is offered on sweatshops, safety, unions, fire, and reforms as well as the Triangle incident.

483. New York State Factory Investigating Commission. *Fourth Report of the Factory Investigating Commission, 1914.* 5 vols. Transmitted to the Legislature February 15, 1915. Albany: J.B. Lyon Company, 1915.

Continues items 484, 485, 486.

484. ————. *Preliminary Report of the Factory Investigating Commission, 1912.* Transmitted to the Legislature March 1, 1912. Albany: The Argus Company, 1912.

Collects evidence regarding factory and store working conditions in New York as part of an extensive survey intended to provide the basis for reform legislation dealing with safeguards of the health, lives, and safety of workers, as well as length of the workday and week, and conditions of labor.

485. ————. *Second Report of the Factory Investigating Commission, 1913.* Transmitted to the Legislature January 15, 1913. Albany: J.B. Lyon Company, 1913.

Continues item 484.

486. ————. *Third Report of the Factory Investigating Commission, 1914.* Transmitted to the Legislature February 14, 1914. Albany: J.B. Lyon Company, 1914.

Continues items 484 and 485.

487. Persons, C.E. "Women's Work and Wages in the United
     States." *Quarterly Journal of Economics*, 29 (Febru-
     ary 1915): 201-34.

     Argues that women receive low wages because they are
     immobile, young, inexperienced, temporary workers whose
     wages only supplement family income. Moreover, women
     face competition from immigrants who are willing to ac-
     cept low wages and poor working conditions. Possible
     solutions include minimum wage laws, industrial educa-
     tion, immigration restriction, and raising the legal
     working age.

488. Peterson, Agnes L. *A Survey of the Shoe Industry in
     New Hampshire.* U.S. Department of Labor, Women's Bu-
     reau. Bulletin No. 121. 1935. 100 pp.

     Describes the shoe manufacturing trade, with emphasis
     on irregularity of employment, and hence earnings, as
     well as hazardous working conditions.

489. Pidgeon, Mary Elizabeth. *Wages of Women in 13 States.*
     U.S. Department of Labor, Women's Bureau. Bulletin
     No. 85. 1931. 211 pp.

     Argues that "geographic location and industrial de-
     velopment of a State and the standards in the industries
     that prevailed there" influence women's wages more than
     fluctuating business conditions.

490. ————. *Women in Industry: A Series of Papers to Aid
     Study Groups.* U.S. Department of Labor, Women's Bu-
     reau. Bulletins No. 91 and 164. 1931, 1935, 1938.
     79, 85 pp.

     Synthesizes data on women workers, their character-
     istics, employment and lack of it, conditions of labor,
     wages, hours, and similar topics organized as brief
     stimuli to group information and discussion.

491. Rich, Frances Ivins. *Wage-Earning Girls in Cincinnati:
     The Wages, Employment, Housing, Food, Recreation and
     Education of a Sample Group.* Cincinnati: Helen S.
     Trounstine Foundation and the Y.W.C.A., 1927. 79 pp.

     Shows that significant numbers of young women earn
     less than a living wage. This practice cannot be jus-
     tified on the ground that working girls live at home
     since 20 percent do not and, of those who do, two-thirds
     contribute regularly to their families. Moreover, these

women need proper housing facilities, earnings sufficient to acquire healthful food and adequate recreation, and educational development.

492. Schweitzer, David J. *A Brief Summary of Investigations and Inquiries Made Between the Years 1905 and 1915 by Government and Private Agencies into Typical Industries Prevalent in the State of New York and Affording Work to Large Numbers of Women.* New York: Council of Jewish Women, Department of Immigrant Aid, 1916. 45 pp.

Brings together statistical information on the hours, seasons, processes, and other conditions of labor in various industries.

493. Smalz, Rebecca G., and Arcadia N. Phillips. *Hours and Earnings in the Leather-Glove Industry.* U.S. Department of Labor, Women's Bureau. Bulletin No. 119. 1934. 32 pp.

Describes factory and home workers who make leather gloves in New York, the Middle West, and California with emphasis on their hours and wages, as the basis for developing an NRA code.

494. "Some Facts Regarding Unorganized Working Women in the Sweated Industries." *Life and Labor,* 5 (January 1915): 4.

Summarizes highlights of information on candy, paper box, canning, and department store workers from the Preliminary Report of the New York State Factory Investigating Commission (item 484).

495. Stein, Leon. *The Triangle Fire.* Philadelphia: J.B. Lippincott Company, 1962. 224 pp.

Reconstructs the circumstances under which 146 garment workers died as a result of fire in the Asch Building, headquarters of the Triangle Shirtwaist Company, on 25 March 1911.

496. Sullivan, Mary Loretta. *Women in Texas Industries: Hours, Wages, Working Conditions, and Home Work.* U.S. Department of Labor, Women's Bureau. Bulletin No. 126. 1936. 81 pp.

Collects data showing that women workers in Texas have long work days and weeks and low wages with significant differences by ethnicity.

497. Sutherland, Arthur T. *Earnings and Hours in Pacific
     Coast Fish Canneries.* U.S. Department of Labor, Wo-
     men's Bureau. Bulletin No. 186. 1941. 30 pp.

     Compiles descriptive and statistical information on
     hours, wages, length of season, types of work, and
     workers in canneries.

498. ———. *Hours and Earnings in Certain Men's-Wear In-
     dustries.* U.S. Department of Labor, Women's Bureau.
     Bulletin Nos. 163-1 to 6. 1938-1939. 27, 10, 8, 9,
     29, 22 pp.

     Summarizes the hourly and weekly hours and earnings
     of women employed in various aspects of the manufacture
     of men's clothing.

499. ———. *Wages and Hours in Drugs and Medicines and in
     Certain Toilet Preparations.* U.S. Department of Labor,
     Women's Bureau. Bulletin No. 171. 1939. 19 pp.

     Describes the workers, tasks, hourly and weekly earn-
     ings, method of payment, hours, and training of opera-
     tives manufacturing drugs, medicines, and beauty products.

500. Taussig, F.W. "Minimum Wages for Women." *Quarterly
     Journal of Economics*, 30 (May 1916): 411-42.

     Argues that wages of working women can be best im-
     proved by a public regulating commission which would
     eliminate wage-depressing employers and apply the best
     practices to the social and industrial situation as a
     whole.

501. Tentler, Leslie. "Occupational Segregation and the
     Female Work Experience, 1900-1930." Paper, Third
     Berkshire Conference on History of Women, Bryn Mawr
     College, 10 June 1976.

     Argues that the work force participation aspect of
     working-class culture shows an unambiguous sex-segregated
     experience with male dominance and female dependence.
     In the labor force, women have frequently been unskilled,
     in search of work, and subject to petty discriminations;
     and they have rarely challenged these conditions.

502. Trax, Lola Carson. "Working Women in Maryland." *Life
     and Labor*, 3 (April 1913): 100-4.

     Reports statistics on numbers, wages, hours, and work-
     ing conditions of women in Maryland. These women lack

organization and should follow the example of white goods workers in New York.

503. van Kleeck, Mary. *Facts about Wage-Earners in the United States Census*. New York: The New York School of Philanthropy, 1915. 39 pp.

Extracts census data regarding sex ratio of occupational and age groups, nativity and race, size of manufacturing establishments, and weekly hours of labor.

504. *Wages of Candy Makers in Philadelphia in 1919*. U.S. Department of Labor, Women-in-Industry Service. Bulletin No. 4. 1919. 46 pp.

Pleads for the candy trade itself to establish a sanitary board representing management, workers, and the public to survey the industry and recommend reasonable standards. Moreover, workers in this industry should have the protection of the minimum wage since their income is low, although improving, and their work is irregular.

505. Willett, Mabel Hurd. *The Employment of Women in the Clothing Trade*. New York: Columbia University Press, 1902. 207 pp.

Argues that it is possible to improve conditions for garment workers through spontaneous increase in the size of shops or the number of factories, more rigid interpretations of existing laws, and trade unionism.

506. *Women in Alabama Industries: A Study of Hours, Wages, and Working Conditions*. U.S. Department of Labor, Women's Bureau. Bulletin No. 34. 1924. 86 pp.

Examines Alabama's industrialization which is comparatively new but will continue to grow, thereby requiring attention to regulation of the circumstances under which women work. Alabama does not limit daily or weekly hours; women lack protection regarding ventilation, lighting, posture, and sanitation; and wages fail to pay for minimum living expenses.

507. *Women in Arkansas Industries: A Study of Hours, Wages, and Working Conditions*. U.S. Department of Labor, Women's Bureau. Bulletin No. 26. 1923. 86 pp.

Shows that Arkansas remains primarily agrarian, with industrial employment for women still in its infancy; with a lack of pressure on business, there is no incen-

tive to extend working hours beyond the legal limitation.
Working conditions (cleanliness, sanitation, seating),
however, are unsatisfactory, and both hours and working
conditions need better inspection.

508. *Women in the Candy Industry in Chicago and St. Louis:*
      A Study of Hours, Wages and Working Conditions in
      1920-1921. U.S. Department of Labor, Women's Bureau.
      Bulletin No. 25. 1923. 72 pp.

      Finds Chicago more attractive than St. Louis in offer-
      ing superior hours, wages, and working conditions in the
      candy manufacturing industry. Postwar depression and
      seasonal employment reduced wages; piece workers earned
      more than time workers, but in general, wages remained
      inadequate.

509. *Women in Delaware Industries: A Study of Hours, Wages,*
      and Working Conditions. U.S. Department of Labor,
      Women's Bureau. Bulletin No. 58. 1927. 156 pp.

      Demonstrates that Delaware has a low standard of legal
      protection for employed women, but many employers have
      better hours than those required by law, except in res-
      taurants and the canning industry. Wages are lower than
      in other states, and plant conditions are generally poor
      except in canneries where sanitation is better.

510. *Women in Florida Industries.* U.S. Department of Labor,
      Women's Bureau. Bulletin No. 80. 1930. 113 pp.

      Shows that hours tend to be longer and wages lower in
      Florida than the recommended standards; working condi-
      tions such as ventilation, strain, and sanitation need
      improvement.

511. *Women in the Fruit-Growing and Canning Industries in*
      the State of Washington: A Study of Hours, Wages, and
      Conditions. U.S. Department of Labor, Women's Bureau.
      Bulletin No. 47. 1926. 223 pp.

      Summarizes information on a sample of women working
      in the outdoor fruit and indoor canning industries, in-
      cluding reasons for working, migrants, housing, time
      worked, earnings, sanitation and service facilities,
      labor turnover, industrial accidents and diseases.

512. *Women in Georgia Industries: A Study of Hours, Wages,*
      and Working Conditions. U.S. Department of Labor,
      Women's Bureau. Bulletin No. 22. 1922. 89 pp.

Concludes that working conditions for women are very poor in Georgia including inadequate wages, excessively long working hours, "a conspicuous lack of the essentials of decency and comfort" in sanitary and service equipment. The statistical evidence displayed here should convince the community or State to create standards and provide for their enforcement.

513. *Women in Illinois Industries: A Study of Hours and Working Conditions.* U.S. Department of Labor, Women's Bureau. Bulletin No. 31. 1926. 108 pp.

Collects information to show that women in Chicago and elsewhere in Illinois frequently worked less than the ten-hour day stipulated by law, but many women experienced turnover, absence for personal reasons, and lost time because of slack work. Working conditions varied but often failed to meet satisfactory levels for health and comfort.

514. *Women in Kentucky Industries, 1937.* U.S. Department of Labor, Women's Bureau. Bulletin No. 162. 1938. 84 pp.

Describes hours and earnings for women in factories, retail stores, commercial laundries and dry cleaners, hotels and restaurants in Kentucky.

515. *Women in Kentucky Industries: A Study of Hours, Wages, and Working Conditions.* U.S. Department of Labor, Women's Bureau. Bulletin No. 29. 1923. 114 pp.

Concludes that Kentucky industries rate poorly in hours, wages, and working conditions for female employees; Kentucky is backward in hours legislation, has no minimum wage law, and fails to enforce adequately even the narrow regulations regarding sanitation, ventilation, lighting, seating, and other working conditions.

516. *Women in Maryland Industries: A Study of Hours and Working Conditions.* U.S. Department of Labor, Women's Bureau. Bulletin No. 24. 1922. 96 pp.

Argues that women working in Maryland need more protection including the eight-hour day and forty-eight-hour week, although such reforms are likely to encounter additional resistance in a state with such a long history of industrialization and entrenched antiquated traditions.

517. *Women in Mississippi Industries: A Study of Hours, Wages, and Working Conditions.* U.S. Department of Labor, Women's Bureau. Bulletin No. 55. 1926. 89 pp.

Demonstrates that conditions of women workers in Mississippi require improvement. Despite state law, actual hours worked were excessive; wage standards fall below other states; and plants lack satisfactory sanitation facilities.

518. *Women in Missouri Industries: A Study of Hours and Wages.* U.S. Department of Labor, Women's Bureau. Bulletin No. 35. 1924. 127 pp.

Exhibits Missouri as moderately progressive in regulating hours, but wage rates and regularity could stand improvement.

519. *Women in New Jersey Industries: A Study of Wages and Hours.* U.S. Department of Labor, Women's Bureau. Bulletin No. 37. 1924. 99 pp.

Claims that New Jersey has not established a high standard of legal protection for wage-earning women. New Jersey law permits a ten-hour day and fifty-four-hour week; prohibition of night work is not yet in effect, and there is no minimum wage law.

520. *Women in Ohio Industries: A Study of Hours and Wages.* U.S. Department of Labor, Women's Bureau. Bulletin No. 44. 1925. 137 pp.

Concludes that Ohio is progressive in its limitations on hours but less satisfactory with regard to wages since it lacks a minimum wage law, and significant proportions of employed women in Ohio do not receive a living wage.

521. *Women in Oklahoma Industries: A Study of Hours, Wages, and Working Conditions.* U.S. Department of Labor, Women's Bureau. Bulletin No. 48. 1926. 118 pp.

Says that Oklahoma has eliminated excessively long hours of labor but has not established the 8-hour standard; overall standards of plant equipment affecting convenience and health of workers are inadequate, as are wage rates. Oklahoma is at the beginning of its industrial development and has the opportunity and responsibility to set high standards.

522. *Women in Rhode Island Industries: A Study of Hours,
     Wages, and Working Conditions.* U.S. Department of
     Labor, Women's Bureau. Bulletin No. 21. 1922. 73
     pp.

     Shows that women employed in industry in Rhode Island
     occupy a middle ground, superior to the most backward
     states but inferior to the most progressive. Therefore,
     labor legislation should be amended and increased, for
     example, to make the eight-hour day universal, to es-
     tablish a minimum living wage in industries which do
     not pay subsistence level, and to create a sanitary
     code as well as better service facilities.

523. *Women in South Carolina Industries: A Study of Hours,
     Wages, and Working Conditions.* U.S. Department of
     Labor, Women's Bureau. Bulletin No. 32. 1923. 128
     pp.

     Demonstrates that the majority of women employed in
     textile and other industries in South Carolina have com-
     paratively poor hours, wages, and working conditions.
     South Carolina regulates hours but still permits the
     sixty-hour week as well as night work; there is no
     minimum wage law and little regulation of working con-
     ditions.

524. *Women in Tennessee Industries: A Study of Hours, Wages,
     and Working Conditions.* U.S. Department of Labor,
     Women's Bureau. Bulletin No. 56. 1927. 120 pp.

     Compiles statistics on wages and earnings, hours and
     rest periods, time lost and overtime, general conditions,
     sanitation, services, and descriptions of the workers.

525. "Women on the Night Shift." *Life and Labor*, 4 (Decem-
     ber 1914): 377-79.

     Condenses volume 2 of the Second Report of the New
     York Factory Investigating Commission (item 485) in
     order to bring factual, statistical information to a
     broader audience than those who read the official re-
     ports. Emphasis is placed on night work and its negative
     effects on women workers.

526. *Women's Employment in Vegetable Canneries in Delaware.*
     U.S. Department of Labor, Women's Bureau. Bulletin
     No. 62. 1927. 47 pp.

     Reprints sections of Bulletin No. 58 (item 509).

527.   *Women's Wages and Hours in Nebraska.* U.S. Department
       of Labor, Women's Bureau. Bulletin No. 178. 1940.
       51 pp.

       Describes hours and earnings for fully and partially
       employed women working in manufacturing, retail stores,
       laundries and dry cleaners, hotels and restaurants,
       beauty parlors, and offices as a basis for formulating
       standards of employment.

528.   *Women's Wages in Kansas.* U.S. Department of Labor,
       Women's Bureau. Bulletin No. 17. 1921. 104 pp.

       Concludes that women workers in Kansas earn insuffi-
       cient hourly, weekly, and annual wages and cannot meet
       their minimum financial obligations, especially to their
       dependents.

529.   "Working Hours of Women in Chicago." *Life and Labor*,
       5 (November 1915): 171-72.

       Claims that half the working women in Chicago would
       be benefitted by a law establishing a nine-hour workday,
       and the other half would benefit from having their hours
       secured by law.

TRADE UNIONS AND WORKER PROTEST

530.   Andrews, Nellie. "Organizing Women." *American Federa-
       tionist*, 36 (August 1929): 976-77.

       Concludes that women are hard to organize in the
       Southern textile industry. Married women cannot attend
       meetings; single girls are too interested in receiving
       wages to appreciate how low the pay is or to organize
       for improvement.

531.   Barnum, Gertrude. "Women in the American Labor Move-
       ment." *American Federationist*, 22 (September 1915):
       731-33.

       Says that trade union women are more interested in
       unionization than in suffrage, social activities, or
       education. Economic freedom has first priority.

532.   Berman, Hyman. "Era of the Protocol: A Chapter in the
       History of the International Ladies' Garment Workers'
       Union, 1910-1916." Ph.D. dissertation, Columbia Uni-
       versity, 1956. 467 pp.

Concludes that protocolism as an effort to get joint
settlement of disputes by cooperation between manufacturers and unions encountered difficulties with a class-
conscious labor force and manufacturers' suspicions about
organized labor's stake in efficient operation. Marxist
union leaders tried to persuade the rank and file that
the protocols were class collaboration.

533. Best, Ethel L. *Conditions of Work in Spin Rooms.* U.S.
Department of Labor, Women's Bureau. Bulletin No. 72.
1929. 39 pp.

Argues that division of labor in spin rooms into tying
threads and cleaning machines was satisfactory from the
viewpoint of employers, but that workers tended to be
absent or leave their jobs more frequently under the
new method.

534. Best, Harry. "Extent of Organization in the Women's
Garment Making Industries of New York." *American
Economic Review,* 9 (December 1919): 776-92.

Claims that the "Protocol" has been violated. The
agreements between garment employers and unions in New
York were intended to protect workers from poor wages
and conditions imposed by subcontractors. But employers
discriminate against union labor and fail to meet protocol requirements regarding conditions of work.

535. Omitted.

536. Bruere, Martha Bensley. "The White Goods Strike."
Life and Labor, 3 (March 1913): 73-75.

Pleads for decent living wage and exposes conditions
in the white goods industry by telling stories of young
Russian and Rumanian Jewesses out on strike.

537. Budish, Jacob M., and George Soule. *The New Unionism
in the Clothing Industry.* New York: Harcourt, Brace
and Howe, 1920. 344 pp.

Shows how difficult it has been to organize women
workers into the trade union movement.

538. Carsel, Wilfred. *A History of the Chicago Ladies' Garment Workers' Union.* Chicago: Normandie House, 1940.
323 pp.

Traces the origins, development, decline, and resurgence of trade unionism among garment workers in Chicago from 1886 to 1939, stressing their struggle "for greater well-being--ever the basic drive of American democracy." For their first thirty years, group activity by workers was small, seasonal, and ineffective. But creation of the Chicago Joint Board of 1914 encouraged solidarity and more effective organization techniques which resulted in a greater voice in the management of the industry.

539. Casper, Bella. "Flower and Feather Workers Take Forward Step." *Life and Labor*, 10 (November 1920): 288-90.

Shows that the small union of flower and feather workers has been a powerful weapon against employers since 1917, winning reduction in hours and enforcement of wage agreements and restrictions on child labor.

540. *Causes of Absence for Men and Women in Four Cotton Mills.* U.S. Department of Labor, Women's Bureau. Bulletin No. 69. 1929. 22 pp.

Claims that women were less likely than men to lose time because of their own illnesses but, when they were ill, lost longer periods of time than men. Men lost significantly more time than women because of accidents, but women lost more time than men because of lack of work.

541. "Chicago at the Front: A Condensed History of the Garment Workers' Strike." *Life and Labor*, 1 (January 1911): 4-13.

Reports on the uprising of garment workers of nine language groups in many separate shops against their "common oppressor" with emphasis on the supportive activities of the Women's Trade Union League.

542. Christman, Elizabeth. "Canvas Glove Workers Win Signal Victory." *Life and Labor*, 6 (March 1916): 40.

Argues that only long struggle and organization will result in the gain of a wage increase without submitting the dispute to a board of arbitration.

543. Cohen, Julius Henry. "Minimizing the Controversy: Industrial Peace in Its Relation to Social and Industrial Efficiency." *Life and Labor*, 3 (April 1913): 105-7.

Supports the Protocol of Peace in the New York garment strikes and asks for recognition that industrial warfare undermines efficiency.

544. Commons, John R. "Women in Unions." *American Federationist*, 13 (June 1906): 383-84.

Shows that women are industrially disadvantaged with low wages and poor unionization because of the competition of immigrant labor and the unwillingness of women to see their work as permanent.

545. Dreier, Mary E. "To Wash or Not to Wash: Aye, There's the Rub." *Life and Labor*, 2 (March 1912): 68-72.

Exposes conditions in the laundry industry in New York City where workers are on strike, with support from the Women's Trade Union League.

546. ———. "The Neckwear Workers and Their Strike." *Life and Labor*, 3 (December 1912): 356-58.

Reports the successful organization and strike of 2,000 women, including abolition of the contract system and partial abolition of home work.

547. Dudley, Amy. "Domestic Workers' Organizations in California." *Life and Labor*, 9 (September 1919): 217-19.

Argues for unionization rather than for protective legislation.

548. "The End of the Struggle." *Life and Labor*, 1 (March 1911): 88-89.

Claims that the sudden end of the Chicago garment workers' strike was a "hunger bargain" achieved without consulting the Women's Trade Union League and others who had supported the strikers. But the net effect of the strike was a sense of solidarity between unorganized immigrant workers and the more Americanized group of organized labor.

549. Falk, Gail. "Women and Unions: A Historical View." *Women's Rights Law Reporter*, 1 (Spring 1973): 54-65.

Concludes that women suffered multiple liabilities in union participation. Male-dominated unions denied women admission, leadership, and organizing supports.

Women suffered divided home and work ties which prevented them from regarding themselves as workers. And low-paid women workers could not afford union dues or money for organizing.

550. Farnham, Rebecca. *Women at Work: A Century of Indus-trial Change.* U.S. Department of Labor, Women's Bu-reau. Bulletin No. 161. 1939. 80 pp.

Revises Bulletin No. 115 (item 369), deleting treat-ment of NRA and adding a section on unions.

551. Field, Amy Walker. "Victory for the Springfield Corset Workers." *Life and Labor,* 5 (November 1915): 168-69.

Reports successful settlement of a strike by women corset workers, supported by men.

552. Filene, Edward A. "The Betterment of the Conditions of Working Women." *Annals of the American Academy of Political and Social Science,* 27 (1906): 613-23.

Argues that unionization could help to solve the difficulties of working women, but women are hard to organize because they are unskilled, unaggressive, tem-porary workers, and face the competition of incoming immigrants. Protective legislation, therefore, is a practical alternative.

553. Franklin, S.M. "Chicago Trade Union Women in Confer-ence." *Life and Labor,* 5 (October 1915): 154-56.

Reports on success in promoting unionization in the past year and urges campaigns among other groups of workers as well as cooperation of state, county, and private agencies to reduce unemployment. Reaffirms commitments to the objectives of the National Women's Trade Union League.

554. ————. "Elizabeth Maloney and the High Calling of the Waitress." *Life and Labor,* 3 (February 1913): 36-40.

Urges women to join trade unions by presenting fa-vorable conditions of organized workers against those before the union.

555. Geisinger, Anna. "What the Union Has Accomplished." *American Federationist,* 36 (August 1929): 983.

Argues that organization has helped wages and working
conditions in the hosiery industry.

556. Gurowsky, David. "Factional Disputes within the
I.L.G.W.U. 1919-1928." Ph.D. dissertation, SUNY at
Binghamton, 1978. 386 pp.

Traces the decline in membership in the International
Ladies Garment Workers Union during the 1920s, as well
as the establishment of an alternative organization,
the Needle Trade Workers Industrial Union, to a factional contest between radicals and conservatives in
the I.L.G.W.U. Right-wing union officials failed to
respond to workers' desires for an aggressive and democratic union and struggled to suppress left-wing challenges. In 1928, the conservatives, aided by the Socialist Party, the American Federation of Labor, and the
courts, ousted the left-wing, which formed a new union.

557. Omitted.

558. Henry, Alice. "Chicago Conference of Women Trade Unionists." *Life and Labor*, 4 (November 1914): 324-29.

Reports on the first city conference of women trade
unionists, organized to address concerns about the limited number of women workers in touch with the union
movement.

559. ———. "The Hart, Schaffner and Marx Agreement."
Life and Labor, 2 (June 1912): 170-72.

Praises the establishment of a Board of Arbitration
which resulted from the 1910-1911 strike of Chicago
garment workers. Argues that labor leaders and rank
and file have lost none of their earlier courage but
now show a greater patience which recognizes the slow
action of social forces.

560. ———. *The Trade Union Woman*. New York: D. Appleton
and Company, 1915. 314 pp.

Proposes unionization as the solution to injustices
which woman suffered as a result of the massive employment in industrialized society. Women workers who have
organized receive much praise, as do sympathetic social
feminists such as the members of the Women's Trade Union
League.

561. ———. *Women and the Labor Movement*. New York: George
      H. Doran Company, 1923. 241 pp.

      Extends *The Trade Union Woman* (item 560) beyond 1915.

562. Herron, Belva Mary. "Labor Organization among Women."
      University of Illinois Bulletin, 2 (1905): 16-24.

      Shows that women customarily entered the printing
      trade as regular workers with regular pay after six-
      week tuition in typesetting while men served a four-
      year apprenticeship. Therefore, women learned only to
      set plain type while men had the opportunity to be worth
      more to employers. Women were not in competition with
      men except in setting straight matter and in that they
      compared well in accuracy but could not do the same
      quantity of work as men in the same time.

563. ———. *The Progress of Labor Organizations Among Wo-
      men, Together with Some Considerations Concerning
      Their Place in Industry*. Urbana: University of
      Illinois Press, 1905. 79 pp.

      Argues that A.F. of L. union locals, especially the
      typographers and cigar-makers, are sex-segregated, and
      organizers have failed to reach women as well as men.
      Women's lack of skill and their failure to take their
      industrial condition seriously, combined with their
      sense of temporary employment and reluctance to identify
      with the laboring classes, all make them poor candidates
      for unionization.

564. Hockman, Julius. "Organizing the Dressmakers." *Amer-
      ican Federationist*, 36 (December 1929): 1462-67.

      Says that manufacturers have sometimes supported or-
      ganization in order to counter uncontrolled competition
      by sweat shops. Moreover, despite difficulties in or-
      ganizing seasonal workers of varied ethnicity, the In-
      ternational Ladies Garment Workers Union has made sig-
      nificant gains in reducing hours and obtaining minimum
      wage scales for workers.

565. Hodges, James Andrew. "The New Deal Labor Policy and
      the Southern Cotton Textile Industry, 1933-1941."
      Ph.D. dissertation, Vanderbilt University, 1963. 502
      pp.

      Demonstrates that a majority of Southern cotton tex-
      tile workers remained unorganized and that collective

bargaining was the exception rather than the rule. NRA boards as mediators were unable to bring collective bargaining to the industry; C.I.O. organizations used provisions of the Wagner Act to establish collective bargaining, but the successor Textile Workers of America failed to establish a really significant union movement.

566. "Hold the Fort: The Chicago Garment Workers' Strike." *Life and Labor*, 1 (February 1911): 48-51.

Reports the agreement ending the long strike of garment workers in Chicago; emphasizes the victory of their right to organize. Moralizes on the judicious views of older and more experienced trade unionists over those of hot-headed foreigners.

567. Janiewski, Dolores. "Race, Class, and the Sexual Division of Labor: The Difficulties of Collective Action in Durham in the 1930s." Paper, Fourth Berkshire Conference on History of Women, Mt. Holyoke College, 24 August 1978.

Concludes that unions among tobacco and textile workers failed because they did not deal with the ways in which workers' lives were already organized. The weakness of class-based strategies rests in the fact that community and class do not coincide.

568. Johnson, Agnes. "What the Boot and Shoe Workers' Union Means to Its Women Members." *Life and Labor*, 10 (April 1920): 102-3.

Pleads for unionization by displaying the benefits won, including the eight-hour day, forty-four- or forty-eight-hour week, and great increases in wages for women shoe workers since the inception of the union in 1895.

569. Kenneally, James J. *Women and American Trade Unions*. St. Albans, Vt.: Eden Press Women's Publications, 1978. 240 pp.

Argues that the Women's Trade Union League was "the most effective champion of women workers for nearly half a century," largely because "male dominated unions frequently were reluctant to espouse the cause of women." Working women were forced to struggle not only against exploitation by management but against sexism which denied them full partnership in unions.

570. ————. "Women and Trade Unions 1870-1920: The Quandary
      of the Reformers." *Labor History*, 14 (Winter 1973):
      42-55.

      Argues that traditional attitudes on a domestic role
      for women overrode the limited support which early labor
      unions gave to women's rights and unionization for fe-
      male workers. Under pressure from groups like the Wo-
      men's Trade Union League, the American Federation of
      Labor gave nominal support to women workers but showed
      greater interest in protective legislation. By 1920
      the federal government had established a Women's Bureau
      in the Department of Labor, 6.6 percent of women workers
      were organized, and women constituted 8 percent of trade
      union membership.

571. Kessler-Harris, Alice, ed. "The Autobiography of Ann
      Washington Craton." *Signs*, 1 (Summer 1976): 1019-37.

      Examines Craton's career as an organizer of garment
      workers for the Amalgamated Clothing Workers in the
      1920s and 1930s. A native-born, college-educated re-
      former, Craton had to appeal to Jewish workers despite
      her lack of knowledge of Yiddish, integrate herself into
      the culture and style of the anthracite region, and find
      ways for women to support unionization "by inviting them
      to do what they knew best"--feed rather than picket.

572. ————. "Organizing the Unorganizable: Three Jewish
      Women and Their Union." *Labor History*, 17 (Winter
      1976): 5-23. Reprinted in *Class, Sex, and the Woman
      Worker*, edited by Milton Cantor and Bruce Laurie.
      Westport, Conn.: Greenwood Press, 1977. Pp. 144-65.

      Explores the tensions which female union activists
      of the early twentieth century experienced between their
      commitment to a trade union movement hostile to female
      workers and a feminist movement led largely by women
      who did not work for wages. When class consciousness
      conflicted with feminism, they decided in terms of the
      working class and assumed traditional sex roles.

573. ————. "Where Are the Organized Women Workers?" *Fem-
      inist Studies*, 3 (Fall 1975): 92-110.

      Argues that women workers failed to become union mem-
      bers in large numbers early in the twentieth century
      because male unions virtually excluded them; women had
      limited labor-force opportunities and dared not risk

employer wrath; and a combination of paternalism, bene-
volence, and protective legislation was pressed on them
to substitute for unionization. Resistance to unionization stemming from cultural background, traditional
roles, and social expectations could have been overcome
had the external forces been more open to the organization of women workers.

574. Kirstein, George G. *Stores and Unions: A Study of the
     Growth of Unionism in Dry Goods and Department Stores*.
     New York: Fairchild Publications, 1950. 246 pp.

     Shows the ambivalence of the Retail Clerks Association
     toward women workers as members in the early days. "The
     female invasion of retailing" raised the problems of
     whether women should be kept out of the industry or, if
     that was impossible, of making sure that their standards
     did not undermine "those won by men." World War I solved
     the dilemma, since the number of women in retailing
     equalled that of men in 1921.

575. Kotchin, Morris. "The Ladies Garment Industry." *Amer-
     ican Federationist*, 36 (December 1929): 1472-77.

     Argues that the garment unions have had a struggle
     against the sweat shop on the one hand and communist
     extremism on the other. Cooperation between the Inter-
     national Ladies Garment Workers Union and "progressive"
     jobbers, however, has helped both to establish union
     standards and to limit competition.

576. Levin, Louis. *The Women's Garment Workers Union: A
     History of the International Ladies Garment Workers
     Union*. New York: B.W. Huebsch, Inc., 1924. 608 pp.

     Says that the signing of the Protocol of Peace in
     1910 constituted a "revolution" in which the "women's
     garment trades have been an industrial experiment sta-
     tion."

577. Lindsey, Matilda. "Southern Women in Industry." *Amer-
     ican Federationist*, 36 (August 1929): 973-75.

     Asserts that the American Federation of Labor and the
     Women's Trade Union League attempted to encourage the
     growth of trade unionism as industry has developed in
     the South. Women have responded to these efforts, some-
     times being the first to strike.

578. McCreesh, Carolyn Daniel. "On the Picket Line: Militant
     Women Campaign to Organize Garment Workers, 1880-
     1917." Ph.D. dissertation, University of Maryland,
     1975. 351 pp.

     Concludes that the entry of middle-class women into
     the trade union movement ultimately failed because of
     ideological differences, allies' condescension toward
     working women, and draining conflicts with male union
     leaders. But "talented and energetic women emerged
     from the workers' ranks" and by 1917 unprecedented num-
     bers of women had joined the two leading garment in-
     dustry unions.

579. MacLean, Annie Marion. "Trade Unionism Versus Welfare
     Work for Women." *Popular Science Monthly*, 87 (July
     1915): 50-55.

     Says that welfare work depends upon a paternalistic
     employer and weakens labor's chances to improve indus-
     trial conditions by their own efforts.

580. Maher, Amy G. "Women Trade Unionists in the United
     States." *International Labor Review*, 11 (March 1925):
     366-80.

     Credits the Women's Trade Union League with most or-
     ganization of women in the twentieth century, while the
     American Federation of Labor discriminated against wo-
     men workers.

581. Marot, Helen. *American Labor Unions*. New York: Holt
     and Co., 1914. 275 pp.

     Argues that women workers are not discriminated
     against if they want to become unionized, but they are
     not encouraged to take an active part in directing the
     union. The real problem is not so much discrimination
     as the position of women with both domestic and indus-
     trial ties.

582. ———. "Organization of Women." *American Labor Unions*.
     New York: Holt and Company, 1914. Pp. 65-77.

     Asserts that women do not suffer discrimination in
     admission to trade unions, although they are difficult
     to organize because of lack of skill and longevity.
     Once organized, women are militant unionists but have
     no opportunities for leadership within their unions.

583. ———. "Trade Unions and the Minimum Wage Boards."
     American Federationist, 22 (November 1915): 966-69.

     Pleads for unionization as preferable to protective
     legislation for women workers. Minimum wages, in prac-
     tice, become the maximum.

584. Matthews, Lillian R. *Women in Trade Unions in San
     Francisco*. Berkeley: University of California Press,
     1913. 100 pp.

     Argues that unionization is better than intrusive
     "social work" as a means of improving wages and shop
     conditions. Union membership also conveys intangible
     benefits of educational and social improvement.

585. Meltzer, Milton. *Bread—And Roses: The Struggle of
     American Labor, 1865-1915*. New York: Alfred A. Knopf,
     1967. 231 pp.

     Shows that women entered industry in significant num-
     bers as cheap labor during the nineteenth century and
     were a fixture in the working class by 1900.

586. Moskowitz, Henry. "The Power for Constructive Reform
     in the Trade Union Movement." *Life and Labor*, 2
     (January 1912): 10-15.

     Lobbies for the preferential union shop.

587. Negler, Isidore. "Wages, Hours and Employment." *Amer-
     ican Federationist*, 36 (December 1929): 1468-71.

     Concludes that unionization has substantially bene-
     fitted dressmakers. Comparison of wages and hours over
     a seventy-year period reveals significant improvements.
     The major remaining problem rests on the seasonal nature
     of the industry.

588. Nestor, Agnes. "The Organization of Women Workers."
     Life and Labor, 1 (November 1911): 342-43.

     Lists recommendations of the Committee on Organization
     to the Third Biennial Convention of the National Women's
     Trade Union League, and argues for activities unionizing
     women workers of different nationalities, constructive
     work after strikes, continued fight for the enforcement
     of agreements reached, and women's leadership and ac-
     tivity in unions.

589. Newman, Pauline M. "From the Battlefield." *Life and
     Labor*, 1 (October 1911): 292-97.

     Reports on inspiring ten-week resistance of six thou-
     sand cloakmakers in Cleveland in the face of the manu-
     facturers' refusal of arbitration and harassment by
     guards and bullies.

590. ———. "The Need of Cooperation Among Working Girls."
     Life and Labor, 4 (October 1914): 312-13.

     Asserts that the individual is helpless because she
     is powerless and that cooperation among working girls
     is absolutely necessary. Solidarity is necessary to
     require enforcement of laws which deal with poor work-
     ing conditions.

591. Nienburg, Bertha M. *Conditions in the Millinery Industry
     in the United States.* U.S. Department of Labor, Wo-
     men's Bureau. Bulletin No. 169. 1939. 128 pp.

     Argues that the millinery industry needs a strong
     union of employees and a strong association of employers,
     working cooperatively to deal first with conditions of
     obtaining materials and selling completed work, and then
     with regularizing seasons and style caprice in coopera-
     tion with women consumers.

592. Norland, John M. "Women in the Timber Industry." *Life
     and Labor*, 9 (May 1919): 113.

     Traces organization of women timber workers. Argues
     for trade unionism rather than a company union.

593. O'Farrell, M. Brigid, and Lydia Kleiner. "Anne Sullivan:
     Trade Union Organizer." *Frontiers*, 2 (Summer 1977):
     29-36.

     Transcribes the autobiographical oral history of Anne
     Sullivan who worked in Massachusetts textile mills in
     the 1920s and 1930s, organized for the Textile Workers
     Union of America, served on state and regional joint
     boards, and directs A.F.L.-C.I.O. COPE in Springfield,
     Massachusetts. Sullivan believes that organizing was
     her most important function "because we had *nothing*."

594. "On the Picket Line." *Life and Labor*, 3 (March 1913):
     71-73.

     Offers first-hand accounts of the abusive treatment
     suffered by strikers at the hands of the police and
     courts.

595. O'Reilly, Leonora. "The Story of Kalamazoo." *Life and Labor*, 2 (August 1912): 228-30.

Reports on the strike of corset workers in Michigan after employers refused to deal with the union and discharged its most active members.

596. O'Reilly, Mary. "The Waist and Dress Makers' Strike." *Life and Labor*, 7 (March 1917): 38-39.

Exposes harassment techniques including injunctions, arrests, and strikebreakers used against Chicago waist and dress makers.

597. Perkins, G.W. "Women and the Cigar Industry." *Life and Labor*, 11 (October 1921): 254-55.

Argues that a strong union in one trade is an asset to the whole labor movement, and appeals to women to identify with the working class as victims of greed and capitalism.

598. Peterson, Joyce Shaw. "A Social History of Automobile Workers before Unionization, 1900-1933." Ph.D. dissertation, University of Wisconsin at Madison, 1976. 339 pp.

Concludes that mass production not only required adjustment on the part of skilled craftsmen who had been working in the auto industry but also by new workers recruited from pre-industrial agricultural labor. Skilled workers had been the backbone of early unionization efforts in other crafts, but for unionization to succeed among automobile workers, it had to be directed toward a new majority of unskilled labor as well as compete with relatively high wages and company welfare plans.

599. Pope, Liston. *Millhands and Preachers: A Study of Gastonia*. New Haven: Yale University Press, 1942. 369 pp.

Analyzes the relationship between Protestant churches and the North Carolina cotton textile industry from the post-Civil War period to the 1930s. Little specific attention is paid to women, although conditions of life, labor, and protest are shown for the mill villages of Gaston County.

600. "Porcelain Workers Win Better Conditions." *Life and Labor*, 3 (March 1913): 80.

Reports on a successful strike in Trenton, New Jersey, to obtain a $5-per-week minimum wage.

601. "Position of the Trade Union Women." *Survey*, 23 June 1917, p. 277.

Argues that women have shifted from casual to permanent and from unskilled to skilled labor as a result of World War I. The National Women's Trade Union League, therefore, wants the American Federation of Labor to include females in its delegation to the International Labor Congress at the peace negotiations. In addition, American immigration laws should continue to restrict the entry of coolie labor.

602. Post, Louis F. "Labor and the Law." *Life and Labor*, 1 (January 1911): 27-30.

Attempts to educate working women about the injunction, which arose from property rights but is being applied to human rights by judges who are acting as dictators.

603. Potter, Frances Squire. "The Educational Value of the Women's Trade Union." *Life and Labor*, 1 (February 1911): 36-40.

Says that trade unionism for women will be inevitable, given the movement of masses of women in industry. Espouses unionization both for the sense of discipline it conveys and for its benefits in teaching about civic participation.

604. Poyntz, Juliet Stuart. "The Unity Movement--The Soul of the Union." *Life and Labor*, 7 (June 1917): 96-98.

Uses the New York Dressmakers' Unity House in the Catskill Mountains and Unity Center in the city to show union concern for the physical and social well-being of organized women workers.

605. "Protest of the Working Women of New York." *Survey*, 31 (14 February 1914): 605-6.

Argues that unemployed women see capitalist ownership, child labor, and long hours as the causes of their problems. A meeting of unemployed women, sponsored by the New York Women's Trade Union League, demanded that local and state government provide them with jobs.

606. Rabinowitz, Dorothy. "The Case of the I.L.G.W.U." In
     The World of the Blue-Collar Worker, edited by Irving
     Howe. New York: Quadrangle Books, New York Times
     Book Company, 1972. Pp. 49-60.

     Examines the rank and file of the garment industry,
     showing them to be low-paid and oppressed. When the
     union succeeded in achieving an increase in wage-level,
     manufacturers moved to depressed areas to escape organiza-
     tion and find cheap labor. The industry has always been
     fiercely competitive and labor-squeezing; more recently,
     it has also become very mobile. These considerations
     shed light on the sadness of charges against the
     I.L.G.W.U. of discrimination in wages, nepotism, and
     lack of leadership opportunity for minorities.

607. Rischin, Moses. "The Jewish Labor Movement in America:
     A Social Interpretation." *Labor History*, 5 (Fall
     1963): 227-47.

     Presents older Jewish unionists as transition figures
     for newer immigrants to become Americanized. As the
     momentum of revolution in Eastern Europe slackened,
     Eastern European Jews in America became the nucleus of
     the great labor movement of the 1930s which fought for
     democratization of American industry. Jewish labor
     leaders acted as spokesmen for less articulate and less
     experienced new immigrants.

608. Robins, Mrs. Raymond. "Freedom Through Organization."
     American Federationist, 22 (September 1915): 727-29.

     Asserts that organization alone will not solve the
     problems of working women. They must also become part
     of the trade union movement.

609. Schacht, John Norten. "The Rise of the Communications
     Workers of America: Union Organization and Centrali-
     zation in the Telephone Industry, 1936-1947." Ph.D.
     dissertation, University of Iowa, 1977. 473 pp.

     Concludes that centralization of union activities
     among telephone workers was a practical response of the
     leadership of the National Federation of Telephone Work-
     ers to the neglect of telephone labor problems by the
     Bell System and the War Labor Board. Unification was
     spurred by experience with bargaining, strikes, strike
     threats, and undercutting by other unions.

610. Schatz, Ronald. "Union Pioneers: The Founders of Local
     Unions at General Electric and Westinghouse, 1933-
     1937." *Journal of American History*, 66 (December
     1979): 586-602.

     Argues that both men and women who founded early local
     unions of electrical workers were atypical of the in-
     dustry's workforce. The men belonged to the upper
     stratum of workers; the women had more personal inde-
     pendence than their family-bound co-workers.

611. Schneiderman, Rose. "The White Goods Workers of New
     York: Their Struggle for Human Conditions." *Life and
     Labor*, 3 (May 1913): 132-36.

     Reports on the conversion of the New York white goods
     industry into an organized trade in five weeks during a
     successful strike. Asserts that competition among manu-
     facturers and individual workers has been replaced by
     conference and cooperation.

612. Scott, Melinda. "The Way to Freedom." *American Federa-
     tionist*, 22 (September 1915): 729-31.

     Believes that only trade unionism and suffrage can
     solve the problems of women. Female participation in
     strikes proves women's serious attitude toward the labor
     movement.

613. Seidman, Joel. *The Needle Trades*. New York: Farrar and
     Rinehart, 1942. 356 pp.

     Argues that unionization has raised garment and other
     needle trades workers from "the degradation of the
     sweatshop" to "important and respected positions in the
     social and economic life of the United States." But it
     would be disastrous for the unions "to become content
     with past achievements and rest on their laurels."

614. Sigman, Morris. "Ladies' Garment Workers Gain." *Amer-
     ican Federationist*, 30 (September 1923): 742-43.

     Says that unionization of women garment workers has
     made satisfactory progress, and organized workers have
     made gains such as the forty-hour week despite many in-
     junctions against them. The union now hopes to combat
     subcontracting.

615. Sive-Tomashefsky, Rebecca. "Identifying a Lost Leader:
     Hannah Shapiro and the 1910 Chicago Garment Workers'
     Strike." *Signs*, 3 (Summer 1978): 936-39.

Praises Hannah Shapiro as the initiator of the walkout
from Hart, Shaffner and Marx because of a one-quarter
of a cent cut in the piece-work rate. She recalled herself at seventeen as fearless and responsive to the
righteousness of the workers' struggle but unsympathetic
to socialism.

616. Stein, Leon, ed. *Out of the Sweatshop: The Struggle
for Industrial Democracy.* New York: Quadrangle Books,
New York Times Book Company, 1977. 367 pp.

Reprints contemporary descriptions of conditions of
life and labor in the garment trades at the turn of the
century as well as accounts of organizing and strike
efforts of the I.L.G.W.U. throughout the twentieth century. Despite the unlikelihood of organizing immigrants
with language problems, tenement lifestyles, and in-
dividualistic ambitions, "the improbabilities were overcome" and the Protocol of Peace set a pattern for labor-
management relations in the garment industry.

617. "Successor to the Protocol of Peace." *Life and Labor,*
5 (August 1915): 137-39.

Shows techniques used by the Chicago Women's Trade
Union League to organize women in the Chicago stockyards.

618. Teller, Charlotte. "Women in Unions: Cloth Hat and Cap
Makers." *American Federationist,* 13 (April 1906):
222-24.

Asserts that women liners and trimmers in the cloth
hat industry have self-initiated and self-governing
unionization. Women make up about 20 percent of the industry's workers and are segregated by task.

619. Tumbler, Bee. "Women in Industry." *American Federationist,* 35 (July 1928): 824-25.

Argues that minimum wage laws provide only subsistence
and leave employers legal opportunities to pay less.
Unionization, on the other hand, would provide women
workers with power to obtain and enforce agreement regarding conditions not regulated by law, such as overtime and factory sanitation.

620. A Union Man's Wife. "To the Wives of Union Men." *Life
and Labor,* 1 (September 1911): 259.

Appeals to women consumers to demand union-made goods
when they buy supplies, and argues that when women see
what their husbands' unions have gained, they should
urge their daughters to join.

621. "Uprising in the Needle Trades in New York." *Life and*
     Labor, 3 (March 1913): 69-71.

     Defends strikers, calls for an investigation of the
     trade, and argues that seasoned trade unionists tried
     for eighteen months to avert a strike but manufacturers
     had not learned from other industrial uprisings.

622. Valesh, Eva McDonald. "Women and Labor." *American*
     Federationist, 2 (October 1896): 221-23.

     Argues that women workers are forced to accept long
     hours and low wages because they work for economic nec-
     essity; but their low pay drives down men's wages.
     Unionization and improvement in men's wages would reduce
     the necessity for women to work. Moreover, women should
     be protected from the physical hazards of being employed
     because they bear the future of the society.

623. Van Osdell, John Garrett, Jr. "Cotton Mills, Labor, and
     the Southern Mind: 1880-1930." Ph.D. dissertation,
     Tulane University, 1966. 297 pp.

     Concludes that Southern textile workers saw themselves
     as partners of the mill owners in the rehabilitation of
     the industrialized New South, and, therefore, they re-
     sisted unionization which appeared to be Northern and
     alien. Changes came in 1929 with the introduction of
     more efficient methods which appeared to threaten the
     position of millworkers as partners. Hence, the strikes
     of 1929-31. But misconceptions about the strikers, es-
     pecially communists at Gastonia, led to the conclusion
     that all unions seemed Bolshevik. The situation was
     eventually resolved by the abandonment of innovation
     and the return to the traditional system.

624. Vorse, Mary Heaton. *Labor's New Millions*. New York:
     Modern Age Books, 1938. 312 pp.

     Includes the story of the Women's Emergency Brigades
     and the women's auxiliaries in an account of C.I.O.
     unionization in the rubber, steel, auto, textile, agri-
     culture, and cannery industries.

625. Walsh, Frank P. "Women and Labor." *Life and Labor*, 5 (November 1915): 165.

Argues that all legislation and reform are hopeless without trade unionism, that union men should assist in organizing women in American industry, and that women as cheap labor will cease to be a threat to men when they organize.

626. Weinstock, Anna. "Boston News Stand Girls Fight for Rights." *Life and Labor*, 11 (January 1921): 5-9.

Appeals to public opinion to support newsstand girls who have been subjected to firing for unionization and the injunction even though they have not struck.

627. "Why I Joined My Union and What It has Done for Me." *Life and Labor*, 10 (December 1920): 312-25.

Describes the benefits of unionization, by working women who won a contest.

628. "Why No Woman on A.F. of L. Executive Council?" *Life and Labor*, 3 (July 1918): 138.

Argues that the increased presence of women in industry and growth of labor organization among women make it natural for women to seek more adequate representation in the union governing body.

629. Withington, Anne. "The Lawrence Strike." *Life and Labor*, 2 (March 1912): 73-77.

Supports conservative A.F.L.-style trade unionism rather than tactics of the Industrial Workers of the World.

630. Wolfe, F.E. "Admission of Women," in *Admission to American Trade Unions*. Baltimore: Johns Hopkins Press, 1912. Pp. 74-95.

Argues that entrance of women into modern industrial life grows out of manufacturing processes previously carried on in the home by women. Women have achieved only minimal effectiveness as trade unionists since they lack interest in long-term wage and benefits issues, are not sufficiently aggressive for encountering employers, tend to do low-skill work, and encounter male opposition to their employment.

631. Wolfson, Theresa. "Wages of Organized Women Workers."
      American Federationist, 32 (September 1925): 811-13.

      Shows union wages to be preferable to wages set by
      minimum-wage commissions.

632. ————. *The Woman Worker and the Trade Union.* New
      York: International Publishers, 1926. 224 pp.

      Concludes that women workers can be organized. The
      1920 census data indicates that women were becoming a
      permanent part of the labor force but constituted a de-
      clining percentage of union members, traceable in part
      to the difficulties of organizing women workers (high
      turnover, for example) and in part to insensitivity of
      the organizers.

633. Wolman, Leo. "Women in Trade Unions in 1920 and 1910."
      The Growth of American Trade Unions 1880-1923. New
      York: National Bureau of Economic Research, 1924.
      Pp. 97-100.

      Presents statistics on the marked proportional rise
      in female membership in trade unions between 1910 and
      1920. Nearly a quarter of the increase came from new
      organizations of clothing workers, textile workers, and
      telephone operators. Clothing workers account for the
      largest percentage of women in unions.

634. Yudelson, Sophia. "Women's Place in Industry and Labor
      Organizations." *Annals of the American Academy of
      Political and Social Science*, 24 (September 1904):
      343-53.

      Argues that industrialization made possible a new
      independence for women working outside the household,
      but women's wages are considerably lower than men's.
      Therefore, women sought admission to trade unions, which
      men resisted until they faced the realities of women's
      permanent presence in the work force. Women are now
      welcomed into unions.

635. ————. "Women in Unions." *American Federationist*,
      13 (January 1909): 19-21.

      Says that employers use the labor of home workers to
      undermine action by factory workers to improve their
      conditions.

WOMEN'S TRADE UNION LEAGUE

636. Boone, Gladys. *The Women's Trade Union Leagues in
    Great Britain and the United States of America.* New
    York: Columbia University Press, 1942. 283 pp.

    Records the origins, establishment, and history of
    W.T.U.L. in England and America with particular atten-
    tion to the United States in a heavily factual treatment.

637. Davis, Allen F. "The Women's Trade Union League: Ori-
    gins and Organization." *Labor History*, 5 (Winter
    1964): 3-17.

    Opposes the general belief that Progressives preferred
    to help workers through government action rather than
    labor unions. The Women's Trade Union League shows a
    pro-labor attitude of social workers and illustrates the
    cooperation between reformers and some labor leaders.
    While the W.T.U.L. could claim no spectacular successes,
    it did its best work in encouraging and supporting wo-
    men's unions at the local level.

638. Dell, Margery. "The National Women's Trade Union League
    of America." *Life and Labor*, 2 (November 1912): 345-
    46.

    Appeals for organization of all workers into trade
    unions; shows recent benefits resulting from good or-
    ganization such as working agreements by New York laun-
    dry workers and furriers, the Illinois ten-hour law,
    and the Massachusetts minimum wage commission.

639. Dreier, Mary. "Tenth Anniversary of the New York Women's
    Trade Union League." *Life and Labor*, 4 (June 1914):
    187-88.

    Traces the first ten years of local League with em-
    phasis on unionization activities. Argues to benefits
    of strength such as the necessity to secure favorable
    laws and see that they are enforced.

640. Dye, Nancy Schrom. *As Equals and as Sisters: Feminism,
    the Labor Movement, and the Women's Trade Union
    League of New York.* Columbia: University of Missouri
    Press, 1980. 224 pp.

    Shows how the New York W.T.U.L. failed to motivate
    women to be militant, outspoken unionists, to integrate

women on an equal basis into the mainstream of the American labor movement, and to create an egalitarian cross-
class alliance because the W.T.U.L. emphasized A.F.L.-
type craft unionism which was inappropriate to unskilled
and semi-skilled women workers, the women themselves
presented insurmountable problems, especially their dif-
fusion, and the workers and allies could not effect an
ideological synthesis of unionism and feminism. After
1913, therefore, the W.T.U.L. directed its efforts to-
wards suffrage and protective legislation.

641.   ————. "Creating a Feminist Alliance: Sisterhood and
        Class Conflict in the New York Women's Trade Union
        League, 1903-1914." *Feminist Studies*, 2 (1975): 24-
        38. Reprinted in *Class, Sex, and the Woman Worker*,
        edited by Milton Cantor and Bruce Laurie. Westport,
        Conn.: Greenwood Press, 1977. Pp. 225-45.

        Concludes that the New York W.T.U.L. failed to achieve
        an egalitarian cross-class coalition of workers and
        allies, facing tensions arising out of dual commitments
        to labor as a whole and the women's movement as a whole,
        as well as internal difficulties between the members.

642.   ————. "Feminism or Unionism? The New York Women's
        Trade Union League and the Labor Movement." *Feminist
        Studies*, 3 (Fall 1975): 111-25.

        Argues that the New York W.T.U.L. had difficulty in
        creating unions for women which were both "effective,
        stable labor organizations" and at the same time "met
        the W.T.U.L.'s feminist objectives of giving women op-
        portunities for self-assertion and responsibility."
        Unions had to be acceptable to A.F. of L. standards
        which rejected independence, and the W.T.U.L. failed
        to go beyond the narrow craft definition of unionism
        which the A.F. of L. represented.

643.   Endelman, Gary E. "Solidarity Forever: Rose Schneider-
        man and the Women's Trade Union League." Ph.D. dis-
        sertation, University of Delaware, 1978. 304 pp.

        Portrays Rose Schneiderman not only as a labor leader
        but also as a political activist. She grew to prefer
        government assistance over self-help, breaking with the
        tradition of voluntary action to support the creation
        of a welfare state. In particular, she favored "govern-
        ment planning as an antidote to industrial disarray."

644. Franklin, S.M. "The Fifth Biennial Convention." *Life and Labor*, 5 (July 1915): 116-32.

Urges immigrant women to become naturalized and men trade unionists to work for suffrage.

645. Jacoby, Robin Miller. "Feminism and Class Consciousness in the British and American Women's Trade Union League, 1890-1925." In *Liberating Women's History: Theoretical and Critical Essays*, edited by Berenice A. Carroll. Urbana: University of Illinois Press, 1976. Pp. 137-60.

Argues that the British W.T.U.L. worked "within sexually mixed, class-based contexts" to achieve improvement for women, while the American League attempted to work across class lines. The Americans, however, failed to transcend their class divisions.

646. ————. "The Women's Trade Union League and American Feminism." *Feminist Studies*, 3 (Fall 1975): 126-40. Reprinted in *Class, Sex, and the Woman Worker*, edited by Milton Cantor and Bruce Laurie. Westport, Conn.: Greenwood Press, 1977. Pp. 203-24.

Argues that the association of the W.T.U.L. and the suffrage movement was tenuous at best and never represented "a genuine achievement of sisterhood on a cross-class basis." The W.T.U.L. did more for the women's movement than the women's movement did for female workers.

647. Kennedy, Susan Estabrook. "The Want It Satisfies Demonstrates the Need of It: A Study of *Life and Labor* of the Women's Trade Union League." *International Journal of Women's Studies*, 3 (July/August 1980): 391-406.

Examines the changing themes and emphases in the magazine issued by the W.T.U.L. from 1911 to 1921. The articles and editorial opinion parallel the shifting focus of the W.T.U.L. from trade unionism to suffrage and protective legislation.

648. "League Organizes Washington Committee." *Life and Labor*, 8 (May 1918): 91-92.

Reports on the establishment of a chapter of the W.T.U.L. in Washington for the dual purpose of serving

as a center for nationwide propaganda regarding women
workers, and helping unions to reach unorganized women
workers.

649. McDowell, Mary. "The National Women's Trade Union
      League." *Survey*, 23 (16 October 1909): 101-7.

      Says that the problems of working women should receive
      immediate redress through legislation. But the long-
      term solution rests in freedom to enter new occupations
      and acquire new skills.

650. Newman, Pauline M. "Out of the Past--Into the Future."
      Life and Labor, 11 (June 1921): 171-74.

      Summarizes the work of the Philadelphia W.T.U.L. on
      behalf of working women, including organization, educa-
      tion, and legislation.

651. Peck, Mary Gray. "Frances Squire Potter." *Life and
      Labor*, 4 (May 1914): 131-33.

      Eulogizes reformer and "ally" of the W.T.U.L.; traces
      her activities from suffrage to the labor movement.

652. Perkins, Frances. "Women Workers." *American Federa-
      tionist*, 36 (September 1929): 1073-79.

      Advises the W.T.U.L. to direct its efforts toward or-
      ganizing the growing numbers of women entering the trade
      and transportation industries, and toward eliminating
      the distinction between blue- and white-collar workers.
      Part-time workers threaten the wages of full-time em-
      ployees and are difficult to organize, although their
      numbers are growing.

653. Robins, Margaret Dreier. "Self-government in the Work-
      shop: The Demand of the Women's Trade Union League."
      Life and Labor, 2 (April 1912): 108-10.

      Argues that the unorganized woman worker is a "tragic
      underbidder" in the labor market and calls for united
      action by workers in unions, not merely for the benefits
      to wages and hours, but for the initiative, social
      leadership, and sense of independence which it will
      bring.

654. ————. "Women in Industry." *Survey*, 31 (December 27,
      1913): 351.

Asserts that workers are unaware of their rights and
of protective laws; and, therefore, they need training
and organization. The W.T.U.L. trains women organizers
and encourages public education to inform workers of
laws enacted for their benefit.

655. Robins, Mrs. Raymond. "Opening Address to the Sixth
Biennial Convention of the National Women's Trade
Union League of America." *Life and Labor*, 7 (July
1917): 103-6.

Argues that World War I will be the final test for
democracy, the worth of labor, and the rise of woman as
women move from casual to permanent employment, from
unskilled and unimportant workers to trained and essential factors in the economic life of the world. Urges
organization of women workers and attention to postwar
unemployment.

656. Scott, Melinda. "Fourth Biennial Outlines Organizational Work." *Life and Labor*, 3 (September 1913):
273-76.

Urges organization of women in trade unions, attempts
to reach the rank and file, women's activities within
their own unions; reports results of recent strike work
in New York and Chicago.

657. "Ten Years of Work by the Chicago League." *Life and
Labor*, 4 (March 1914): 93-94.

Summarizes the first ten years of the Chicago branch
of the W.T.U.L. and emphasizes the necessity and benefits of organization of women into trade unions.

PROTECTIVE LEGISLATION

658. Anderson, Mary. "Women's Wages." *American Federationist*, 32 (August 1925): 681-83.

Attempts to prove that minimum wage laws are necessary because, where they do not exist, wages are very
low, which has a negative impact on women's families
and on men's wages. "Equal pay for equal work" should
be established for each occupation regardless of the
worker performing the task.

659. Andrews, Irene Osgood. "The Courts and Women's Work."
Life and Labor, 2 (April 1912): 123.

Reports court rulings which uphold limitations on
women's working hours.

660.   Baer, Judith A. *The Chains of Protection: The Judicial
       Response to Women's Labor Legislation.* Westport,
       Conn.: Greenwood Press, 1978. 238 pp.

       Shows how laws initially propounded as limitations on
       employers for the benefit of women workers had, by the
       1960s, become restrictions on the employed females.
       But legislation of the 1960s and judicial verdicts of
       the 1970s have invalidated sex-specific state labor
       laws.

661.   Baker, Elizabeth Faulkner. *Protective Labor Legislation.*
       New York: Columbia University Press, 1925. 467 pp.

       Argues that unskilled women need protection while
       protective legislation can be used negatively against
       skilled women.

662.   Berch, Bettina Eileen. "Industrialization and Working
       Women in the Nineteenth Century: England, France, and
       the United States." Ph.D. dissertation, University
       of Wisconsin at Madison, 1976. 376 pp.

       Concludes that protective legislation did not improve
       the living and working conditions of employed women.
       Rather, it established an ideology that women are mar-
       ginal workers, providing a modern domestic reserve labor
       force.

663.   Beyer, Clara M. *History of Labor Legislation for Women
       in Three States.* U.S. Department of Labor, Women's
       Bureau. Bulletin No. 66-1. 1929. 133 pp.

       Asserts that "the overpowering urge toward social
       justice" led to considerable labor legislation between
       1911 and 1914, especially laws affecting women workers
       in Massachusetts, New York, and California which regu-
       late hours, wages, and working conditions. Factors
       contributing to the passage of these laws included or-
       ganized labor; factory inspectors and other enforcement
       officials; bureaus of labor statistics; special legis-
       lative study groups; governors; employers; social,
       civil, philanthropic, and church groups; factual stu-
       dies; and the spirit of the time.

664.   Brandeis, Louis D., and Josephine Goldmark. *Women in
       Industry: Decision of the United States Supreme Court*

in Curt Muller vs. State of Oregon Upholding the Con-
stitutionality of the Oregon Ten Hour Law for Women
and Brief for the State of Oregon. New York: Reprinted for the National Consumers' League, 1908.
121 pp.

Argues that the State has the right to regulate the
"liberty" to purchase or sell labor, ordinarily protected under the Fourteenth Amendment, when that restriction on "liberty" relates to the public health,
safety, or welfare. To permit women to work in a factory or laundry more than ten hours in one day endangers
public health, safety, morals, or welfare.

665. Breckenridge, Sophonisba P. "Legislative Control of
      Women's Work." *Journal of Political Economy*, 14
      (February 1906): 107-9.

      Says that protective legislation discriminates against
      women. Contrary to the assumption that women as a
      class benefit from laws which establish health and safe-
      ty standards or prevent immoral conduct in places of
      employment, such regulations actually limit employment
      opportunities for women.

666. Brown, Emily C. *Women in Industrial Home Work.* U.S.
      Department of Labor, Women's Bureau. Bulletin No. 79.
      1930. 18 pp.

      Urges states to study the existence and practices of
      home work as a basis for establishing regulation and
      control as well as enforcement of existing restrictions
      on health, child labor, and the like.

667. Buchanan, Sara Louise, *et al. The Legal Status of Wo-*
      men in the United States of America: Final Report,
      Giving Summary for All States Combined; Reports for
      States and Territories; Revisions. U.S. Department
      of Labor, Women's Bureau. Bulletins Nos. 157, 157-A,
      157-1 to 157-2. 1938-1962. 89, 16, 31, 105 pp.

      Compiles and abstracts laws regarding the civil and
      political rights of women including contracts, property,
      estates, marriage, divorce, domicile, and public office.

668. Byrne, Harriet A. *Women's Employment in West Virginia.*
      U.S. Department of Labor, Women's Bureau. Bulletin
      No. 150. 1937. 27 pp.

      Presses West Virginia to pass labor legislation deal-
      ing with the sixth of its female population who are

gainfully employed. Hours, though unregulated, were
not long; but wages fell below recommended standards
and hourly earnings decreased from 1935 to 1936, although weekly earnings rose.

669. Candela, Joseph L., Jr. "The Struggle to Limit the
      Hours and Raise the Wages of Working Women in Illinois,
      1893-1917." *Social Service Review*, 53 (March 1979):
      15-34.

Says that Progressive reformers worked for protective
labor legislation because they believed that industrial
conditions were especially difficult for working women.
Reformers viewed women as mothers or potential mothers
and had children's welfare in mind when they struggled
for minimum wage and hours limitation for employed females.

670. Correll, Marie. *State Requirements for Industrial
      Lighting: A Handbook for the Protection of Women Work-
      ers, Showing Lighting Standard and Practices*. U.S.
      Department of Labor, Women's Bureau. Bulletin No.
      94. 1932. 62 pp.

Claims that satisfactory lighting affects workers'
comfort and health, reduces accidents, and improves the
quantity and quality of work done; but state codes do
not come up to the levels required in the American Standard Code.

671. *The Development of Minimum-Wage Laws in the United
      States, 1912 to 1927*. U.S. Department of Labor,
      Women's Bureau. Bulletin No. 61. 1928. 635 pp.

Analyzes the terms, impact, and current status of
state minimum wage legislation including construction
and methods of operation, costs of administration,
changes for women workers, and court decisions.

672. *The Effect of Minimum-Wage Determinations in Service
      Industries: Adjustments in the Dry-Cleaning and Power-
      Laundry Industries*. U.S. Department of Labor, Women's
      Bureau. Bulletin No. 166. 1938. 44 pp.

Pleads for minimum-wage orders to bring about more
efficient business management, protect fair employers
from price undercutting. These orders do not produce
lessened employment unless other factors such as technological changes are present, do not lead to the sub-

stitution of men for women workers, but they materially raise pay rates and total earnings for women workers, including skilled workers.

673. *The Effects of Labor Legislation on the Employment Opportunities of Women.* U.S. Department of Labor, Women's Bureau. Bulletin No. 65. 1928. 498 pp.

Argues that "the real forces that influence women's opportunity are far removed from legislative restriction of their hours or conditions of work." These forces include division and simplification of processes, technology, the supply and cost of labor, and the general psychology of the times. Thus, women have not been hurt by restrictive legislation.

674. *The Eight-Hour Day in Federal and State Legislation.* U.S. Department of Labor, Women's Bureau. Bulletin No. 5. 1919. 14 pp.

Summarizes places where women workers are affected by the eight-hour day and/or limitations on the number of days or hours worked per week as well as occupations for women falling under these regulations.

675. *Employment in Service and Trade Industries in Maine.* U.S. Department of Labor, Women's Bureau. Bulletin No. 180. 1940. 30 pp.

Urges Maine to pass a minimum-wage law because women workers in Maine receive earnings below the cost of living, are paid less than men, and are subject to irregular employment. In addition, the Maine law permits long hours of labor by contemporary standards.

676. *The Employment of Women in Hazardous Occupations in the United States.* U.S. Department of Labor, Women's Bureau. Bulletin No. 6. 1919. 8 pp.

Summarizes states and industries in which laws regulate the employment of women and all workers as well as compulsory reporting of industrial diseases and workmen's compensation laws which include industrial diseases.

677. Erickson, Ethel. *Employment of Women in Tennessee Industries.* U.S. Department of Labor, Women's Bureau. Bulletin No. 149. 1937. 63 pp.

Concludes that Supreme Court invalidation of the National Industrial Recovery Act influenced a reduction

in hourly wages, but weekly earnings increased because
of longer hours and steadier work.

678. Gleason, Caroline J. (Sister Miriam Theresa). *Oregon
      Legislation for Women in Industry*. U.S. Department
      of Labor, Women's Bureau. Bulletin No. 90. 1931.
      37 pp.

      Examines the characteristics of wage-earning women in
      Oregon as well as wage and hour legislation and decisions
      of the industrial welfare commission.

679. Goldmark, Josephine. *Fatigue and Efficiency: A Study
      in Industry*. New York: Russell Sage Foundation, Sur-
      vey Associates, 1912. 302 pp.

      Opposes night work for women and favors scientific
      management, based on analysis of the physical and chem-
      ical effects of speed and strain in industry.

680. ————. "The Necessary Sequel of Child-Labor Laws."
      American Journal of Sociology, 11 (November 1905):
      312-25.

      Asserts that most working women are under twenty years
      of age and cannot protect themselves against exploita-
      tion or dangerous working conditions. A few states have
      passed protective laws, but the Supreme Court has in-
      validated limitations on hours.

681. ————. "Workingwomen and the Laws: A Record of Neglect."
      *Annals of the American Academy of Political and Social
      Science*, 28 (September 1906): 63-78.

      Shows that state laws to protect the rapidly increas-
      ing numbers of employed women are meagre and insuffi-
      cient. Existing legislation deals primarily with night
      work and length of the workday, but virtually no atten-
      tion is paid to conditions of labor, particularly in
      sweatshops and home work.

682. Hager, Alice Rogers. "Occupations and Earnings of Wo-
      men in Industry." *Annals of the American Academy of
      Political and Social Science*, 143 (May 1929): 65-73.

      Argues that law will not eliminate women's wage in-
      equality. An educated public opinion will be necessary
      for the step-by-step establishment of equality of oppor-
      tunity and equality of payment for work done.

683. *Health Problems of Women in Industry.* U.S. Department of Labor, Women's Bureau. Bulletin No. 18. 1921. 6 pp.

Pleads for the standards espoused by the Women's Bureau such as the eight-hour day, no night work, a living wage based on occupation rather than sex, and decent working conditions which fall under the power of the State to protect health.

684. Hill, Ann Corinne. "Protection of Women Workers and the Courts: A Legal Case History." *Feminist Studies*, 5 (Summer 1979): 247-73.

Claims that protective legislation is based on the faulty premise that all women should be covered because many women need protection; the same simplistic logic protects women but excludes men and minorities who actually need protection.

685. Holcombe, A.N. "The Effects of the Legal Minimum Wage for Women." *Annals of the American Academy of Political and Social Science*, 69 (January 1917): 34-41.

Asserts that minimum wage laws result in increased wages and more regular employment for women. They do not cause the replacement of women by male employees.

686. Hopkins, Mary D. *The Employment of Women at Night.* U.S. Department of Labor, Women's Bureau. Bulletin No. 64. 1928. 86 pp.

Argues that night work is harmful to the worker and that the United States should follow the example of other leading industrial nations in suppressing it.

687. Hunt, Vilma R. "A Brief History of Women Workers and Hazards in the Workplace." *Feminist Studies*, 5 (Summer 1979): 274-85.

Shows how identification of health and safety hazards to women in the workplace has, ironically, led to the exclusion of women from such occupations rather than the improvement of safety for all workers.

688. Hutchinson, Emilie J. *Women's Wages: A Study of the Wages of Industrial Women and Measures Suggested to Increase Them.* New York: Columbia University Press, 1919. 181 pp.

Argues that no single measure can solve the problems of women's inadequate wages and irregular employment, but minimum-wage legislation, trade unionism, and vocational education will all help.

689. *The Installation and Maintenance of Toilet Facilities in Places of Employment.* U.S. Department of Labor, Women's Bureau. Bulletin No. 99. 1933. 86 pp.

Claims that boards of public health deal only with establishments where food is handled; therefore, additional state regulations are necessary to control toilet facilities for other kinds of workers. Moreover, many states lack any statutory regulation, while others have laws that are seriously weakened by vague language.

690. Johnsen, Julia E., comp. *Special Legislation for Women.* Vol. IV, no. 7 of The Reference Shelf. New York: H.W. Wilson Company, 1926. 142 pp.

Sets out arguments on both sides of the debate over protective legislation vs. equal rights for women.

691. Johnson, Ethel M. "The Problem of Women in Industry." *American Federationist*, 33 (August 1926): 974-77.

Urges legislation as the only adequate protection for women workers who receive low wages because they perform unskilled work.

692. Kelley, Florence, and M. March. "Labor Legislation for Women and Its Effect on Earnings and Conditions of Labor." *Annals of the American Academy of Political and Social Science*, 143 (May 1929): 286-300.

Says that women workers are often adolescents who need legislative protection of wages and hours. The Woman's Party opposes such laws while the National Women's Trade Union League supports them.

693. *Labor Laws for Women in Industry in Indiana.* U.S. Department of Labor, Women-in-Industry Service. Bulletin No. 2. 1919. 29 pp.

Argues that in view of wartime and postwar changes in conditions of labor for women in Indiana, the state should require the eight-hour day, establish minimum sanitation and comfort standards in factories, include at least one woman on the industrial board to administer labor laws, and establish a special bureau for women in industry.

694. Lattimore, Eleanor L., and Ray S. Trent. *Legal Recognition of Industrial Women.* New York: Industrial Committee of War Work Council of National Board of Y.W.C.A., 1919. 91 pp.

   Argues for legislation to protect women from the negative results of factory production replacing domestic production. Women who entered work under abnormal industrial conditions should have their permanency of employment protected; women do not work for pin money.

695. Lemons, J. Stanley. "Social Feminism in the 1920s: Progressive Women and Industrial Legislation." *Labor History*, 14 (Winter 1973): 83-91.

   Shows how social feminists such as the League of Women Voters, the National Consumers' League, the National Women's Trade Union League, and others continued to fight for reform, especially protective legislation for women and children, in the 1920s. If they were thwarted by business, conservatives, the courts, and more radical feminists, they at least kept the issues of protection alive until the New Deal.

696. ———. *The Woman Citizen: Social Feminism in the 1920s.* Urbana: University of Illinois Press, 1973. 266 pp.

   Claims that the progressive traditions and concerns of social feminism slowed in the 1920s, but they neither failed nor died out. Social feminists concerned themselves with broad reforms such as citizenship, education, and protective legislation to ease the plight of industrial workers. These commitments brought them into conflict with hard-core feminists who opposed protection and favored an equal rights amendment.

697. Lieberman, Jacob Andrew. "Their Sisters' Keepers: The Women's Hours and Wages Movement in the United States, 1890-1925." Ph.D. dissertation, Columbia University, 1971. 514 pp.

   Argues that success in reforming women's hours of labor led to the campaign for minimum-wage laws. Investigations in the 1880s revealed appalling conditions in the sweatshop system, including poor health and destitution of many women operatives; well-to-do, educated women undertook reform which succeeded in getting hours regulated in thirty-nine states by 1913, inspiring the social Progressives to work for minimum-wage laws. Extensive participation of women in World War I led the federal government to establish the Women's Bureau.

698.   MacLean, Annie Marion. "Factory Legislation for Women
       in the United States." *American Journal of Sociology*,
       3 (September 1897): 183-205.

       Summarizes factory labor legislation as it applies to
       women, including hours, sanitation, and factory inspec-
       tion.

699.   Mann, Annette. *Women Workers in Factories: A Study of
       Working Conditions in 275 Industrial Establishments
       in Cincinnati and Adjoining Towns.* Cincinnati: Con-
       sumers' League, 1918.   45 pp.

       Shows that working conditions need improvement, that
       the minimum initial wage paid to women and girls is
       very low, and that the child labor laws are violated.
       Among the recommendations are abolition of home work and
       prohibition of the employment of women on night shifts.

700.   Mason, Lucy Randolph. *The Shorter Day and Women Workers.*
       Richmond, Va.: Virginia League of Women Voters, 1922.
       26 pp.

       Opposes excessive hours of labor as a threat to health;
       the nine-hour day would help.

701.   ————. *Standards for Workers in Southern Industry.*
       N.p.: National Consumers' League, 1931.   46 pp.

       Pleads for the limitation of hours of labor, especially
       for women.

702.   Mettert, Margaret Thompson. *State Reporting of Occu-
       pational Disease, Including a Survey of Legislation
       Applying to Women.* U.S. Department of Labor, Women's
       Bureau.   Bulletin No. 114.   1934.   99 pp.

       Says that occupational disease prevention will be
       helped by elimination of harmful substances from manu-
       facturing processes, coverage of diseases on the same
       basis as accidents in workmen's compensation laws, and
       complete and standardized reporting of cases of disease.

703.   ————. *Summary of State Reports of Occupational Dis-
       ease with a Survey of Preventive Legislation, 1932 to
       1934.*   U.S. Department of Labor, Women's Bureau.   Bul-
       letin No. 147.   1936.   42 pp.

       Continues Bulletin No. 114 (item 702).

704. Mies, Frank P. "Statutory Regulation of Women's Employ-
     ment--Codification of Statutes." *Journal of Political
     Economy*, 14 (December 1906): 104-18.

     Summarizes state laws regulating employment of women
     including hours, night work, rest and meal times, sani-
     tation, working conditions, and dangerous industries.

705. Millis, H.A. "Some Aspects of the Minimum Wage." *Jour-
     nal of Political Economy*, 22 (February 1914): 132-59.

     Argues that men are competitive and, therefore, do not
     need the minimum wage; but women lack skills, mobility,
     and organization. However, industrial education for
     women and restriction of cheap immigrant labor, as well
     as the minimum wage, would improve the situation for
     women workers.

706. Mulligan, Jean Elizabeth. "Three Federal Interventions
     on Behalf of Childbearing Women: The Sheppard-Towner
     Act, Emergency Maternity and Infant Care, and the
     Maternal and Child Health and Mental Retardation Plan-
     ning Amendment of 1963." Ph.D. dissertation, University
     of Michigan, 1976. 301 pp.

     Claims that Congressional action began in an effort to
     prevent pregnancy-related deaths in some women. Preg-
     nancy underwent a changed definition with new emphasis
     on pathology, death, or disability. But Congress has
     not yet attended fully to the social, economic, and
     medical dimensions of pregnancy for all childbearing
     women.

707. Nestor, Agnes. "The Trend of Legislation Affecting Wo-
     men's Hours of Labor." *Life and Labor*, 7 (May 1917):
     81-82.

     Lists laws and terms whereby states regulate hours of
     work.

708. Nienburg, Bertha, and Bertha Blair. *Factors Affecting
     Wages in Power Laundries*. U.S. Department of Labor,
     Women's Bureau. Bulletin No. 143. 1936. 82 pp.

     Shows that wage rates vary by city, that there is no
     consistency between retail prices paid by the public and
     the wage rates of women operatives, and wages were higher
     because of the President's Reemployment Agreement and
     the Code of Fair Competition under the National Indus-

trial Recovery Act, even though they were not legally
in effect.

709. *Night-Work Laws in the United States.* U.S. Department
      of Labor, Women's Bureau. Bulletin No. 7. 1920.
      4 pp.

      Summarizes state laws which limit the number of hours
      which women may work at night, including eight per night
      and forty-eight per week, eight per night within fixed
      hours, twelve per night and prohibitions of night work
      for women in certain occupations.

710. O'Toole, Kitty. "Protective Legislation for Women."
      Life and Labor, 1 (December 1911): 356-57.

      Reports recommendations of the Legislative Committee
      to the Third Biennial Convention of the National Women's
      Trade Union League. Emphasizes the necessity to educate
      women workers about existing labor laws and the need of
      others, advocates a voluntary social police force to
      see that laws are enforced, stresses need to counter
      judicial nullification of protective laws, and suggests
      techniques for procuring more such legislation.

711. Patterson, James T. "Mary Dewson and the American Min-
      imum Wage Movement." *Labor History*, 5 (Spring 1964):
      134-52.

      Examines Mary Dewson's career and especially her
      struggle for minimum-wage legislation to illustrate the
      interactive commitments of the social justice and wo-
      men's rights movements.

712. Persons, Charles E., Mabel Parton, Mabelle Moses, *et al.*
      *Labor Laws and Their Enforcement, with Special Refer-
      ence to Massachusetts*, edited by Susan M. Kingsbury.
      New York: Longmans, Green and Co., 1911. 419 pp.

      Pleads for protective legislation for industrial
      workers by tracing the history of factory legislation,
      especially the Massachusetts labor laws between 1902
      and 1912.

713. Pidgeon, Mary Elizabeth. *Employed Women under N.R.A.
      Codes.* U.S. Department of Labor, Women's Bureau.
      Bulletin No. 130. 1935. 144 pp.

      Argues that the NRA has influenced an increase in
      wages and employment, shortened hours of work, and has

advanced the establishment of standards for the employment of women. However, the codes are limited to industries in interstate or foreign commerce, which covers only half of employed women. And the codes are not clearly defined enough regarding lowered minimum wages and provision for workers who deserve more than the minimum.

714. ————. *Summary of State Hour Laws for Women and Minimum-Wage Rates.* U.S. Department of Labor, Women's Bureau. Bulletin No. 137. 1936. 54 pp.

Asserts that minimum-wage laws have raised the depressed wages of large numbers of women receiving the lowest pay, and lists wages and hours legislation by state, industry, and terms of laws.

715. ————. *Variations in Wage Rates under Corresponding Conditions.* U.S. Department of Labor, Women's Bureau. Bulletin No. 122. 1935. 57 pp.

Documents that workers performing the same task do not get the same wages; even where the work period, product, and size of locality are the same, wages vary from plant to plant and even within the same plant. Minimum-wage requirements and their enforcement often bring considerable improvement in workers' earnings.

716. Pinchot, Cornelia Bryce. "Women Who Work." *Survey,* 62 (15 April 1929): 138-39.

Asks for social and protective legislation for employed women. The professional woman may benefit from the equal rights advocated by the Woman's Party, but industrial women suffer exploitation and unrestricted competition with other unskilled women. Therefore, working-class women need legislative protection until they learn the value of organization.

717. *Proceedings of the Women's Industrial Conference: January 11, 12, and 13, 1923.* U.S. Department of Labor, Women's Bureau. Bulletin No. 33. 1923. 190 pp.

Collects the addresses of speakers such as Mary van Kleeck, Margaret Dreier Robins, Maud Swartz, Melinda Scott, and Agnes Nestor to the conference called by the Women's Bureau to discuss problems of women in industry, such as what industry and women mean to each other, health standards, wages, labor legislation for women, and the need for its enforcement.

718.   "Regulation of Women's Working Hours in the United
       States." *American Labor Legislation Review*, 8 (De-
       cember 1918): 339-54.

       Claims that laws limiting working hours are necessary
       for racial survival, since potential mothers should not
       have their strength unduly drained.

719.   Robins, Margaret Dreier. "Fatigue and Efficiency: A
       New Defense for Shorter Hours." *Life and Labor*, 2
       (October, November, December 1912): 297-99, 324-26,
       367-68.

       Reviews Josephine Goldmark's *Fatigue and Efficiency*
       with heavy quotation from the original. Workers can
       produce more effectively if they are not rendered in-
       efficient by excessively long hours.

720.   ————. "The Minimum Wage." *Life and Labor*, 3 (June
       1913): 168-72.

       Pleads for the minimum wage to decrease drain on
       public charity and to avoid prostitution.

721.   Ryan, Rev. John A. "Guaranteeing a Living Wage by Law."
       Life and Labor, 2 (March 1912): 84-85.

       Demands the minimum-wage law, using the example of
       Australia since 1896, statistics on wages, and the argu-
       ment that the resulting improvement in conditions of
       living would enable employees to produce more.

722.   Sayin, Afife Fevzi. "Industrial Home Work in Pennsyl-
       vania: A Study of the Home Work System in the Knitted
       Outerwear and the Women's Apparel Industries." Ph.D.
       dissertation, Bryn Mawr College, 1945. 174 pp.

       Concludes that home work has declined and, where it
       still exists, enjoys better conditions since 1925, es-
       pecially since the Fair Labor Standards Administration.
       Home work in knitted outerwear and the women's apparel
       industries has become largely the occupation of married
       white women of the lower social strata.

723.   Smith, Ethel M. "Raising the Pay of Washington's Women
       Workers." *Life and Labor*, 9 (August 1919): 191-93.

       Reports that the District of Columbia minimum-wage
       board has announced the highest minimum wage for women
       working in stores and the printing trade to date, and
       the law makes that wage mandatory.

724. Smith, Florence P. *Chronological Development of Labor Legislation for Women in the United States.* U.S. Department of Labor, Women's Bureau. Bulletin No. 66-II. 1929. Revised 1931. 173 pp.

Compiles listings by state of laws limiting daily and weekly hours, providing rest periods and days, regulating night work, regulating or prohibiting employment of women in certain occupations, and dealing with physical conditions of working women.

725. ———. *Labor Laws for Women in the States and Territories: Hours, Home Work, Prohibited or Regulated Occupations, Seats, Minimum Wage.* U.S. Department of Labor, Women's Bureau. Bulletin No. 98. 1932. 67 pp.

Revises Bulletin No. 63 (item 735).

726. ———. *State Labor Laws for Women.* U.S. Department of Labor, Women's Bureau. Bulletin No. 156. 1938, 1940. 16, 18, 45 pp. (Part I: Summary, December 31, 1937; revised, December 31, 1940; Part II: Analysis of Hour Laws for Women Workers.)

Summarizes state laws regulating daily and weekly hours, rest periods and days, night work, seating, home work, minimum wage, and prohibition and regulation of women's work in certain occupations.

727. ———. *State Labor Laws for Women: Hours, Home Work, Prohibited or Regulated Occupations, Seats, Minimum Wage.* U.S. Department of Labor, Women's Bureau. Bulletin No. 144. 1937. 93 pp.

Revises Bulletin No. 98 (item 725).

728. ———. *State Minimum-Wage Laws and Orders: An Analysis; Supplements.* U.S. Department of Labor, Women's Bureau. Bulletin Nos. 167, 167-1, and 167-2. 1939-1941. 34, 15, 13 pp.

Compiles and abstracts laws providing for minimum wages or their determination by conferences or wage boards.

729. *Some Effects of Legislation Limiting Hours of Work for Women.* U.S. Department of Labor, Women's Bureau. Bulletin No. 15. 1921. 26 pp.

Asserts that laws regulating hours of labor for women will not lead to their dismissal; on the contrary, women

are more likely to be retained where protected by law.
Reduction of the total number of hours worked did not
reduce amounts produced, after a period of adjustment.

730. *Special Study of Wages Paid to Women and Minors in Ohio
      Industries Prior and Subsequent to the Ohio Minimum
      Wage Law for Women and Minors.* U.S. Department of
      Labor, Women's Bureau. Bulletin No. 145. 1936.
      83 pp.

      Claims that women work to support themselves and their
      dependents but receive wages which have no relationship
      to the value of the work they perform or to the cost of
      living. They have been powerless to remedy their situa-
      tion themselves, but the application of the minimum-wage
      law to the laundry and dry-cleaning industries illus-
      trates its benefits to women employees.

731. *Standards and Scheduled Hours of Work for Women in In-
      dustry: A Study Based on Data from 13 States.* U.S.
      Department of Labor, Women's Bureau. Bulletin No. 43.
      1925. 68 pp.

      Argues that shorter hours of labor increase efficiency
      and aid individual and national welfare; more progressive
      legal standards in more states would force employers to
      comply with maximum-hour limitations.

732. *Standards for Employment of Women in Industry, Recom-
      mended by the Women's Bureau.* U.S. Department of
      Labor, Women's Bureau. Bulletin No. 173. 1939.
      9 pp.

      Pleads for the establishment of specific standards of
      hours of work, wages, working conditions, industrial
      home work, and employer-employee relations, developed
      by employers, labor, and government in response to
      changing conditions. Standards are needed because many
      female wage-earners are also mothers and homemakers,
      because women working under low standards become un-
      willing undercutters of men, and because women need
      public concern and control since their bargaining power
      is weaker than men's.

733. *Standards for the Employment of Women in Industry.*
      U.S. Department of Labor, Women's Bureau. Bulletin
      No. 3. 1918, 1919, 1921, 1928. 8 pp.

      Argues that increasing employment of women in industry
      and women's relatively weaker economic condition require

standards to safeguard industrial efficiency and the
health of women such as the eight-hour day, time for
meals and rest, and comfort and sanitation, as well as
prohibition of night work and employment in occupations
more injurious to women than to men. Management, workers, and official agencies should cooperate in establishing these conditions.

734. *State Laws Affecting Working Women*. U.S. Department of
Labor, Women's Bureau. Bulletin No. 16. 1921. 51 pp.

Summarizes state laws regulating daily and weekly
hours of labor, rest days and periods, night work, home
work, wages, and pensions. Not a single state covers
all the possible types of legislation for regulating
women's hours of labor.

735. *State Laws Affecting Working Women: Hours, Minimum Wage,
Home Work*. U.S. Department of Labor, Women's Bureau.
Bulletin Nos. 40 and 63. 1924, 1927. 51 pp.

Summarizes state legislation regulating length of the
working day and week, rest days and periods, time for
meals, night work, and minimum wage; with charts, maps,
and cross-index by state.

736. Stone, Edna L. *List of References on Minimum Wage for
Women in the United States and Canada*. U.S. Department of Labor, Women's Bureau. Bulletin No. 42.
1925. 42 pp.

Collects citations of books, pamphlets, and articles
from official and other sources relating to minimum wage
in general and in the states which have adopted minimum-
wage laws.

737. *Summary: The Effects of Labor Legislation on the Employment Opportunities for Women*. U.S. Department of
Labor, Women's Bureau. Bulletin No. 68. 1928. 22 pp.

Reprints chapter II of Bulletin 65 (item 672).

738. Webster, George W. *A Physiological Basis for the Shorter Working Day for Women*. U.S. Department of Labor,
Women's Bureau. Bulletin No. 14. 1921. 20 pp.

Asserts that hours and conditions of labor should be
based on scientific evidence, that fatigue impedes efficiency and increases accidents, and that scientific
study should provide the basis for establishing standards of hours in industry dependent upon its physical
and psychological strains.

739. Weiss, Caroll. "What the Wisconsin Decision Means to
      the Working Woman." *Life and Labor*, 7 (April 1917):
      65.

      Discusses state regulation of hours of labor.

740. Werthein, Elsa. "The Firetrap in Chicago." *Life and
      Labor*, 4 (February 1914): 36-40.

      Lists violations of industrial safety in argument to
      have the building department turned into a division of
      public safety.

741. Omitted.

742. Omitted.

WOMEN'S BUREAU

743. Obenauer, Marie L. "What Is the United States Bureau
      of Labor Statistics Doing for Women in Industry?"
      Life and Labor, 6 (May 1916): 67-70.

      Demands accurate and relevant information on wage-
      earning women because the public needs to be awakened
      to the necessity for studies of women and legislation
      to bring justice to their conditions of employment.
      Argues for the creation of an independent Women's Divi-
      sion within the Department of Labor.

744. Sealander, Judith A. "The Women's Bureau, 1920-1950:
      Federal Reaction to Female Wage Earning." Ph.D. dis-
      sertation, Duke University, 1977. 303 pp.

      Shows how the Women's Bureau tried to improve the
      working and earning situations of American women through
      reform, advocacy of trade unionization, and association
      with foreign and international women's organizations.
      But in the years 1920 to 1950, members of the Women's
      Bureau were caught in their dual role of Outsiders as
      Insiders, reformers within government; they "contributed
      to the problem even as they sought a solution."

745. "Senate Bill 5408." *Life and Labor*, 6 (May 1916): 40.

      Reports on a bill for the establishment of a Women's
      Division in the Department of Labor to investigate and
      report on all matters regarding the welfare of wage-
      earning women, especially the adjustment of modern in-

dustrial mechanism and management to the physical and nervous organization of women and the influence of industrial employment on home life.

746. Smith, Ethel M. "At Last--A National Women's Labor Bureau." *Life and Labor*, 8 (August 1918): 159-60.

Applauds the establishment of the Women-in-Industry Service to oversee conditions of wage-earning women, a bureau which the Women's Trade Union League had been advocating since 1909.

747. "Trade Union Women Serving Uncle Sam." *Life and Labor*, 8 (October 1918): 213-15.

Publicizes how trade unionists and reformers assumed federal posts relating to treatment of women workers in World War I.

748. van Kleeck, Mary. "The Government and Women in Industry." *American Federationist*, 25 (September 1918): 788-90.

Claims that concern for the welfare of the many women entering the labor market during World War I has led the federal government to establish the Women-in-Industry Service within the Department of Labor. Working women should be represented in the councils of trade unions as a vehicle for their cooperation with the Women-in-Industry Service in seeking such improvements as equal pay, adequate working conditions, and collective bargaining.

F. HISTORICAL CONDITIONS

WORLD WAR I

749. "Are Many Women Replacing Soldiers in Industrial Work." *Current Opinion*, 64 (January 1918): 60-61.

Argues that many women hold war jobs but there has been little significant substitution of women for men in wartime industrial employment. Women do not receive the same wages as men for doing the same tasks.

750. "Democracy a Taunt or a Reality--Which?" *Life and Labor*, 7 (August 1917): 119.

Attacks the veneer of patriotism which appeals to women and young girls to replace men in industry but at
lower wages.

751.   "Female Labor Arouses Hostility and Apprehension in
       Union Ranks." *Current Opinion*, 65 (April 1910): 292-
       94.

Says that World War I does not require the extensive
employment of women in the United States as it has in
Europe. Employment of women demoralizes male workers
and may lead to their rebellion.

752.   Funk, Bertha. "The Girl in the Gas Mask Plant." *Life
       and Labor*, 9 (April 1919): 90-91.

Urges organization of women workers as the best protection and help in getting their rights; reports that
the war brought temporary relief from low wages but also
meant long hours and bad conditions.

753.   Goldmark, Josephine C. "Some Considerations Affecting
       the Replacement of Men by Women Workers." *Monthly
       Review*, 6 (January 1918): 56-64.

Shows that women have moved into occupations previously held by men; this has reduced prejudices against women's inexperience. But new roles require safeguards
such as equal wages and restrictions on lifting, industrial poisoning, fatigue, and night work.

754.   "Gravity of the Woman Labor Problem after the War."
       Current Opinion, 66 (January 1919): 61-62.

Claims that women will want to retain good-paying jobs
after World War I and employers may continue to employ
them.

755.   Greenwald, Maurine Weiner. "Women, War and Work: The
       Impact of World War I on Women Workers in the United
       States." Ph.D. dissertation, Brown University, 1977.
       260 pp.

Concludes that World War I accelerated long-term
trends in sex-segregated organization of work. Some of
these innovations are directly related to the development of corporate capitalism in the early twentieth century.

756. ————. "Women Workers and World War I: The American
   Railroad Industry, A Case Study." *Journal of Social
   History*, 9 (December 1975): 154-77.

   Uses occupational and personal data on women railway
   workers from 1917 to 1919 to show national changes in
   the patterns of women's work from 1910 to 1930. Generally the expansion of the female labor force was due
   to a gain in numbers in occupations already designated
   as women's work, such as clerical and service tasks.

757. Harney, Esther. "Boston's Shine Girls." *Life and
   Labor*, 7 (December 1917): 186-88.

   Warns that women who substitute for men workers during
   the war should not permit themselves to be exploited in
   humiliating jobs.

758. *Industrial Opportunities and Training for Women and
   Girls*. U.S. Department of Labor, Women's Bureau.
   Bulletin No. 13. 1920. 48 pp.

   Argues that increase in the number of wage-earning
   women, demonstrated capabilities of trained women workers in wartime, more industrial training courses available to women, decrease in male immigrant labor, and
   expansion of peacetime industries ought to encourage
   women and girls to acquire marketable industrial skills
   especially in machine shops, assembling and finishing
   products, optical and instrument factories, and sheet
   metal shops.

759. Krivy, Leonard Philip. "American Organized Labor and
   First World War, 1917-1918: A History of Labor Problems and the Development of a Government War Labor
   Program." Ph.D. dissertation, New York University,
   1965. 375 pp.

   Concludes that World War I saw increased centraliza-
   tion and efficiency in the successive boards and agencies which dealt with labor problems. Lack of planning
   at first meant dependency on pre-1917 agencies of state
   and local government, but inefficiencies and lack of
   real assistance led to establishment of several labor
   adjustment boards, which were replaced by the central-
   ized War Labor Administration in January 1918.

760. Lape, Esther E. "Women in Industry." *New Republic*, 25
   (26 January 1921): 251-53.

Expects that the entry of women into new occupations
during World War I will mean the permanent opening of
such jobs to females. In industries with unsafe or un-
healthful working conditions, women would prefer legislation to regulate the conditions rather than laws limiting the employment of women in those fields.

761. "League Members Called to Larger Service." *Life and
        Labor*, 8 (August 1918): 158.

Uses the appointment of Mary Anderson as assistant to
the chief of the Women's Division of the Department of
Labor to advocate principles of equal pay and full citizenship for women.

762. Malan, Nancy E. "How Ya Gonna Keep 'Em Down?: Women
        and World War I." *Prologue*, 5 (Winter 1972): 209-39.

Argues that World War I represents the first organized
effort to involve large numbers of women in war activities. While some women were urged to expand traditional
activities, others were recruited into jobs previously
held by men. Although most such workers were replaced
by returning veterans at the conclusion of the war,
postwar employment of women represented about a 50 percent increase over prewar employment.

763. "The Menace of Great Armaments." *Life and Labor*, 4
        (September 1914): 260-63.

Urges women workers to unite in opposing war; "this
is no people's war."

764. Morrison, Harry L. "Trade Organizations and War Prob-
        lems--Laundry Workers' International Union." *American
        Federationist*, 24 (September 1917): 732-33.

Shows that women and girls already dominated the laundry industry before the war; therefore, women have not
replaced men in wartime in that occupation. But wartime
increases in the cost of living encouraged workers to
organize the union, which obtained a wage increase.

765. *The New Position of Women in American Industry*. U.S.
        Department of Labor, Women's Bureau. Bulletin No. 12.
        1920. 158 pp.

Claims that women in industry rendered real service
during World War I, that the number of women workers in
war-production industries increased markedly while the

number of women in traditional woman-employing industries decreased, and that women received training in skilled vocations by the employing firms and over the objections of organized labor. Wartime success in training skilled women workers accounts for their remaining in most crafts and industries after the war and should encourage larger use of female labor in the future.

766. *The Occupational Progress of Women: An Interpretation of Census Statistics of Women in Gainful Occupations.* U.S. Department of Labor, Women's Bureau. Bulletin No. 27. 1922. 37 pp.

Says that publicity given to women entering traditionally male occupations in wartime gave a false impression of the numbers, proportions, and occupations of employed females. Census data indicates only a slight change in the proportion of women employed in nonagricultural pursuits but a significant change in distribution of occupations, with a great decrease among women working in domestic and service tasks and a corresponding increase in clerical, teaching, and nursing work where women were already established but are now showing impressive numbers.

767. *Proposed Employment of Women During the War in the Industries of Niagara Falls, N.Y.* U.S. Department of Labor, Bureau of Labor Statistics, Women-in-Industry Service. Bulletin No. 1. 1919. 16 pp.

Opposes permitting industries in the Niagara region to employ women at night despite wartime necessity, since adequate safety precautions have not been taken to protect workers in those hazardous occupations. In view of the need for labor, however, management of those plants should be urged to work toward safety and sanitation by extending the scope of the New York State Workmen's Compensation law to include occupational diseases.

768. Thorne, Florence C. "Trend toward Equality." *American Federationist*, 24 (February 1917): 120-21.

Argues that women workers have an opportunity to achieve freedom as a result of the increased demand for their labor during the war. Since men will not voluntarily acknowledge women's equal abilities in work, women must demand "equal pay for equal work" for themselves.

769. ————. "Women's War Service." *American Federationist*,
      24 (June 1917): 455-56.

      Urges women to seek greater opportunity and indepen-
      dence as a result of their work opportunities of World
      War I. But women should demand "equal pay for equal
      work" since employers do not intend to pay women as
      much as the men who previously held the same jobs.

770. "Uniforms to Be Taken Out of Sweatshops." *Life and
      Labor*, 7 (October 1917): 158.

      Reports that Secretary of War Newton D. Baker will
      not buy clothing made under unfair or unsanitary con-
      ditions.

771. van Kleeck, Mary. "Federal Policies for Women in In-
      dustry." *Annals of the American Academy of Political
      and Social Science*, 81 (January 1919): 87-94.

      Argues that women were a permanent part of the indus-
      trial work force even before World War I, but the war
      proved that with proper training, supervision, and ad-
      ministration, they could move into any industry. Con-
      tinuance of female employment in industry after the war
      will depend on federal and state laws and policies re-
      gulating their wages, hours, and conditions of labor.

772. "Women Conductors of Detroit Hold Jobs." *Life and
      Labor*, 9 (February 1919): 40, 46.

      Reports compromise to permit women streetcar conduc-
      tors who took jobs during World War I to keep them but
      not to allow other women to be hired.

GREAT DEPRESSION

773. Adams, Grace. *Workers on Relief*. New Haven: Yale Uni-
      versity Press, 1939. 344 pp.

      Analyzes the promise and confusion of the W.P.A. and
      other New Deal measures for the unemployed during the
      Great Depression. Case studies do not single out women;
      illustrations and examples are men.

774. Benham, Elisabeth D. *The Woman Wage Earner: Her Situa-
      tion Today*. U.S. Department of Labor, Women's Bureau.
      Bulletin No. 172. 1939. 56 pp.

Shows that women in a wide variety of manufacturing
and service occupations have weekly earnings significantly below the cost of living, and unemployment has
hit certain groups, such as semi-skilled factory workers, especially hard.

775. Bennett, Sheila Kishla, and Glen H. Elder, Jr. "Women's
      Work in the Family Economy: A Study of Depression
      Hardship in Women's Lives." *Journal of Family His-
      tory*, 4 (Summer 1979): 153-76.

Argues that deprived middle-class households in the
1930s oriented subsequent generations of women toward
a more prosperous life style and the security provided
by women's employment outside the home; these desires
represent an extension of family responsibilities.
Economic pressures in adulthood, rather than background
in the Depression, shaped the worklife of low-status
women, however.

776. Blackwelder, Julia Kirk. "Women in the Work Force:
      Atlanta, New Orleans, and San Antonio, 1930 to 1940."
      Journal of Urban History, 4 (May 1978): 331-58.

Claims that women's participation in the labor force
is determined by "a complicated pattern of cultural attitudes, financial needs, and individual perceptions of
employment opportunities."

777. Blair, Bertha. *Women in Arkansas Industries*. U.S.
      Department of Labor, Women's Bureau. Bulletin No.
      124. 1935. 45 pp.

Concludes that the heavy unemployment rate of women
in Arkansas (over 35 percent) as well as their responsibilities for supporting themselves and their families
have resulted in serious reductions in those families'
standards of living as well as their increasing depen-
dence on outside assistance and public relief.

778. Byrne, Harriet A. *The Effects of the Depression on
      Wage Earners' Families: A Second Survey of South Bend*.
      U.S. Department of Labor, Women's Bureau. Bulletin
      No. 108. 1936. 31 pp.

Asserts that social security legislation is necessary
because of the impact of unemployment of both men and
women as a result of technological changes and of the
Depression.

779. ————. *Women Unemployed Seeking Relief in 1933*. U.S.
      Department of Labor, Women's Bureau. Bulletin No.
      139. 1936. 19 pp.

      Describes women seeking relief in Chicago, Cleveland,
      Minneapolis, and St. Paul: there was no uniformity of
      age, most were native-born and white, most were widowed
      or divorced or separated, most were unemployed for in-
      dustrial reasons, and many had held a job other than
      their usual employment after losing their regular job.

780. ————, and Cecile Hillyer. *Unattached Women on Relief
      in Chicago, 1937*. U.S. Department of Labor, Women's
      Bureau. Bulletin No. 158. 1938. 84 pp.

      Examines the non-family women on relief as primarily
      older and white, as self-supporting or financially in-
      dependent before applying for relief because of loss of
      employment or ill health or other misfortune. Their
      living conditions were wretched, and they were forced
      to spend food money on other necessities.

781. Hewes, Amy, ed. *Women Workers in the Third Year of the
      Depression*. U.S. Department of Labor, Women's Bureau.
      Bulletin No. 103. 1933. 13 pp.

      Argues that extended unemployment results in lower
      incomes, inability to save and depletion of existing
      savings, the necessity of borrowing to meet emergencies,
      and a declining standard of living for the women workers
      and their families.

782. LaFollette, Cecile Tipton. *A Study of the Problems of
      652 Gainfully Employed Married Women Homemakers*. New
      York: Bureau of Publications, Teachers College, Colum-
      bia University, 1934. 208 pp.

      Opposes discharging married women workers as a solu-
      tion to depression by analyzing their economic status
      and contributions to family income.

783. McElvaine, Robert Stuart. "Thunder without Lightning:
      Working Class Discontent in the United States, 1929-
      1937." Ph.D. dissertation, State University of New
      York at Binghamton, 1974. 338 pp.

      Concludes that depression conditions led laborers,
      white-collar workers, and farmers to see their common
      difficulties and to become increasingly class conscious.
      Examination of ten thousand letters to public figures

as well as contemporary opinion surveys and sociological studies show an overwhelming sentiment for the country to move leftward, although they veered to Franklin Roosevelt and the New Deal rather than the Socialist or Communist Parties.

784. Manning, Caroline, and Arcadia N. Phillips. *Wage-Earning Women and the Industrial Conditions of 1930: A Survey of South Bend.* U.S. Department of Labor, Women's Bureau. Bulletin No. 92. 1932. 81 pp.

Compiles information on characteristics and conditions of employed women in South Bend and Mishawka, indicating that, on average, these women lost 5.9 hours in time and $4.45 in earnings per week over a year earlier.

785. Miller, Frieda S. "Women's Place—What Will Determine It?" *American Federationist,* 39 (March 1932): 287-90.

Asserts that women have become a permanent part of the industrial labor force. More women are employed in non-agricultural areas; they have entered new occupations. Depression unemployment ought not to be excuse for reviving old prejudices against employed women.

786. Nienburg, Bertha M. *Reemployment of New England Women in Private Industry.* U.S. Department of Labor, Women's Bureau. Bulletin No. 140. 1936. 118 pp.

Argues that industries and services can be developed to re-employ many unemployed factory, clerical, and professional women. For example, potential markets could be developed for sporting goods, staple fabric for wool gloves, low-to-medium-priced canned fish, novel salt and spiced products, household equipment, child care, and household services such as catering.

787. Pidgeon, Mary Elizabeth. *Employment Fluctuations and Unemployment of Women: Certain Indications from Various Sources, 1928-31.* U.S. Department of Labor, Women's Bureau. Bulletin No. 113. 1933. 236 pp.

Claims that general economic and business conditions are the main cause of unemployment of the approximately 18.9 percent of women normally gainfully employed. The greatest impact of such unemployment is seen in manufacturing industries (a third) and in domestic and personal service (a fourth). Significant numbers of these

women hold responsibility for the financial support of
others as well as themselves.

788.   ————. *Trends in the Employment of Women, 1928-36.*
        U.S. Department of Labor, Women's Bureau. Bulletin
        No. 159. 1938. 48 pp.

        Demonstrates that women form a slightly larger pro-
        portion of employed persons than in 1930 in general,
        although they have suffered relative losses in such
        trades as textiles and foods. Both women and men ex-
        perienced some increase in manufacturing employment,
        and the two sexes generally had similar changes in the
        general direction of employment in an industry, although,
        where they differed, employment declined for women and
        advanced for men.

789.   Scharf, Lois. *To Work and to Wed: Female Employment,
        Feminism, and the Great Depression.* Westport, Conn.:
        Greenwood Press, 1980. 240 pp.

        Argues that pressures of the Depression decade erased
        any positive arguments which feminists had made advocat-
        ing employment for married as well as unmarried women.
        Married women workers experienced discrimination from
        government, employers, professions, and vocational
        guidance. Society continued to assume that married wo-
        men belong at home.

790.   Sullivan, Mary Loretta. *Employment Conditions in De-
        partment Stores in 1932-33.* U.S. Department of Labor,
        Women's Bureau. Bulletin No. 125. 24 pp.

        Describes hours, schedules, wages, and earnings of
        women employed in department stores and similar retail
        businesses.

791.   Westin, Jeane. *Making Do: How Women Survived the '30s.*
        Chicago: Follette Publishing Company, 1976. 329 pp.

        Records women's reminiscences of how they coped with
        the hardships of the Great Depression.

V. RECENT AMERICA: SINCE 1940

A. PERSONAL

792. *The American Woman, Her Changing Role: Worker, Homemaker, Citizen; Report of the 1948 Women's Bureau Conference.* U.S. Department of Labor, Women's Bureau. Bulletin No. 224. 1948. 207 pp.

Reprints speeches from the conference, on such topics as legislation and working conditions, status of women, interaction of work and home obligations, and unions.

793. Chafe, William H. *The American Woman: Her Changing Social, Economic, and Political Role, 1920-1970.* New York: Oxford University Press, 1972. 351 pp.

Argues that woman's "place" is derived from the division of spheres of responsibility and that, while some crucial changes for women took place in the context of World War II, in fact, only those things changed which did not challenge the traditional economic and sexual status quo.

794. Diner, Hasia R. *Women and Urban Society: A Guide to Information Sources.* Detroit: Gale Research Company, 1979. 138 pp.

Lists and summarizes books, articles, and dissertations which analyze women undergoing urbanization throughout the world, including such subjects as family structure, fertility, employment, adjustment, behavior, associations, politics, and reform. Argues that literature tends to be contemporary; the works of demographers, anthropologists, political scientists, economists, and psychologists lack historical analysis.

795. Ferris, Abbott L. *Indicators of Trends in the Status of American Women.* New York: Russell Sage Foundation, 1971. 451 pp.

Collects data on numbers, education, marital status,
fertility, labor force status, employment, income, organizational membership, recreation, and health of women
in general, with limited attention to families and persons below the poverty level.

796. Flora, Cornelia Butler. "The Passive Female: Her Comparative Image by Class and Culture in Women's Magazine Fiction." *Journal of Marriage and the Family*,
33 (August 1971): 435-44.

Exposes the image of female passivity which pervaded
magazine fiction directed at working-class and middle-
class women in the United States and Latin America.
Cultural differences influence degrees of emphasis on
passivity; Latin American fiction, for example, stresses
passivity more than U.S. fiction does.

797. Frymer-Blumfield, Hanita. "The Maintenance of Ethnic
Identity among Jewish Women in an Urban Setting."
Ph.D. dissertation, American University, 1977.
141 pp.

Concludes that "in the United States the retention of
ethnic identification is primarily a function of self
ascription fostered by social interaction at the primary
group level." For the forty Jewish women interviewed
in the Washington, D.C., area, personal friendship and
institutional affiliations reinforced ethnic affilia-
tion.

798. Hartman, Susan M. "Prescriptions for Penelope: Literature on Women's Obligations to Returning World War
II Veterans." *Women's Studies*, 5 (1978): 223-39.

Shows how women were pressured by women's magazines
and by doctors to become "feminine" as a means of helping veterans to reorient themselves to domestic society.
These obligations were imposed in addition to the re-
quirement that women give up jobs to returning veterans.

799. Lasson, Kenneth. *The Workers: Portraits of Nine American Jobholders*. New York: Grossman Publishers,
1971. 269 pp.

Allows workers to describe their own lifestyles, work
experiences, and attitudes. A waitress traces her
career from a tenant farm through two marriages, acquisition of skills, and voluntary choice of employment as
a waitress.

800. Linden, Fabian, assisted by Helen Axel. *Women: A Demo-graphic, Social and Economic Presentation.* New York: The Conference Board, 1973. 40 pp.

Summarizes current statistics on women's place in the population, age, longevity, marriage and divorce, women heads of households, children, education, labor force participation, income distribution, family income and wives' contribution to it, occupations, professions, and professional degrees.

801. Myrdal, Gunnar. *An American Dilemma: The Negro Problem and Modern Democracy.* New York: Harper and Bros., Publishers, 1944. Appendix 5, pp. 1073-78.

Compares the disadvantages of women and children with those of blacks. Women are limited by procreation, Negroes by unassimilability.

802. O'Neill, William L. "Introduction." *Women at Work.* Chicago: Quadrangle Books, 1972. Pp. v-xix.

Points up similarities in the lives of working-class women at the turn of the century and of lower-middle-class women of the early 1970s. Also contains items 229 and 909.

803. United States. Bureau of the Census. *A Statistical Portrait of Women in the U.S.* Washington, D.C.: Government Printing Office, 1976. 90 pp.

Compiles statistics on female population, longevity, health, residence, marital and family status, education, labor force participation, income, voting, and crime.

804. United States. President's Commission on the Status of Women. *American Women: The Report of the President's Commission on the Status of Women and Other Publications of the Commission,* edited by Margaret Mead and Frances Bagley Kaplan. New York: Charles Scribner's Sons, 1965. 274 pp.

Surveys the contemporary conditions of women in general with regard to education, social insurance, law, leadership, citizenship, employment, labor standards, and protective legislation.

ATTITUDES

805. Balswick, Jack O. "Attitudes of Lower Class Males to-
      ward Taking a Male Birth Control Pill." *Family Co-
      ordinator*, 21 (April 1972): 195-99.

      Says that lower-class men's fear of emasculation pre-
      judices them against either birth control pills for men
      or vasectomies.

806. Kelley, Eleanor, Evelyn Good, and Sarah Walter. "Work-
      ing Class Adolescents' Perceptions of the Role of
      Clothing in Occupational Life." *Adolescence*, 9
      (Summer 1974): 185-98.

      Surveys a sampling of working-class teenagers regard-
      ing clothing. They see clothes not only as functional
      but also as "an item to be manipulated to create an
      impression and influence other people." White girls
      were more likely than white boys or than black boys and
      girls to hold this view.

807. LeMasters, E.E. *Blue-Collar Aristocrats: Life-Styles
      at a Working-Class Tavern.* Madison: University of
      Wisconsin Press, 1975. 218 pp.

      Examines conversations of men and women in a working-
      class tavern that reveal mutual suspicion, a double
      standard of permissible sexual activity, and overall
      fatalism about personal relationships between the sexes.

808. Levison, Andrew. *The Working-Class Majority.* New York:
      Coward, McCann and Geoghegan, 1974. 319 pp.

      Claims that blue-collar people are not becoming con-
      servative but are basically liberal, and the working
      class has not become lower middle class, either in in-
      come or in attitudes. "Most women are married and
      therefore live in the class and culture of their hus-
      bands."

809. McLaughlin, Gerald W., W. Kevin Hunt, and James R.
      Montgomery. "Socioeconomic Status and Career Aspira-
      tions and Perceptions of Women Seniors in High School."
      Vocational Guidance Quarterly, 25 (December 1976):
      155-62.

      Argues that socioeconomic status affects women's
      orientation toward work aspirations in a manner similar
      to its effect on men. Women in the lower socioeconomic

groups tended to favor community colleges and technical schools and stressed security as a major job goal.

810. Philliber, William W., and Dana V. Hiller. "A Research Note: Occupational Attainments and Perceptions of Status Among Working Wives." *Journal of Marriage and the Family*, 41 (February 1979): 59-62.

Concludes that wives of men with working-class jobs do not alter their self-concept of social status based on their own job attainments; women married to men with middle-class jobs do.

811. Wasserman, Susan A. "Values of Mexican-American, Negro, and Anglo Blue-Collar and White-Collar Children." *Child Development*, 42 (December 1971): 1624-28.

Explores value-orientation of a sampling of ethnic children. Girls have lower humanitarian values than blue-collar boys but higher values than white-collar boys; however, the girls' responses did not differ according to socioeconomic status.

B. HOME AND FAMILY

812. Dowdall, Jean A. "Women's Attitudes toward Employment and Family Roles." *Sociological Analysis*, 35 (Winter 1974): 251-62.

Shows that not all working-class women share the same assumptions about the relationship between family responsibilities and women's employment. Religion is not a significant influence, but nationality is, among non-high school graduates and non-white-collar families.

813. Ferree, Myra Marx. "Working-Class Jobs: Housework and Paid Work as Sources of Satisfaction." *Social Problems*, 23 (April 1976): 431-41.

Argues that contrary to general belief, working-class housewives are more dissatisfied than women employed outside the household. Housework yields less of a sense of competence, social connectedness, and self-determination than does paid employment. While more working-class women seek jobs because of financial need, they also do so to satisfy basic social and psychological needs.

814. Handel, Gerald, and Lee Rainwater. "Changing Family
     Roles in the Working Class." In *Blue-Collar World:
     Studies of the American Worker*, edited by Arthur B.
     Shostak and William Gomberg. Englewood Cliffs, N.J.:
     Prentice-Hall, Inc., 1964. Pp. 70-76.

     Concludes that working-class family life has been
     heavily influenced by increased economic prosperity and
     security in the last thirty years and by increased spa-
     tial mobility of individuals and families which breaks
     up close-knit social networks. Therefore upper-lower-
     class couples focus more on the nuclear family and are
     shifting away from highly segregated conjugal roles to-
     ward greater mutual involvement. Working-class parents
     are also showing a greater interest in the individual
     child.

815. ———. "Persistence and Change in Working-Class Life
     Style." In *Blue-Collar World: Studies of the Amer-
     ican Worker*, edited by Arthur B. Shostak and William
     Gomberg. Englewood Cliffs, N.J.: Prentice-Hall, Inc.,
     1964. Pp. 36-41.

     Says that some working-class behaviors and attitudes,
     such as those in education and housing, have superficial
     similarities to those of the middle class, "but they
     have a different meaning for the working class than they
     do for the middle class." In the areas of family life
     and social participation, the working class is divided
     into traditional and modern; the modern group resembles
     lower-middle-class values. Working-class people spend
     like the middle class on hard goods but not on other
     expenditures, especially services.

816. Hayghe, Howard. "Families and the Rise of Working
     Wives--An Overview." *Monthly Labor Review*, 99 (May
     1976): 12-19.

     Asserts that increased labor-force participation by
     married women increases income, which provides the fam-
     ily with adequate food, housing, and educational oppor-
     tunities that would not be available otherwise.

817. Hinday, Virginia Aldise. "Parity and Well-Being among
     Low-Income Urban Families." *Journal of Marriage and
     the Family*, 37 (November 1975): 789-97.

     Argues that the number of children influences income
     level, public assistance, and maternal employment.

While poverty is not caused by children, larger numbers of children hurt a mother's ability to operate a household efficiently and hamper the family's opportunity to save.

818. Howell, Joseph L. *Hard Living on Clay Street: Portraits of Blue Collar Families.* Garden City, N.Y.: Anchor Press/Doubleday, 1973. 381 pp.

Offers a realistic description of blue-collar families showing their range and complexity of social and economic stability. The ineffectual, sickly, drunken man's family appears in contrast to the less poor and more stabilized family observed during 1970-1971 in a suburb of Washington, D.C.

819. Kolko, Gabriel. "The Structure of the Working Class and the Working Wife." In *The American Working Class: Prospects for the 1980s*, edited by Irving Louis Horowitz, *et al.* New Brunswick, N.J.: Transaction Books, 1979. Pp. 94-113.

Claims that increases in the number and proportion of employed females indicates that their husbands are suffering from unemployment or inadequate wages. But it becomes increasingly difficult for the working class to resolve its economic problems by the entry of more wives into the labor market because they cannot be absorbed unless the cost of female labor is further cheapened.

820. Komarovsky, Mirra. *Blue Collar Marriage.* New York: Random House, 1962. 397 pp.

Presents a sociological investigation of the working class rather than basing primary assumptions, especially about marriage and education, on middle-class respondents. Case studies in 1958 and 1959 involve fifty-eight respondents, white, native-born of native parents, Protestant, not over forty years old, parents of at least one child, and highest education high school graduates in a community five miles from a city of half a million and less than twenty miles from a metropolis, with industrial development dating from a mid-nineteenth-century mill.

821. Levitan, Sar A., ed. *Blue-Collar Workers: A Symposium on Middle America.* New York: McGraw-Hill, 1971. 393 pp.

Explores working-class feelings on alienation from the
American Dream. Wives work because of working-class income pressures, and consume in ways to protect their
own value to their families.

822. McEaddy, Beverly Johnson. "Women Who Head Families: A
     Sociological Analysis." *Monthly Labor Review*, 99
     (June 1976): 3-9.

     Shows that families headed by women are more likely to
     be poor than families headed by men. The only solution
     is female employment in skilled occupations which pay
     higher salaries.

823. Myrdal, Alva, and Viola Klein. *Women's Two Roles: Home
     and Work*. London: Routledge and Kegan Paul, Ltd.,
     1956, 1968. 213 pp.

     Examines society's dual claims on women, regeneration
     and economic progress. Modern economy cannot afford,
     nor can democratic ideology tolerate, a large section of
     the population living by the efforts of others; there-
     fore, a fairer re-distribution of work and leisure be-
     tween the sexes is necessary, but this depends on re-
     forms to allow women to reconcile family and professional
     life.

824. Nelson, Elizabeth Ness. "Women's Work--Jobs and House-
     work." Ph.D. dissertation, University of California
     at Los Angeles, 1975. 384 pp.

     Claims that employed women tend to be "quite satisfied
     with their jobs" and less so with housework, although
     nuclear family roles as wives and mothers were more im-
     portant than jobs or housework to the New Jersey women
     interviewed.

825. Ogburn, William Fielding, and Meyer F. Nimkoff. *Tech-
     nology and the Changing Family*. Boston: Houghton
     Mifflin Company, 1955. 329 pp.

     Argues that increasing urbanism and technology have
     altered family size, structure, interrelationships, and
     interactions with external world. Technology has con-
     tributed to the growth of cities, which means separa-
     tion of place of occupation from place of residence.
     Urban employment opportunities for women tend to retard
     marriage; and technology decreases household duties
     after marriage.

826. Patterson, James M. "Marketing and the Working-Class Family." In *Blue-Collar World: Studies of the American Worker*, edited by Arthur B. Shostak and William Gomberg. Englewood Cliffs, N.J.: Prentice-Hall, Inc., 1964. Pp. 76-80.

Concludes that the limited social experience and pervasive anxiety of the working-class family leads them to be overly preoccupied with the stability of basic human relationships and to look to their peers for standards of behavior. Therefore, they spend on immediate-consumption items, strive only for a "common man" level of recognition and respectability, trade where they are known and unthreatened, and purchase recognized brands.

827. Pidgeon, Mary Elizabeth. *Women Workers and Their Dependents*. U.S. Department of Labor, Women's Bureau. Bulletin No. 239. 1952. 117 pp.

Shows how women's earnings make necessary and significant contributions to the support of the American home. Upwards of a fourth of employed women are the only wage-earners in their families and the proportion of working mothers is increasing. Two-thirds of union women interviewed reported using all or most of their earnings to support themselves and others.

828. Rainwater, Lee. *And the Poor Get Children: Sex, Contraception, and Family Planning in the Working Class*. Chicago: Quadrangle Books, Inc., 1960. 202 pp.

Examines the range of attitudes toward family size and contraceptive practices by working-class men and women arranged by income level. The working class tends to resist limitation of family size for a variety of social and psychological reasons.

829. ———. "Making a Good Life: Working-Class Family and Life-Styles." In *Blue-Collar Workers: A Symposium on Middle America*, edited by Sar A. Levitan. New York: McGraw-Hill Book Company, 1971. Pp. 204-29.

Claims that the working class has experienced a steadily increased level of prosperity and security which it expends on mass-market products rather than services in an effort to obtain the good things in life. A sharp division of labor continues, with the husband as provider and the wife as mother-homemaker. Working-class morale is affected by anxiety and a sense of isolation, wondering whether members of the working class are obtaining their share of the American Dream.

830.   ————, Richard P. Coleman, and Gerald Handel. *Workingman's Wife: Her Personality, World and Life Style.* New York: Oceana Publications, Inc., 1969. 238 pp.

Asserts that working-class buying power has increased and that many working-class women handle family consumption; therefore, it would be profitable to understand their psychology and social characteristics. Working-class women are husband-tenders, child-rearers, and housewives who pride themselves on obtaining good value and orient their purchasing toward home and family.

831.   Rosenberg, George S., and Donald F. Anspach. *Working Class Kinship.* Lexington, Mass.: D.C. Heath and Company, 1973. 157 pp.

Concludes that working-class people have some, but not unlimited, choices in selecting from among broad categories of kinship roles for interaction. "Recognition of common descent provides the normative basis for kinship interaction among kindred."

832.   Ross, Heather L., and Isabel V. Sawhill. *Time of Transition: The Growth of Families Headed by Women.* Washington, D.C.: The Urban Institute, 1975. 223 pp.

Explores the increase in female-headed families which have grown ten times as rapidly as two-parent families; 15 percent of all families are now headed by mothers. Therefore, public policy should increase work opportunities and earning levels of women, increase and facilitate the flow of income support payments within the private sector from parents to children, and reform and extend the system of public income maintenance.

833.   Senf, Janet Hilger. "Women's Employment and Kinship Patterns." Ph.D. dissertation, University of Illinois at Chicago Circle, 1977. 190 pp.

Argues that frequency of kin contacts and the nature of relationships depends primarily on geographical proximity and to a lesser extent on work status—full time, part time, or none.

834.   Sexton, Patricia Cayo. "Speaking for the Working-Class Wife." *Harpers Magazine,* 225 (October 1962): 129-33.

Portrays working-class women as deprived and estranged from current society. While working outside the household offers a version of independence, the lifestyle of these women tends toward passivity and a direct routine. Sexton herself, however, represents a combination of self, family, union, and working class which leaves her optimistic about "raising workers to first-class status and creating a more just and dynamic society."

835. ———. "Wife of the 'Happy Worker.'" In *Blue-Collar World: Studies of the American Worker*, edited by Arthur B. Shostak and William Gomberg. Englewood-Cliffs, N.J.: Prentice-Hall, Inc., 1964. Pp. 81-85.

Attacks organized labor as "grossly neglectful of the worker's wife." Unions try to establish communication with women only when their support is needed in a strike situation. Union men resent women's involvement in politics, especially local union elections. But the obvious power of middle-class club-women reveals a great potential for working-class women to offer political and other support to their husbands.

836. Sherman, Lucille Olive. "Women in the Labor Force: Relationships among Occupational Attachments, Family, Statuses, and Poverty." Ph.D. dissertation, University of Georgia, 1973. 158 pp.

Concludes that poverty exists for women in all occupational categories and all family statuses. Southern women are more likely to be in low-income occupational categories.

837. Social Research, Inc. *Working-Class Women in a Changing World: A Review of Research Findings*. New York: MacFadden-Bartell Corporation, 1973. 54 pp.

Claims that Women's Liberation has had a double effect on working-class women, making for new opportunities but also adding to anxieties. This analysis of the young, working-class housewife as a potential consumer points to trends which up-date *Workingman's Wife* by Lee Rainwater *et al.* (item 830).

838. Sweet, James Arthur. "Family Composition and the Labor Force Activity of Married Women in the United States." Ph.D. dissertation, University of Michigan, 1968. 281 pp.

Develops methodologies and categories for examining employment patterns of wives in relation to the composition of their families.

839.   ———. *Women in the Labor Force*. New York: Seminar Press, 1973. 211 pp.

Speculates on the relationship between employment and fertility, including the impact on labor-force activity of marriage, child status, family history, education, economic need, and race.

840.   Tanabe, Patricia Anne White. "Views of Women's Work in Public Policy in the United States: Social Security and Equal Pay Legislation, 1935-1967." Ph.D. dissertation, Bryn Mawr College, Graduate School of Social Work and Social Research, 1973. 155 pp.

Argues that women policy-makers are more likely than men to see women as independent contributors to the society as a whole. Legislation and policy, which is primarily influenced by men, tends to view women as stereotypical mothers and caretakers of children.

841.   Terkel, Studs. "Blue-Collar Wife: Being the Woman in One of America's Scorned Families." *Today's Health*, 50 (February 1972): 48-53, 72.

Examines popular culture portrayals of stereotyped working-class women images which are not only inaccurate but which contribute to anxiety in a rapidly changing and challenging world. Working-class women describe their neighborhoods, their attitudes, and their activism.

842.   Whitehurst, Robert Noel. "Employed Mothers' Influence on Working-class Family Structure." Ph.D. dissertation, Purdue University, 1963. 259 pp.

Concludes that there is little difference in decision-making, conflict in the family, or control of finances between families with working mothers and those with non-working mothers, based on the study of eighty-three mothers in Lafayette, Indiana. But the two groups do display differing value patterns, with working women more likely to value companionship, economic value, standard of living, and fewer children, while the non-working mothers were more traditionally family-oriented.

C. COMMUNITY

843. Bauer, Constance Elizabeth Coe. "Voluntary Associations among Women of Two Classes in Urban Colorado." Ph.D. dissertation, University of Colorado, 1975. 241 pp.

   Argues that subcultural position is not a good explanation for level of participation in voluntary groups.

844. *Employed Mothers and Child Care.* U.S. Department of Labor, Women's Bureau. Bulletin No. 246. 1953. 92 pp.

   Urges provision for child care because it is increasingly important at a time "when married women constitute the largest labor reserve in the country." Committees should examine local needs and provide a central reference service for mothers requiring child care. Employed mothers should have healthful working conditions and hours "on a shift fitted as far as possible to their family needs."

845. Fandetti, Donald V. "Day Care in Working-Class Ethnic Neighborhoods: Implications for Social Policy." *Child Welfare*, 55 (November 1976): 618-26.

   Shows that significant percentages of American-born Poles and Italians do not view an "outside" teacher at a day-care center negatively; the same is true, to a lesser degree, of foreign-born Poles and Italians. On the other hand, institutions sponsored by the Catholic Church would be accepted much more readily than public assistance.

846. ————. "Sources of Assistance in a White, Working-class, Ethnic Neighborhood." D.S.W. dissertation, Columbia University, 1974. 180 pp.

   Claims that working-class ethnic Catholics prefer to turn to family, church, or ethnic voluntary organizations rather than professional or institutional social and mental health services to deal with child care, care of the aged, financial aid, and personal problems.

847. Feldman, Harold, and Margaret Feldman. "Preferences by Low-income Women about Day Care." *Human Ecology Forum*, 4 (Autumn 1973): 16-18.

Says that most low-income women prefer home care rather than nursery school or day care because they believe family care is a better way to deal with sick children, it gives the child more personal attention, and it is more convenient for the mother in location and hours.

848. Fried, Marc, *et al.* *The World of the Urban Working Class.* Cambridge, Mass.: Harvard University Press, 1973. 410 pp.

Argues that the community as well as the physical area was demolished when the city took over a tenement district near the center of Boston in 1958 for slum clearance and urban renewal. The employment experience of women in this district shows that they seek jobs out of overt necessity, and that their lack of education and occupational skills hinders their job search and mobility. But once employed, many such women find both financial and personal satisfaction from working and earning.

849. Gans, Herbert J. "Effects of the Move from City to Suburb." In *The Urban Condition: People and Policy in the Metropolis,* edited by Leonard J. Duhl. New York: Basic Books, Inc., 1963. Pp. 184-98.

Examines the unhappiness of women in suburbia. The working class especially feels an economic pinch and is distressed at being cut off from relatives by distance from the city and lack of public transportation.

850. ————. *The Levittowners: Ways of Life and Politics in a New Suburban Community.* New York: Pantheon Books, 1967. 474 pp.

Includes an analysis of the alienation experienced by working-class women torn from kin relations to live in suburbia. Working-class families are sexually segregated, with men finding organizational social outlets while women tend to depend on relatives who may now live at a distance. Hence, women tend to feel isolated, stay close to home, and view the house as a refuge from a hostile external world.

851. McCourt, Kathleen. *Women and Grass-Roots Politics.* Bloomington: Indiana University Press, 1977. 256 pp.

Examines the emergence of women in large numbers in demonstrations and on picket lines and also in speaking,

organizing, and providing leadership. Active women are
committed to staying in their neighborhoods and usually
join an organization because of the need to confront a
particular problem or because they are invited to join.

852. Peters, Barbara, and Victoria Samuels, eds. *Dialogue
      on Diversity: A New Agenda for American Women*. New
      York: Institute on Pluralism and Group Identity of
      the American Jewish Committee, 1976. 88 pp.

      Asks that women of diverse ethnic, religious, and
      class backgrounds develop a deeper understanding of one
      another's perceptions of differing realities, a better
      sense of how to communicate, and a clearer idea of is-
      sues of mutual concern.

853. Ryan, Joseph A., ed. *White Ethnics: Life in Working-
      Class America*. Englewood Cliffs, N.J.: Prentice-Hall,
      Inc., 1973. 184 pp.

      Examines concepts of white ethnicity and includes some
      neighborhood and lifestyle descriptions.

854. Suttles, Gerald D. *The Social Order of the Slum: Eth-
      nicity and Territory in the Inner City*. Chicago:
      University of Chicago Press, 1968. 243 pp.

      Uses the Addams area of the Near West Side of Chicago
      to examine sharply defined groups segregated by age,
      sex, ethnicity, and residence.

855. Thomas, Carolyn Palmer. "Social Participation of Women:
      Labor, Force, Formal, Informal." Ph.D. dissertation,
      Michigan State University, 1974. 247 pp.

      Concludes that women with a labor force participation
      history are more likely to be involved in clubs and
      neighborhood interaction, at least with friends and
      relatives, than women who have never been employed.

856. Van Gelder, Lindsy. "National Congress of Neighborhood
      Women: When the Edith Bunkers Unite!" *Ms. Magazine*,
      7 (February 1979): 53-56.

      Publicizes the National Congress of Neighborhood Wo-
      men as a persuasive argument against the stereotype of
      the working-class woman as "passive and inarticulate and
      incapable of thinking about the 'larger' issues outside
      her home." It also shows that the Women's Movement need

not be middle class and need not project only a single
brand of feminism.

857.   *Women in Blue-Collar Jobs*. New York: Ford Foundation,
       1976. 28 pp.

       Says that working-class women, who constituted 40
       percent of all workers in 1974, have largely been ig-
       nored until the December 1974 two-day national Confer-
       ence on Women in Blue-Collar Industrial and Service Jobs
       sponsored by the Ford Foundation. While rate of par-
       ticipation by women in the labor force is increasing,
       disparities continue in ratios of pay, sex-related oc-
       cupations, opportunities for training and advancement,
       activity in labor unions, working-class lifestyles, and
       problems of reconciling occupational safety with equal
       opportunity.

                          D. CLASS

858.   Aronowitz, Stanley. *False Promises: The Shaping of
       American Working Class Consciousness*. New York:
       McGraw-Hill Book Company, 1973. 465 pp.

       Argues that women reinforce the authoritarianism of
       society which sustains a social order of hierarchy in
       the American workplace and ethnic fragmentation of the
       labor force which has pitted worker against worker. But
       working-class women suffer double victimization; they
       are subordinate in the factory and in the home.

859.   Berger, Bennett. *Working-Class Suburb: A Study of Auto
       Workers in Suburbia*. Berkeley and Los Angeles: Uni-
       versity of California Press, 1960. 143 pp.

       Examines auto workers in Richmond, California, in the
       1950s; they showed little evidence of socially mobile
       attitudes, a relatively low level of occupational aspi-
       ration, and a low level of organizational or community
       involvement. About half the group studied identified
       themselves as working class, but large minorities de-
       signated themselves and their neighbors as middle-class
       despite low dollar income levels.

860.   Davis, Susan. "Organizing from Within." *Ms. Magazine*,
       1 (August 1972): 92-98.

Speculates that women's caucuses may become a major element for change within corporations since they work to raise consciousness and then address such issues as low salaries, lack of promotion, and disrespect for women regardless of economic status or racial group. Caucuses will have to face and overcome mutual antagonisms between blacks and women in order for both groups to take advantage of recent legislation for equal opportunity.

861. Gardner, Burleigh B. "The Awakening of the Blue Collar Woman." *Intellectual Digest*, 4 (March 1974): 17-19.

Argues that the working-class woman was part of one of the most stable, unchanging groups in society for decades, but she is now emerging as a new social, political, and economic force. The working-class woman has been developing greater self-confidence and enjoys improved material well-being; therefore, she is oriented more toward current freedom and pleasure than toward "the ancient middle-class virtues of hard work and self-denial" attached to upward mobility.

862. Gutman, Robert. "Population Mobility in the American Middle Class." In *The Urban Condition: People and Policy in the Metropolis*, edited by Leonard J. Duhl. New York: Basic Books, Inc., 1963. Pp. 172-83.

Claims that for the working-class wife the move to suburbia constitutes an upward movement in the social scale but creates problems of adjustment to the new social environment, including strain in relations with neighbors.

863. Roby, Pamela, ed. *The Poverty Establishment*. Englewood Cliffs, N.J.: Prentice-Hall, Inc., 1974. 217 pp.

Attacks poverty programs which continue the unequal distribution of resources by preventing its being questioned. Local, state, and federal administrators of poverty programs and legislators are under the control of an upper echelon multi-national corporate elite which shapes the distribution of income and the lives of the poor and others.

864. Samuels, Victoria. *Nowhere to Be Found: A Literature Review and Annotated Bibliography on White Working Class Women*. Working Paper Series No. 13. New York: American Jewish Committee, Institute on Pluralism and

Group Identity, Project on Group Life and Ethnic America, 1975. 29 pp.

Shows that working-class women are largely missing
from the literature on women or on the working class,
and that the only studies really attempting to deal
with them are now out-dated since they pre-date the
Women's Movement. Media images of working-class women
are absent or negative, and images of the Women's Movement are presented by the media as incompatible with
working-class women.

865. Seifer, Nancy. *Absent from the Majority: Working Class
      Women in America.* New York: National Jewish Committee,
      National Project on Ethnic America, 1973. 85 pp.

Opposes the assumption that working-class women or
white ethnics resemble the stereotypes presented of them.
A brief overview of these women since World War II emphasizes their anxieties and points out the beginnings
of their self-action.

866. ————. *Nobody Speaks for Me! Self-Portraits of Amer-
      ican Working Class Women.* New York: Simon and
      Schuster, 1976. 477 pp.

Presents interviews with ten working-class women who
offer a portrait of American diversity in ethnicity,
region, urban/suburban/rural living, employment, income,
age, and relevant issues. They represent a spirit of
communalism, optimism, and involvement in supporting
others that is indicative of the present and future
situation of working-class women.

867. Szymanski, Albert. "Race, Sex, and the U.S. Working
      Class." *Social Problems*, 21 (June 1974): 706-25.

Claims that trends in occupation, income, and education from 1940 to 1970 support both the classical Marxist prediction of increasing homogeneity in the working
class and the neo-Marxist prediction of continuing sexual discrimination. Corporate need for masculine and
feminine personality traits in the labor force per-
petuates the sexual division of labor. But blacks have
been integrated into most levels of the work force in
order to keep white wages down.

868. Tepperman, Jean. *Not Servants, Not Machines: Office
      Workers Speak Out!* Boston: Beacon Press, 1976.
      188 pp.

Says that women office workers are questioning not
only their treatment on the job but their status as
"second-class citizens in every aspect of life." New
activism, such as that of "9 to 5" in Boston, challenges
job conditions and assumptions about employed women, in
the hope of bringing office work into line with other
significant changes in American life because "office
work has lost many of its old advantages in pay and job
security which were supposed to make organizing unnecessary."

E. EMPLOYMENT

869. Agassi, Judith Buber. "Women Who Work in Factories."
      In *The World of the Blue-Collar Worker*, edited by
      Irving Howe. New York: Quadrangle Books, 1972. Pp.
      239-48.

Shows that women workers, who are increasing in numbers, have been sex-typed so that they do not receive
training in industrial craft skills. Moreover, equality
for women workers does not lie in technology or in
socio-biological needs of women as mothers, but in a
re-structuring of outmoded and restrictive norms of
industry which were initially created by and for men
and to which women were expected to conform. Movement
away from rules favoring immobility and uninterrupted
work would not only open employment opportunities to
working mothers, but would benefit the economy and society in general.

870. Albrecht, Stan L. "Social Class and Sex-Stereotyping
      of Occupations." *Journal of Vocational Behavior*, 9
      (December 1976): 321-28.

Concludes that while legal and institutional barriers
to women's employment in non-traditional occupations
are being withdrawn, attitudinal and social-psychological
barriers remain. And these attitudinal barriers occur
more often among those having less education. Education was a more significant factor than social class,
although both of these outweighed sex and religion.

871. *Analysis of Coverage and Wage Rages of State Minimum
      Wage Laws and Orders: August 1, 1965.* U.S. Department

of Labor, Women's Bureau. Bulletin No. 291. 1965.
130 pp.

Abstracts state regulations by occupation.

872. Andreas, Carol. *Sex and Caste in America*. Englewood
     Cliffs, N.J.: Prentice-Hall, Publishers, 1971.
     146 pp.

     Complains that education currently inhibits full de-
     velopment of human potential by sexually based chanel-
     ling, and that economic patterns divide labor by sex
     which is caste-like. Religion, pseudo-science, and the
     nuclear family limit behavior. Working-class women are
     part of the general category of women as oppressed.

873. Arthur, Julietta K. *Jobs for Women over Thirty-Five*.
     New York: Prentice-Hall, Inc., 1947. 253 pp.

     Advises on strategies for women to move into the labor
     market by way of applying present skills. The advantage
     of a factory career is the opportunity to meet a cross
     section of the world.

874. Baetjer, Anna M. *Women in Industry: Their Health and
     Efficiency*. Philadelphia: W.B. Saunders Company,
     1946. 344 pp.

     Claims that women can do the same work as men except
     for excessively muscular jobs, and women lose more time
     from work than men but are absent for shorter periods.
     Evidence of the effect of wartime employment on gyne-
     cological and obstetrical problems is inconclusive.

875. Baker, Sally Hillsman. "Earnings Prospects of Black and
     White Working-Class Women." *Sociology of Work and
     Occupations*, 3 (May 1976): 123-50.

     Concludes that white working-class women have a better
     chance at regular employment and receive higher wages
     than black or Puerto Rican women, both on first employ-
     ment and after several years of work.

876. Bell, Carolyn. "Implementing Safety and Health Regula-
     tions for Women in the Workplace." *Feminist Studies*,
     5 (Summer 1979): 286-301.

     Asks for protection for workers regardless of gender.
     "Protective legislation only becomes restrictive when
     we begin to develop standards that are discriminatory in
     nature toward a particularly susceptible group."

877. Bem, Sandra L., and Daryl J. Bem. *Training the Woman to Know Her Place: The Social Antecedents of Women in the World of Work.* Harrisburg: Pennsylvania Department of Education, 1973. 29 pp.

Shows how society has conditioned women into domestic and inferior occupational roles rather than into careers, and urges guidance counselors not to follow that pattern.

878. Bibb, Robert. "Blue Collar Women in Low-Wage Industries: A Dual Labor Market Interpretation." In *The American Working Class: Prospects for the 1980s,* edited by Irving Louis Horowitz, et al. New Brunswick, N.J.: Transaction Books, 1979. Pp. 125-50.

Argues that working-class women have been trapped in poverty-wage industries by discrimination, labor market segmentation, and the position of the marginal industries in which they find work in the overall economy. A combination of unionization, legislation, and the Equal Rights Amendment could break down these limitations.

879. Bird, Caroline. *Everything a Woman Needs to Know to Get Paid What She's Worth,* edited by Helene Mandelbaum. New York: David McKay Company, Inc., 1973. 304 pp.

Urges women to get out of the female job ghetto, avoid jobs segregated to women since they are, by definition, low-paying. Male jobs should be feminized by taking the women's angle on them; new jobs should be created for women to fill.

880. ———, with Sara Welles Briller. *Born Female: The High Cost of Keeping Women Down.* New York: David McKay Company, Inc., 1968, 1970. 302 pp.

Complains that the contemporary employment picture shows a waste of talent in not allowing full and free opportunity for women as well as men. Sex need not be related to occupation, and there is some trend toward androgyny, that is, sexless jobs.

881. Blake, Judith. "The Changing Status of Women in Developed Countries." *Scientific American,* n.s. 231 (September 1974): 137-47.

Says that the income issue for working women is not so much a matter of wage discrimination as the concentration of women in low-paying occupations and the secondary role of paid employment in their lives. In an unstable situation, women suffer a net loss of status.

882. Blaxall, Martha, and Barbara Reagan, eds. *Women and the
      Work-Place: The Implications of Occupational Segrega-
      tion.* Chicago: University of Chicago Press, 1976.
      326 pp.

      Claims that an occupationally integrated society would
      be preferable to occupational segregation; but societal
      values and goals must be jolted to break the vicious
      cycle of current labor demands.

883. Brady, Dorothy S. "Equal Pay for Women Workers." *Annals
      of the American Academy of Political and Social Science*,
      251 (May 1947): 53-60.

      Asserts that equal pay regardless of the gender of the
      worker is a matter of simple justice to women workers,
      sustains men's wage rates and jobs by discouraging em-
      ployers from substituting cheaper female labor, and in-
      creases consumer purchasing power.

884. Briggs, Norma. "Women Apprentices: Removing the Bar-
      riers." *Manpower*, 1 (December 1974): 3-11.

      Shows how women have been handicapped as workers and
      earners because they are led to believe that they will
      be paid laborers only until marriage and are channelled
      into vocations by sex, particularly being discouraged
      from pursuing technical interests. But the experience
      of women in Wisconsin Apprenticeship shows that women
      can successfully learn technological skills, and ap-
      propriately trained women have a significantly lower
      dropout rate than men.

885. *Careers for Women as Technicians.* U.S. Department of
      Labor, Women's Bureau. Bulletin No. 282. 1961.
      28 pp.

      Says that abundant employment opportunities exist in
      technical occupations "for women and girls who have the
      interest and resolve to prepare for them," although few
      women are currently in the field.

886. *Changes in Women's Occupations: 1940-1950.* U.S. Depart-
      ment of Labor, Women's Bureau. Bulletin No. 253.
      1954. 104 pp.

      Illustrates how women's employment has gradually
      shifted toward "occupations involving specialized skills
      and preparations," and the variety of service occupations
      held by women has broadened. In addition, more older

women are employed, and the proportion of married women
has risen while the proportion of single women has declined among nurses, waitresses, and food industry workers.

887. *Clerical Occupations for Women: Today and Tomorrow.*
U.S. Department of Labor, Women's Bureau. Bulletin
No. 289. 1964. 69 pp.

Argues that "virtually all girls can expect to hold a
paying job, many of them for a significant part of their
lives" and most will find employment in the clerical
field.

888. *Community Household Employment Programs.* U.S. Department of Labor, Women's Bureau. Bulletin No. 221.
1948. 70 pp.

Notes that the drawing off of household workers into
war industries and service trades represented a hardship
on American households; the necessity for recruiting an
adequate supply of domestic workers demonstrates the
importance of effective community employment programs
as well as establishment of standards of wages, hours,
and working conditions for such workers.

889. Coover, Edwin Russell. "Status and Role Change Among
Women in the United States, 1940-1970: A Quantitative
Approach." Ph.D. dissertation, University of Minne-
sota, 1973. 306 pp.

Concludes that although female labor participation
rates have increased significantly since 1940, the distribution of occupations in 1970 was similar to 1940 and
showed a slight retrogression from 1960. Performance
within occupational categories remained mixed, but private household work and farm labor declined while clerical work increased; there has been no significant female penetration into higher status fields.

890. Cross, Susan Deller. *The Rights of Women: The Basic
A.C.L.U. Guide to Woman's Rights.* New York: Avon
Books, 1973. 384 pp.

Pleads for the extension of protective legislation,
lobbying, and lawsuits on behalf of women. Equal protection and equal rights should be applied in employment,
education, mass media, crimes, control of body, divorce,
name change, and the like.

891. Darian, Jean Catherine. "Labor Force Participation of
      Married Women in the United States: An Investigation
      of the Role of Occupation." Ph.D. dissertation, Uni-
      versity of Pennsylvania, 1972. 246 pp.

      Argues that home responsibilities are less inhibiting
      on women working where work makes fewer demands on the
      woman's time; and financial pressure to work has less
      influence on participation where work is interesting and
      pleasant. Changing working conditions have affected the
      size and composition of the female labor force.

892. Davis, Ethelyn. "Careers as Concerns of Blue-Collar
      Girls." In *Blue-Collar World: Studies of the American
      Worker*, edited by Arthur B. Shostak and William Gomberg.
      Englewood Cliffs, N.J.: Prentice-Hall, Inc., 1964.
      Pp. 154-64.

      Claims that working-class girls and young women are
      more motivated by service to others than by occupational
      advancement in seeking work satisfaction. Blue-collar
      girls seek traditional female occupations where they do
      not compete with men.

893. *Earnings of Women in Selected Manufacturing Industries,
      1946.* U.S. Department of Labor, Women's Bureau. Bul-
      letin No. 219. 1948. 14 pp.

      Compiles earnings information for women in union and
      nonunion plants and according to geographical region
      and individual locality for various occupations within
      the textile, footwear, tobacco, paper container, and
      costume jewelry industries.

894. *Employment Opportunities for Women as Secretaries, Ste-
      nographers, Typists, and as Office-Machine Operators
      and Cashiers.* U.S. Department of Labor, Women's Bu-
      reau. Bulletin No. 263. 1967. 30 pp.

      Shows that women dominate clerical occupations, but
      labor shortages have resulted in lowered hiring stan-
      dards, waste, and inefficiency. Improved training and
      standards of skills are needed.

895. *Employment Opportunities for Women in Beauty Service.*
      U.S. Department of Labor, Women's Bureau. Bulletin
      No. 260. 1956. 51 pp.

      Believes that beauty culture will continue to expand
      as an area of employment which has advantages for women

workers because the occupation is not restricted by geographic locality, age, marital status, or physical han-
dicap.

896. Faltermayer, Edmund. "A Better Way to Deal with Unemployment." *Fortune*, 87 (June 1973): 146-49, 236-42.

Argues that the creation of more challenging, better-
paying, part-time jobs for women would strengthen their
attachment to the labor force and possibly counteract
some of the influences of discrimination, wifely adjustment of careers to those of husbands, problems of child
care, and the like.

897. Fitzpatrick, Blanche. *Women's Inferior Education: An
Economic Analysis*. New York: Praeger Publishers, 1976.
189 pp.

Explores the lack of equal opportunities for young
women at every level of academic and vocational education beyond high school; the same is true in employment.
Universities, colleges, and vocational schools set up
barriers which restrict most young women to lesser-paid
skills and lower-paid professions, according to a 1972
study in Massachusetts and a study of twenty states in
1973.

898. Garson, Barbara. *All the Livelong Day: The Meaning and
Demeaning of Routine Work*. Garden City, N.Y.: Doubleday and Company, Inc., 1975. 221 pp.

Pleads for a socialist solution because assembly-line
work is so dull and workers are subjected to the tyran-
nies of the system and of their superiors.

899. *Handbook on Women Workers* (also entitled *Handbook of
Facts on Women Workers*). U.S. Department of Labor,
Women's Bureau. Bulletin Nos. 225, 237, 242, 255,
261, 266, 275, 285, 290, 297. 1948, 1950, 1952, 1954,
1956, 1958, 1960, 1962, 1965, 1975.

Compiles factual data on the numbers, characteristics,
occupations, earnings, and economic responsibilities of
working women as well as pertinent state and federal
legislation, education, training, and their civil and
political status.

900. Hooks, Janet M. *Women's Occupations Through Seven Decades*. U.S. Department of Labor, Women's Bureau. Bulletin No. 218. 1947, 1951. 257 pp.

Concludes that it is increasingly customary for women
to work, that the highest rate of increase in fields in
which women are employed is in clerical jobs, but that
women workers are clustered into relatively few occupational fields.

901. Howe, Louise Kapp. *Pink Collar Workers: Inside the
      World of Women's Work*. New York: G.P. Putnam's Sons,
      1977. 294 pp.

      Argues that the work most American women do is bla-
      tantly undervalued. Most employed women are in tradi-
      tional occupations in which they form the vast majority
      of workers, such as beauticians, salespersons, waitresses,
      office workers, and homemakers. They work because they
      must, at unfulfilling tasks, without respect or recogni-
      tion.

902. Hulett, Josephine, and Janet Dewart. "Household Help
      Wanted--Female." *Ms. Magazine*, 1 (February 1973):
      45-49, 105-7.

      Claims that female domestic employees deserve dignity,
      respect, decent wages and hours, benefits, and good
      working relationships including mutual regard for pri-
      vacy between employer and employee. Women, who have
      been kept divided, must learn to apply pressure on those
      above them in the power structure, not on those below.

903. Hunt, Chester L. "Female Occupational Roles and Urban
      Sex Ratios in the United States, Japan, and the
      Philippines." *Social Forces*, 43 (March 1965): 407-17.

      Shows that the United States has a low urban sex ratio
      because of industrialization and the related demand for
      female labor in urban centers.

904. *The Industrial Nurse and the Woman Worker*. U.S. Depart-
      ment of Labor, Women's Bureau. Bulletin No. 228.
      1949. 48 pp.

      Shows that the nurse in the industrial plant can do
      more than administer first aid; she can discover condi-
      tions within the factory which hamper production such
      as size, noise, confusion, tensions of work force and
      household responsibilities, and suitability of tasks to
      female physical capacity.

905. Jacobson, Dan. "Rejection of the Retiree Role: A Study
      of Female Industrial Workers in Their 50's." *Human
      Relations*, 27 (May 1974): 477-92.

Argues that women blue-collar workers are less likely
than men blue-collar workers to have positive attitudes
toward retirement. Women want to continue working to
retain work-based social ties. Moreover, their lifestyle has changed; it is less home-centered, and they
perceive fewer social options outside the workplace.

906. Jett, Michael. "The Return of Rosie: Blue Collar Occu-
     pations Attract More Women, Mainly for the Money."
     Wall Street Journal, 17 April 1973, p. 1.

     Asserts that women are "returning" to the kinds of
     blue-collar jobs they held temporarily during World War
     II, and that their reason is economic. Legislation of
     the 1960s has given women access to such employment;
     women account not only for more than 40 percent of the
     work force but for nearly two-thirds of the recent in-
     crease in the labor force; and employers are finding
     that women's performance on these jobs is as good as
     men's or better.

907. Kerschbaum, Winifred F. *Night Work for Women in Hotels
     and Restaurants*. U.S. Department of Labor, Women's
     Bureau. Bulletin No. 233. 1949. 56 pp.

     Argues that some night work is necessary in industries
     which are an important source of jobs for women, but
     statutes prohibiting night work for women should be re-
     vised only after careful study to establish adequate
     standards for protection of workers.

908. Kyrk, Hazel. "Who Works and Why." *Annals of the Amer-
     ican Academy of Political and Social Sciences*, 251
     (May 1947): 44-52.

     Concludes that women who are most likely to work are
     single and urban, but married women are also employed.
     Urbanization, number and ages of children, their own
     ages, and their husbands' income influence the deci-
     sions of married women to seek gainful employment.

909. Langer, Elinor. "The Women of the Telephone Company."
     New York Review of Books, 14 (12 and 26 March 1970):
     16-24, 14-22.

     Exposes paternalistic treatment of female employees
     of the telephone company, in particular supervision and
     control of their behavior, both job-related and personal.

910. Lecht, Leonard A. *Occupational Choices and Training
      Needs: Prospects for the 1980s.* New York: Praeger
      Publishers, 1977. 203 pp.

      Forecasts that women's portion of the labor force will
      grow more rapidly than men's or whites' but less than
      nonwhites' by 1985. Historical concentration of women
      in low-skill, low-paid occupations should be offset by
      vocational training, based on realistic planning and
      goal setting.

911. Lederer, Muriel. *Blue-Collar Jobs for Women.* New York:
      E.P. Dutton, 1979. 257 pp.

      Argues that women should acquire skills in order to be
      prepared to meet employer interest in recruiting women
      for well-paying craft jobs. "A skilled trade pays twice
      as much as a traditional women's white-collar job."

912. Levitan, Sar A., and William B. Johnston. *Work is Here
      to Stay, Alas.* Salt Lake City: Olympus Publishing Co.,
      1973. 184 pp.

      Urges that jobs be designed for people. The nature
      of work has changed from agrarian to industrial to
      white collar with increases in the service sector. Blue-
      collar work has experienced gradual but slower improve-
      ment.

913. Lyle, Jerolyn R., and Jane L. Ross. *Women in Industry:
      Employment Patterns of Women in Corporate America.*
      Lexington, Mass.: D.C. Heath and Company, 1973.
      164 pp.

      Shows women concentrated in clerical jobs where they
      are regarded as inexpensive labor. Women suffer dis-
      crimination and sex-typing of jobs.

914. Madden, Janice Fanning. *The Economics of Sex Discrimi-
      nation.* Lexington, Mass.: D.C. Heath and Company,
      1973. 140 pp.

      Claims that the female labor market is unique in that
      it is restricted to traditional occupations in an un-
      favorable occupational structure with wage inferiority.

915. Mancke, Richard B. "Lower Pay for Women: A Case of
      Economic Discrimination?" *Industrial Relations,* 10
      (October 1971): 1316-26.

Concludes that women receive lower wages than men in equivalent jobs and are regularly put in low-paying jobs, not because of sex discrimination, but because firms employing women have higher indirect labor costs. Therefore, the best places for women to seek employment are in jobs where training is brief and cheap.

916. Marshall, Patricia. "Look Who's Wearing Lipstick." *Manpower Magazine*, 4 (December 1972): 2-9.

Portrays women crossing occupational sex barriers to assume jobs traditionally done by males, such as diesel truck driver, police officer, and construction worker.

917. *Maternity Protection of Employed Women*. U.S. Department of Labor, Women's Bureau. Bulletin No. 240. 1952. 50 pp.

Argues that the increasing participation of married women in the labor force makes maternity protection more significant. The United States has little legal provision for pregnancy and maternity disabilities; instead, most protection has been achieved through employer or union industrial plans.

918. Miller, Frieda S. "Women in the Labor Force." *Annals of the American Academy of Political and Social Science*, 251 (May 1947): 35-43.

Asserts that women work to support themselves and others; few are employed by free choice. Many women workers are heads of families; others are members of families which need their income.

919. Minter, Charlotte, and Roseann Cacciola. "The Welder Is a Woman." *Community and Junior College Journal*, 47 (November 1976): 6-7.

Shows that some urban community colleges are beginning "to meet the changing social problems of the urban environment," including the training of women for skilled blue-collar occupations. Women are attracted to such programs because the training programs are brief and the wage potential attractive.

920. Mohr, Jennie. *Industrial Injuries to Women*. U.S. Department of Labor, Women's Bureau. Bulletin No. 212. 1947. 20 pp.

Claims that although frequency of injury is lower for
women than for men, the number and kinds of injuries
sustained indicate the need for safety programs in certain industries, especially slaughtering and meat packing, stamped and pressed metal products, fabricated
metal products, and textiles and cotton yarn.

921. ————. *Maternity Benefits under Union Contract: Health
      Insurance Plans.* U.S. Department of Labor, Women's
      Bureau. Bulletin No. 214. 1947. 16 pp.

Argues that maternity benefits relieve women of part
of their economic burden, but prenatal leaves in the
1940s were three times as long as the time during which
benefits were paid, women used weekly cash benefits
rather than hospitalization and surgical benefits to
which they were entitled, and hospital costs were higher
than the amount paid in benefits.

922. National Manpower Council. *Womanpower.* New York:
      Columbia University Press, 1957. 371 pp.

Examines women as an essential and distinctive part
of manpower resources, and recommends vocational guidance, government placement services, scholarships for
higher education, and better training especially for
the mature woman. The substance of the lives of most
women is fundamentally determined by their functions as
wives, mothers, and homemakers, but great changes are
noted in their emergence into the work force.

923. Nye, Francis Ivan, and Lois Wladis Hoffman, eds. *The
      Employed Mother in America.* Chicago: Rand McNally and
      Company, 1963. 406 pp.

Gathers sociological and socio-psychological research
completed between 1957 and 1962 dealing with why mothers
work, how employed and non-employed mothers interact
with their children and marriages, and how such women
feel about themselves, their health, and their relationships.

924. *Occupations for Girls and Women--Selected References:
      July 1943-June 1948.* U.S. Department of Labor, Wo-
      men's Bureau. Bulletin No. 229. 1949. 102 pp.

Lists books, pamphlets, articles, and reports regarding jobs, training, counseling, and women's status in
work and education.

925. Oppenheimer, Valerie Kincade. *The Female Labor Force in the United States: Demographic and Economic Factors Governing Its Growth and Changing Composition.* Westport, Conn.: Greenwood Press, Publishers, 1976. 197 pp.

Argues that the unprecedented increase in the number of working women since 1940 lies primarily in older women, married with husbands present, who have responded to the expansion of job opportunities.

926. *Part-Time Employment for Women.* U.S. Department of Labor, Women's Bureau. Bulletin No. 273. 1960. 53 pp.

Asserts that most part-time workers are women, that increasing numbers of women are employed in part-time jobs, especially in trade and service industries, and that the trend should continue for women in all age groups.

927. *Part-Time Jobs for Women--A Study in 10 Cities.* U.S. Department of Labor, Women's Bureau. Bulletin No. 238. 1951. 82 pp.

Claims that part-time employment has benefits for both employers and women workers. Employers can obtain "a large labor force for jobs and services that lend themselves to less than full-time hours," as well as cope with "the increasing manpower demands due to the national emergency." Married women can take advantage of part-time work which brings financial gain, uses their skills, and brings them personal satisfaction, while still meeting their family responsibilities.

928. Pidgeon, Mary Elizabeth. *Employment of Women in the Early Postwar Period, with Background of Prewar and War Data.* U.S. Department of Labor, Women's Bureau. Bulletin No. 211. 1946. 14 pp.

Forecasts that despite dramatic postwar declines in the employment of women, larger proportions of the female population may remain in the labor force than before the war.

929. *Progress Toward Equal Pay in the Meat-Packing Industry.* U.S. Department of Labor, Women's Bureau. Bulletin No. 251. 1953. 16 pp.

Publicizes factual descriptions of inequitable pay
situations in the hope that these will permit the problem to be viewed realistically. Women receive lower
earnings because they are concentrated in low-paying
jobs within an industry, have different hours of work,
have less seniority and more limited experience, and
have less opportunity for advancement.

930.   *Report of the National Conference on Equal Pay: March
        31 and April 1, 1952.* U.S. Department of Labor, Wo-
        men's Bureau. Bulletin No. 243. 1952. 25 pp.

Pleads for the principle of equal pay for workers regardless of gender and urges better education to inform
public understanding on the issue. If legislation is
the solution, it should be "rate for the job," but
existing legislation is difficult to enforce. Collective bargaining offers another avenue, but not for the
large numbers of unorganized women workers.

931.   Robinson, Mary V. *Old Age Insurance for Household
        Workers.* U.S. Department of Labor, Women's Bureau.
        Bulletin No. 220. 1947. 17 pp.

Presses for coverage to be extended to household employees under the old-age insurance system under the
Social Security Act, particularly since their employment
carries such liabilities as poor pay, irregularity,
illness and accident, and lack of legal safeguards, yet
they have responsibilities for dependents and many are
heads of households.

932.   Rosenberg, Bernard, and Saul Weinman. "Young Women Who
        Work: An Interview with Myra Wolfgang." In *The World
        of the Blue-Collar Worker*, edited by Irving Howe. New
        York: Quadrangle Books, 1972. Pp. 23-35.

Shows that the restaurant industry provides opportunities for women to work irregular hours, but these low-
paid service jobs are becoming de-skilled and unions are
not addressing the problems of organizing these chain-
restaurants. Further danger to the position of working
women rests in the Equal Rights Amendment which would
negate legislation which favors women.

933.   A *Short-Term Training Program in an Aircraft Engine
        Plant.* U.S. Department of Labor, Women's Bureau.
        Bulletin No. 245. 1953. 11 pp.

Argues that inexperienced women can become productive
machine tool and metal workers with well-organized
training programs. In time of labor shortage such programs are especially useful.

934. Simmons, Adele, et al. *Exploitation from 9 to 5: Report
of the Twentieth Century Fund Task Force on Women and
Employment.* New York: Twentieth Century Fund, 1975.
200 pp.

Demands for greater public and private education as
well as unionization and legislation to enforce civil
rights and fair employment practices regarding women.

935. Smith, Florence P. *State Minimum-Wage Laws and Orders:
1942; An Analysis.* U.S. Department of Labor, Women's
Bureau. Bulletin No. 191. 1942.

Revises Bulletin No. 167 (item 728).

936. Sonenstein, Freya Lund. "The Impact of a Wife's Employment on Working Class Families." Ph.D. dissertation,
Boston University Graduate School, 1976. 371 pp.

Concludes that a wife's employment means greater income, but among white families this "is defined as an
undesirable means of attaining external satisfaction."
Employed wives get less help from their husbands than
women who do not work outside the home; therefore, employed wives are overworked.

937. *State Hour Laws for Women.* U.S. Department of Labor,
Women's Bureau. Bulletin No. 250, revised as No. 277.
1953, 1961. 114, 105 pp.

Abstracts state legislation regulating daily and weekly hours of labor, day of rest, meal and rest periods,
and night work.

938. *State Minimum-Wage Law and Order Provisions Affecting
Working Conditions: July 1, 1942 to April 1, 1959.*
U.S. Department of Labor, Women's Bureau. Bulletin
No. 269. 1959. 141 pp.

Abstracts those portions of state regulations "de-
signed to safeguard the basic minimum-wage rate" such
as overtime pay, split shifts, meal and rest periods,
travel and waiting time, tips and gratuities, deductions
for meals and lodging and uniforms, and other provisions
dealing with working conditions.

939. *State Minimum-Wage Laws and Orders: July 1, 1942-July 1,*
      1950. U.S. Department of Labor, Women's Bureau. Bul-
      letin No. 227. 1950. 65 pp.

      Revised supplement to Bulletin No. 191 (item 935).
      Lists and abstracts minimum-wage legislation and regu-
      lations.

940. *State Minimum-Wage Laws and Orders: July 1, 1942-March*
      1, 1953. U.S. Department of Labor, Women's Bureau.
      Bulletin No. 247. 1953. 84 pp. + charts.

      Claims that "minimum-wage legislation became an ac-
      cepted and important part of our basic social legisla-
      tion" since the late 1930s, with continued and improved
      state laws and orders, including extension of coverage
      to men. State regulations are summarized.

941. *State Minimum-Wage Laws and Orders: July 1, 1942 to*
      July 1, 1958. U.S. Department of Labor, Women's Bu-
      reau. Bulletin No. 267. 1958, 1963. 30, 107 pp.

      Supersedes Bulletin 247 (item 940).

942. *State Minimum-Wage Order Provisions Affecting Working*
      Conditions: July 1, 1942 to June 1, 1955. U.S. De-
      partment of Labor, Women's Bureau. Bulletin No. 259.
      1955. 75 pp.

      Abstracts regulations affecting various occupations,
      to accompany the analysis in Bulletin No. 247 (item 940).

943. *The Status of Women in the United States: 1953.* U.S.
      Department of Labor, Women's Bureau. Bulletin No.
      249. 1953. 26 pp.

      Argues that the "Korean emergency, like the two World
      Wars, gave impetus to women's employment," accelerating
      a long-term trend of women holding jobs outside the
      home. Growing proportions of married women and of old-
      er women are in the labor force. Women have moved from
      less remunerative occupations to those offering better
      pay and working conditions. Women workers have experi-
      enced "a substantial increase in wage rates."

944. Sullivan, Teresa A. *Marginal Workers, Marginal Jobs:*
      The Underutilization of American Workers. Austin:
      University of Texas Press, 1978. 229 pp.

      Includes arguments that the underutilization of women
      workers may stem from their lack of education, from the

narrow demand for women's labor which channels both
training and utilization. Moreover, "women may also
find nonparticipation a feasible alternative to under-
utilization more often than men do."

945. Sweet, James A. "Labor Force Reentry by Mothers and
Young Children." *Social Science Research*, 1 (June
1972): 189-210.

Argues that women with low incomes are most likely to
return to work. Nurses, private household workers, and
teachers are more likely than sales workers and clerical
workers to return to employment.

946. Thomas, David Lloyd. "An Investigation of the Process
by Which Women Become Employed." Ph.D. dissertation,
University of Iowa, 1963. 372 pp.

Concludes that a woman's employment depends upon her
qualifications, her motivation, and the prospective employer's knowledge of them. Women who are employed frequently work because of enjoyment, desire to increase
income, concern with family responsibilities, and their
perception of attractive job opportunities.

947. Tobias, Sheila, and Lisa Anderson. *What Really Happened
to Rosie the Riveter? Demobilization and the Female
Labor Force, 1944-47.* MSS Modular Publications,
module 9, 1973. 36 pp.

Examines the cases of female war workers who did not
leave their jobs voluntarily at the end of World War II
but were forced out of their higher-skilled and better-
paid wartime employment. Since most worked from necessity, they reverted to lower-level means of earning
or suffered unemployment which led them to the welfare
rolls.

948. *Toward Better Working Conditions for Women: Methods and
Policies of the National Women's Trade Union League
of America.* U.S. Department of Labor, Women's Bureau.
Bulletin No. 252. 1953. 71 pp.

Summarizes the activities of the N.W.T.U.L. which "was
made up primarily of working women themselves, together
with others who understood their needs." The League
sought public recognition of women workers' problems
and approval of efforts to solve them, while it also
"sought to develop among working women themselves ini-

tiative, self-reliance, fellowship, and a knowledge of
the economic backgrounds of their employment."

949.   *Training Mature Women for Employment: The Story of 23
       Local Programs.* U.S. Department of Labor, Women's
       Bureau. Bulletin No. 256. 1955. 46 pp.

       Claims that mature women can learn new skills and se-
       cure jobs using them. But the women must be willing to
       learn, the community to supply training as well as coun-
       seling and placement, and employers to hire competent
       workers regardless of age.

950.   *Training Opportunities for Women and Girls: Preemploy-
       ment Courses, Initial Training Programs.* U.S. Depart-
       ment of Labor, Women's Bureau. Bulletin No. 274.
       1960. 64 pp.

       Argues that dynamic technological change has created
       new opportunities for women workers, but it also re-
       quires that they develop skills while planning their
       vocational futures to take full advantage of such op-
       portunities. Public trade and high schools, junior and
       community colleges, private business and technical
       schools, as well as in-service training and apprentice-
       ship, can help women to prepare for employment.

951.   *Typical Women's Jobs in the Telephone Industry.* U.S.
       Department of Labor, Women's Bureau. Bulletin No.
       207A. 1947. 49 pp.

       Compiles descriptions of tasks in traffic, accounting,
       and commercial departments of the telephone industry.

952.   Weil, Mildred Wishnatt. "A Study of the Factors Affect-
       ing the Role and Role Expectations of Women Participat-
       ing or Planning to Participate in the Labor Force."
       Ph.D. dissertation, New York University, 1959.
       152 pp.

       Concludes that a wife's participation in the labor
       force is significantly affected by the career orienta-
       tion of the wife and the favorable attitude of the hus-
       band.

953.   West, Karen. "How to Get a Blue Collar." *Ms. Magazine*,
       5 (May 1977): 62-65.

       Claims that many women are drawn to careers in the
       trades where they find "the promise of higher wages, a

sense of self-sufficiency and independence, and the satisfaction of acquiring a set of skills which will build something that endures." But such women face problems of training, apprenticeships, hiring, and on-the-job hassles including abuse and physical molestation.

954. *The Woman Telephone Worker*. U.S. Department of Labor, Women's Bureau. Bulletin No. 207. 1946. 38 pp.

Shows that jobs are sex-segregated in the telephone industry; women, who make up almost three-fourths of the labor force, hold most of the operating and clerical positions, while men do most of the plant jobs. The telephone operator's job requires more training, skills, and strains than routine clerical jobs; job reclassification would facilitate collective bargaining.

955. *Women Telephone Workers and Changing Technology*. U.S. Department of Labor, Women's Bureau. Bulletin No. 286. 1963. 46 pp.

Examines the influence of technology on women's employment opportunities in the telephone industry with the conversion from manual to dial operations, and continued automation will change some jobs, eliminate others, and provide new job opportunities. Conversion to automatic equipment is less likely to produce larger layoffs than transfer to positions vacated by attrition. But automation may also realign job structure and open new opportunities such as clerical occupations. Women should not anticipate much hiring or promotion into occupations traditionally dominated by men, however.

956. *Women Workers after V-J Day in One Community: Bridgeport, Connecticut*. U.S. Department of Labor, Women's Bureau. Bulletin No. 216. 1947. 34 pp.

Says that almost all of the women who constitute a third of the Bridgeport labor force work to support themselves or themselves and others. But they have suffered unemployment or a narrowed range of available occupations since the war, are earning less, and have inadequate placement, vocational training, and vocational counseling.

957. *Women Workers in Power Laundries*. U.S. Department of Labor, Women's Bureau. Bulletin No. 215. 1947. 67 pp.

Estimates that displaced women war workers will return
to previous occupations such as commercial laundries; it
is, therefore, necessary to know the nature of occupations, earnings, prices, productivity, hours, and physical working conditions in that industry.

958. *Women's Jobs: Advance and Growth.* U.S. Department of
Labor, Women's Bureau. Bulletin No. 232. 1949.
88 pp.

Popularizes Bulletin No. 218 (item 900).

959. Wool, Harold, and Bruce Dana Phillips. *The Labor Supply
for Lower-Level Occupations.* New York: Praeger Publishers, 1976. 383 pp.

Argues that the withdrawal of groups which have traditionally held low-paid, low-status jobs (blacks, immigrants, rural outmigrants) creates opportunities for
women to find employment in demeaning occupations.

960. *Working Women's Budgets in Twelve States/Thirteen
States.* U.S. Department of Labor, Women's Bureau.
Bulletin No. 226 and Revised. 1948, 1951. 33, 41 pp.

Asserts that cost of living is a principal basis for
state minimum-wage legislation; and, therefore, tabulates
costs of housing, food, clothing, living essentials,
taxes, savings, and private insurance.

961. Young, Esther. "Individuality in a Factory." *American
Behavioral Scientist,* 16 (September-October 1972):
65-74.

Claims that women working on an assembly line have no
opportunity to express individuality except by learning,
which to them does not mean adjusting to the job so
much as creating their own ways of doing the job. However, women tend to internalize management and male
views of their sex-typed jobs which makes them vulner-
able to self-hatred for such individuality.

TRADE UNIONS AND WORKERS PROTEST

962. Abicht, Monika Maria. "Women's Leadership Roles in Two
Selected Labor Unions in the United States and Belgium:
A Comparative Descriptive Study." Ed. D. dissertation,
University of Cincinnati, 1976. 191 pp.

Argues that attitudes must change, especially among
women before union women can participate more fully in
union leadership in either country. Women in two blue-
collar labor unions in 1975-76 not only showed low rates
of holding leadership positions, but tended to have
negative views of their female leaders.

963. Berquist, Virginia A. "Women's Participation in Labor
Organizations." *Monthly Labor Review*, 97 (October
1974): 3-9.

Shows that the numbers of women in unions have increased, but women are joining the labor force in greater
numbers than they are joining unions. Moreover, there
is still no significant increase in women in leadership
positions within unions.

964. Conway, Mimi. *Rise Gonna Rise: A Portrait of Southern
Textile Workers*. Garden City, N.Y.: Anchor Press/
Doubleday, 1979. 228 pp.

Demonstrates that whatever benefits were attached to
early paternalistic operation of the mills did not sur-
vive their acquisition of J.P. Stevens. Deteriorating
conditions, machine speed-up, and health hazards encouraged some workers to support unionization and compensation for brown lung; resistance came primarily from
older white workers who feared loss of their jobs.

965. Cook, Alice H. "Women and American Trade Unions." *Annals of the American Academy of Political and Social
Science*, 375 (January 1968): 124-32.

Concludes that unions have not significantly changed
their attitudes or practices regarding women workers
from those held in the 1940s.

966. Dickason, Gladys. "Women in Labor Unions." *Annals of
the American Academy of Political and Social Science*,
251 (May 1947): 70-78.

Argues that the increase in female membership in
unions results from increased wartime employment, industrial rather than craft organizing, declining prejudices and membership restrictions within unions, and
the efforts of the Women's Trade Union League. Unions
have reduced discrimination against women regarding
wages, hours, and standards; they have negotiated
maternity-leave benefits and increased education.

967. Hillman, Bessie. "Gifted Women in the Trade Unions."
      In *American Women: The Changing Image*, edited by
      Beverly Benner Cassara. Boston: Beacon Press, 1962.
      Pp. 99–115.

      Says that women can and should assume executive re-
      sponsibilities in the labor movement. Women already
      serve well as shop stewards and local union officers;
      immediate opportunities lie in professional staff posi-
      tions. Female occupancy of significant numbers of union
      presidencies and other executive offices will come in
      the next generation.

968. LeGrande, Linda H. "Women in Labor Organizations: Their
      Ranks Are Increasing." *Monthly Labor Review*, 101
      (August 1978): 8–14.

      Shows that women's membership in trade unions increased
      much more rapidly than their representation in official
      and leadership positions between 1956 and 1976. Occu-
      pation and industry of female employees explain why the
      proportion of working women has risen faster than the
      proportion who join unions: most women are in white-
      collar occupations which have low unionization.

969. Raphael, Edna E. "Working Women and Their Membership
      in Labor Unions." *Monthly Labor Review*, 97 (May 1974):
      27–33.

      Claims that union membership makes women less disad-
      vantaged. The earnings gap between men and women workers
      is narrower for female union nembers. But the propor-
      tion of working women who belong to labor unions de-
      clined in the late 1960s.

970. ————. "Working Women and Their Membership in Labor
      Unions." In *The American Working Class: Prospects
      for the 1980s*, edited by Irving Louis Horowitz. New
      Brunswick, N.J.: Transaction Books, 1979. Pp. 114–24.

      Argues that declining labor union membership among
      women blue-collar workers accounts for an increasing
      disparity in wages between men and women union members.
      Union women, on the other hand, are reluctant to support
      equal rights legislation, fearing the loss of protection.
      And the Women's Liberation Movement has come late and
      tenuously to join efforts with women in the labor move-
      ment. But some women union activists have established
      vehicles to press both union and the law toward con-
      structive recognition of women's interests.

971. Troger, Anne Marie. "Organizing That Works." *Quest: A Feminist Quarterly*, 1 (Fall 1974): 24-34.

Anticipates that the Coalition of Labor Union Women can provide a much needed link between middle- and working-class women in the Women's Movement as well as improve general working conditions. C.L.U.W.'s multiunion strategy seeks to transcend the inefficiency of traditional trade unionism to deal with bread-and-butter issues which require airing in a larger political framework. And C.L.U.W. can activate "a collective sense of unity among working women" to fulfill their "self defined economic and political needs."

972. Wertheimer, Barbara, and Anne Nelson. "The American Woman at Work." *Personnel Management*, 6 (March 1975): 20-23, 40-41.

Estimates that there are more working women and more women trade union members but not more women union officials. A study of New York City locals indicates that women need self-confidence and programs to further their individual educational goals before they will actively seek and receive leadership roles in unions.

973. ———. *Trade Union Women: A Study of Their Participation in New York City Locals*. New York: Praeger Publishers, 1975. 178 pp.

Shows that women are under-represented in leadership positions in unions and proposes action to encourage their participation, especially education programs.

974. Withorn, Ann. "The Death of C.L.U.W." *Radical America*, 10 (March-April 1976): 47-51.

Claims that the Coalition of Labor Union Women deteriorated from a widely based mass organization within the trade unions into "a paper organization dominated by union bureaucrats who cannot mobilize large numbers of trade-union women for even the most narrow goals." The initial leadership sought only "recognition," "more status for themselves and for other potential women bureaucrats," and failed to develop either an alternative vision of trade unionism or broad feminist goals.

F. HISTORICAL CONDITIONS

WORLD WAR II

975. Anderson, Karen. "The Impact of World War II in the
      Puget Sound on the Status of Women and the Family."
      Ph.D. dissertation, University of Washington, 1975.
      245 pp.

      Concludes that World War II served as a catalyst for
      social change in the status and roles of women in the
      Puget Sound area. Women found increasing employment in
      manufacturing, but economic opportunities became limited
      with postwar reestablishment of discriminatory policies.
      Nevertheless, a significant number of women chose to
      remain in the work force.

976. Anderson, Mary Kay. *Employment of Women in the Manu-
      facture of Cannon and Small Arms in 1942.* U.S. Depart-
      ment of Labor, Women's Bureau. Bulletin No. 192-3.
      1943. 36 pp.

      Says that the comparative lightness of the work in
      small-arms manufacture makes those occupations more ac-
      ceptable for women who could form up to 75 percent of
      the work force, while women could represent up to 40
      percent of total employees in cannon manufacturing.

977. Anthony, Susan B., II. *Out of the Kitchen--Into the
      War: Woman's Winning Role in the Nation's Dream.* New
      York: Stephen Day, Inc., 1943. 246 pp.

      Asks women to become anti-fascist fighters in World
      War II by taking jobs in industry. Women can be lib-
      erated from their homes to take their "place in the war
      today and in the work of the world tomorrow."

978. Baker, Melva Joyce. "Images of Women: The War Years,
      1941-1945: A Study of the Public Perceptions of Wo-
      men's Roles as Revealed in Top-Grossing War Films."
      Ph.D. dissertation, University of California at Santa
      Barbara, 1978. 323 pp.

      Concludes that World War II "strengthened rather than
      weakened Americans' attachment to women's traditional
      roles in society." Home, family, church, marriage, and
      romance were staple fare; war jobs were only a patriotic
      sacrifice on the part of housewife-mother heroines.

979. Banning, Margaret Culkin. *Women in Defense.* New York:
      Duell, Sloan and Pearce, 1942. 243 pp.

      Uses claims of great gains made by women in World War
      I to encourage their patriotic participation in World
      War II.

980. Benham, Elisabeth D. *Employment Opportunities in Char-
      acteristic Industrial Occupations of Women.* U.S. De-
      partment of Labor, Women's Bureau. Bulletin No. 201.
      1944. 50 pp.

      Argues that women are highly employable in occupations
      which require deftness, accuracy, patience, attention
      to detail, and close following of instructions, as de-
      monstrated by prewar employment of some women and the
      great wartime increase in numbers and range of tasks
      done by women.

981. Campbell, D'Ann Mae. "Wives, Workers and Womanhood:
      America During World War II." Ph.D. dissertation,
      University of North Carolina at Chapel Hill, 1979.
      294 pp.

      Concludes that the strong family orientation of Amer-
      ican women of the 1940s led them to resist media and
      government appeals to change their roles and plans dur-
      ing the war. "The suburban, family-centered society
      that emerged after the war was what American women wanted
      and demanded."

982. Carr, Lowell Julliard, and James Edson Sterner. *Willow
      Run: A Study of Industrialization and Cultural Inade-
      quacy.* New York: Harper and Brothers, Publishers,
      1952. 406 pp.

      Claims that the proportions of women employed in the
      World War II Willow Run bomber plant were not typical of
      either the bomber work force or of female participation
      in the war. Whatever tasks these women performed, they
      experienced traditional differentiation in which office
      workers were socially better off than production workers
      but economically disadvantaged.

983. Clawson, Augusta H. *Shipyard Diary of a Woman Welder.*
      New York: Penguin, 1944. 181 pp.

      Urges improvement in training to eliminate women quit-
      ting work in shipyards shortly after being trained and

entering employment. A Special Agent for Training Women
for War Production in the Vocational Division of the
United States Office of Education describes her experiences during training and on the job.

984. Clive, Alan. "Women Workers in World War II: Michigan
      as a Test Case." *Labor History*, 20 (Winter 1979):
      44-72.

      Shows that the study of women war workers in Michigan
      confirms Eleanor Straub's thesis that World War II failed
      to make visible changes in the status of American women,
      rather than Chester W. Gregory's claims of war-based
      emancipation.

985. *Employment and Housing Problems of Migratory Workers
      in New York and New Jersey Canning Industries, 1943.*
      U.S. Department of Labor, Women's Bureau. Bulletin
      No. 198. 1944. 35 pp.

      Says that work, earnings, housing, and other issues
      were misrepresented to workers when they were recruited;
      these problems, as well as transportation, feeding, and
      child care should be rectified.

986. *The Employment of and Demand for Women Workers in the
      Manufacture of Instruments--Aircraft, Optical and
      Fire-Control, and Surgical and Dental.* U.S. Depart-
      ment of Labor, Women's Bureau. Bulletin No. 189-4.
      1942. 20 pp.

      Demonstrates how tasks in instrument manufacture are
      being broken down and no longer require the work of men
      classed as all-around skilled instrument makers. The
      British experience has disproven attitudes that women
      lack mechanical ability, interest, or aptitude.

987. *Employment of Women in Army Supply Depots in 1943.*
      U.S. Department of Labor, Women's Bureau. Bulletin
      No. 192-8. 1945. 33 pp.

      Claims that women can be employed more extensively
      and more effectively in army supply depots if careful
      consideration is given to job placement, training, di-
      vision and simplification of tasks, wider use of lifting
      devices, provision of sanitation and safety facilities,
      upgrading and wage reclassification, and use of women
      in personnel and supervisory jobs.

988. *Employment of Women in the Manufacture of Artillery Ammunition.* U.S. Department of Labor, Women's Bureau. Bulletin No. 189-3. 1942. 17 pp.

Shows women being used extensively in tasks dealing with small components and processes broken down into many operations; they could be used to assist in setting-up and adjusting machines if they develop sufficient skill through vocational courses or training within industry.

989. *Employment of Women in the Manufacture of Small-Arms Ammunition.* U.S. Department of Labor, Women's Bureau. Bulletin No. 189-2. 1942. 11 pp.

Asks that women be substituted in part for men in some tasks of small-arms ammunition manufacture, particularly where the work is done by automatic machinery and requires only short training periods.

990. Erickson, Ethel. *Women's Employment in Aircraft Assembly Plants in 1942.* U.S. Department of Labor, Women's Bureau. Bulletin No. 192-1. 1942. 23 pp.

Shows that the dramatic increase in female employment in aircraft assembly, as well as the range of new and upgraded jobs women perform, demonstrates that industrial capability is not based on sex and that women can do highly skilled and responsible work if they receive training and encouragement.

991. ————. *Women's Employment in the Making of Steel, 1943.* U.S. Department of Labor, Women's Bureau. Bulletin No. 192-5. 1944. 39 pp.

Asserts that much work in the steel industry is beyond the limited physical strength of women, and since returning veterans will have seniority and priority on postwar jobs, it is unfair to ask women to do heavy and dangerous tasks and dissipate their strength on temporary employment.

992. Gregory, Chester W. *Women in Defense Work During World War II: An Analysis of the Labor Problem and Women's Rights.* New York: Exposition Press, 1974. 243 pp.

Argues that the war period was a major step toward self-emancipation from second-class status for women. Significant psychological and sociological reasons caused

several million women to take over many new jobs for-
merly held exclusively by men.

993.   Harnish, Francis E.P. *Women's Employment in Foundries,*
        1943. U.S. Department of Labor, Women's Bureau.
        Bulletin No. 192-7. 1944. 28 pp.

        Urges that women be employed in foundries where tasks
        can be broken down to prevent heavy lifting or where
        skills can be diluted. But, ordinarily, the long learn-
        ing process, degree of strength needed, health hazards
        from silica and metallic dust, and likelihood that men
        will reclaim jobs at the end of the war make it unlike-
        ly that foundries will represent significant opportu-
        nities for long-term occupational gains by women work-
        ers.

994.   Holcomb, Josephine Chandler. "Women in the Labor Force
        in the United States, 1940-1950." Ph.D. dissertation,
        University of South Carolina, 1976. 300 pp.

        Concludes that the only traceable gain for women
        workers from World War II was an increase in numbers
        of participants. Quality of work, place and occupa-
        tions in the labor force, and public attitudes toward
        their employment remained unchanged. Historians have
        exaggerated the positive impact of the war on women.

995.   Newman, Dorothy K. *Employing Women in Shipyards.* U.S.
        Department of Labor, Women's Bureau. Bulletin No.
        192-6. 1944. 83 pp.

        Notes that the unprecedented influx of women workers
        into wartime ship building raises serious problems of
        training, safety, personnel, and medical programs which
        require planning and standards governing their employ-
        ment and working conditions such as cooperation of men
        supervisors and workers, suitability of tasks, sched-
        ules and shifts, and safe work practices.

996.   —————, and Martha J. Ziegler. *Employment of Women in*
        the Machine-Tool Industry, 1942. U.S. Department of
        Labor, Women's Bureau. Bulletin No. 192-4. 1943.
        42 pp.

        Claims that contrary to traditional opinion, women
        can be trained for a wide variety of tasks in machine-
        tool manufacture and that the full employment of men
        makes such recruitment and training of women necessary,
        assuming the interest and cooperation of management.

997. Pidgeon, Mary Elizabeth. *"Equal Pay" for Women in War
      Industries.* U.S. Department of Labor, Women's Bureau.
      Bulletin No. 106. 1942. 26 pp.

      Argues that wage rates, including the entrance rate,
      should be the same for women as for men. Most occupa-
      tions and processes are not sex-determined; women work
      as efficiently as men; and additional plant costs re-
      lating to the employment of women are insignificant.
      Wage rates should be set for the job, not the worker.

998. Quick, Paddy. "Rosie the Riveter: Myths and Realities."
      Radical America, 9 (July-August 1975): 115-31.

      Demonstrates that Rosie the Riveter was neither a
      happy housewife who did patriotic factory work, nor an
      angry freedom-seeker who returned reluctantly to home
      and family at war's end, but a working-class woman re-
      quired by economic necessity to seek employment and at-
      tracted by relatively high wartime wages. After the
      war she continued to work, at lower wages and in service
      or clerical jobs rather than in industry, but still
      because of financial need.

999. Robinson, Mary V. *Recreation and Housing for Women
      War Workers: A Handbook on Standards.* U.S. Depart-
      ment of Labor, Women's Bureau. Bulletin No. 190.
      1942. 40 pp.

      Urges communities to assume responsibility to help
      women war workers solve problems regarding their living
      arrangements and leisure-time pursuits, and urges that
      the women themselves should participate in planning
      and conducting programs and that at least minimum stan-
      dards should prevail. Basic requirements as well as
      additional considerations for rural areas and large
      cities are listed.

1000. Rupp, Leila J. *Mobilizing Women for War: Germany and
      American Propaganda, 1939-1945.* Princeton: Princeton
      University Press, 1978. 243 pp.

      Concludes that although Americans and Nazis shared
      a traditional view of women in the home, the United
      States mobilized more women for war work, primarily
      because of stronger economic incentives. Postwar at-
      titudes changed slowly with increased peacetime employ-
      ment of women.

1001. Seidman, Joel. *American Labor from Defense to Recon-*
      version. Chicago: University of Chicago Press, 1953.
      307 pp.

      Examines the impact of World War II on employment and
      occupations, with incidental comments on women workers
      such as warnings against wearing tight sweaters or
      dating bosses.

1002. *State Labor Laws for Women in Wartime Modifications:*
      December 15, 1944. U.S. Department of Labor, Women's
      Bureau. Bulletin Nos. 202-1 to 202-5. 1945-1946.
      110, 43, 12, 26, 60 pp.

      Lists, abstracts, and summarizes legislation on hours,
      plant facilities, regulation of conditions, prohibition
      of female employment in certain tasks, maternity, and
      industrial home work.

1003. Straub, Eleanor Ferguson. "Government Policy Toward
      Civilian Women during World War II." Ph.D. disser-
      tation, Emory University, 1973. 393 pp.

      Exposes the dichotomy between the glossy image of the
      woman war worker and the reality of meager changes in
      women's status. Prosecution of the war took priority
      over response to pressures from special interest groups.
      Those few gains made in wartime were not permanent,
      largely because the war produced little awareness among
      women of their common problems.

1004. ————. "United States Government Policy toward Civil-
      ian Women during World War II." *Prologue,* 5 (Winter
      1973): 240-54.

      Argues that American women who participated in World
      War II neither had a significant influence on the pol-
      icies which ruled them as workers nor enjoyed much im-
      provement in status. Although women were portrayed as
      cultural heroines for their support of the war, es-
      pecially by accepting war industry jobs, government,
      which recruited six million such workers, saw them only
      as temporary, emergency employees and did not develop
      rational policies to deal with this new presence in the
      work force. Nor did women themselves constitute an ef-
      fectively organized force to influence such a policy.

1005. ————. "Women in the Civilian Labor Force." Paper,
      National Archives 1976 Conference on Women's History,
      Washington, D.C., 23 April 1976.

Shows how private industry, the federal government, and the media consciously glamorized employment opportunities for women in order to attract them into the labor force to meet employment needs of World War II.

1006. Trey, J.E. "Women in the War Economy--World War II."
       The Review of Radical Political Economics, 4 (July
       1972): 41-57.

Concludes that "women were manipulated as a group into a completely new role which required a completely new conception of themselves, yet they never changed their consciousness to fit that new role." Women remained "women" even in the factory; they were not permitted to develop a self-concept as "workers."

1007. Valentine, Frances W. *Successful Practices in the Em-
       ployment of Nonfarm Women on Farms in the Northeast-
       ern States, 1943*. U.S. Department of Labor, Women's
       Bureau. Bulletin No. 199. 1944. 44 pp.

Points out the necessity for using women as agricultural workers although they have no experience in such tasks; but this situation required adequate recruitment, placement, and general supervision as well as adequate pay, time to adjust to the work, rest periods, suitable clothing, sanitation, safety, and health protection.

1008. ————. *Women's Emergency Farm Service on the Pacific
       Coast in 1943*. U.S. Department of Labor, Women's
       Bureau. Bulletin No. 204. 1945. 36 pp.

Claims that both growers and women workers were satisfied with the experiment of using nonfarm women in agriculture and food-processing work, although improvement is needed in training and supervision.

1009. von Miklos, Josephine. *I Took a War Job*. New York:
       Simon and Schuster, 1943. 223 pp.

Says that in wartime "the crux of the matter is that there is a job to be done to which we have been called," and describes her own transition from fashion photographer to munitions worker.

1010. *Womanpower Committees during World War II: United
       States and British Experience*. U.S. Department of
       Labor, Women's Bureau. Bulletin No. 244. 1953.
       73 pp.

Concludes that the Women's Advisory Committee to the
War Manpower Commission (1942-1945) held to a moderate
position "between the extremes of feminism and subser-
vience to reaction." Women's input was stronger in
staff positions or in review of materials than in
policy-making, but the Committee made an outstanding
contribution in developing cooperation with women's
organizations to obtain "participation by women in women's problems."

1011. *Women During the War and After: Summary of a Compre-*
       hensive Study. Bryn Mawr, Pa.: Carola Woerishoffer
       Graduate Department of Social Economy and Social Re-
       search, Bryn Mawr College, 1945. 57 pp.

       Shows the impact of participation in World War II on
       employment, family, children, housing, and housekeeping.

1012. *Women Workers in Some Expanding Wartime Industries: New*
       Jersey, 1942. U.S. Department of Labor, Women's Bu-
       reau. Bulletin No. 197. 1943. 44 pp.

       Claims that the large and rapid expansion of war pro-
       duction has been accompanied by planning to produce
       plant conditions which promote worker efficiency, and
       additional attention to conditions and facilities is
       needed.

1013. *Women Workers in Ten War Production Areas and Their*
       Postwar Employment Plans. U.S. Department of Labor,
       Women's Bureau. Bulletin No. 209. 1946. 56 pp.

       Argues that women worked and plan to continue to work
       because they carry heavy economic responsibilities at
       home, and that their work in industries producing di-
       rectly for war purposes gave them significantly higher
       take-home earnings than women in other industries. But
       the numbers of women greatly exceed the numbers of wo-
       men employed in the same areas and occupations in 1940.

1014. *Women's Factory Employment in an Expanding Aircraft*
       Production Program. U.S. Department of Labor, Wo-
       men's Bureau. Bulletin No. 189-1. 1942. 12 pp.

       Claims that women can work effectively in all depart-
       ments of the aircraft industry but particularly in pro-
       duction. To allay fears of personnel managers about
       men and women working side by side in shops, women
       might receive trial employment in subassembly and bench-

work departments with light repetitive work, thus re-
leasing men for heavier work.

1015. *Women's Wartime Hours of Work: The Effect on Their
Factory Performance and Home Life.* U.S. Department
of Labor, Women's Bureau. Bulletin No. 208. 1947.
187 pp.

Argues that total production cannot be increased by
lengthening the scheduled hours for women workers much
beyond 48 per week, because women will not work longer
hours for any extended period, even in wartime.

1016. *Women's Wartime Jobs in Cane-Sugar Refineries.* U.S.
Department of Labor, Women's Bureau. Bulletin No.
192-9. 1945. 20 pp.

Says that wartime increases in the employment of women in cane-sugar refineries represents not only a
growth in the number of women performing traditional
tasks but also the opening of new operations to female
employees. The continuation of such employment after
the war was uncertain, however.

1017. *Women's Work in the War.* U.S. Department of Labor,
Women's Bureau. Bulletin No. 193. 1942. 10 pp.

Shows that women are available for war jobs, are
sought for industrial and other occupations, and are
receiving training in plants throughout the country;
but standards are necessary to control the conditions
of labor and a number of states have passed wartime
laws regulating hours, rest periods, night work, Sunday
work, holidays, and overtime pay.

1018. *Your Questions as to Women in War Industries.* U.S. Department of Labor, Women's Bureau. Bulletin No. 194.
1942. 10 pp.

Notes that women are employed in war industries in
unprecedented numbers and in new kinds of skilled tasks
for which they are receiving training. This extensive
employment of women underscores the need for standards
to establish proper conditions under which they can
work with greatest efficiency and for adequate minimum
wages which will prevent the use of women to undercut
men.

1019. Ziegler, Martha J. *Women's Employment in Artillery
Ammunition Plants, 1942.* U.S. Department of Labor,
Women's Bureau. Bulletin No. 192-2. 1942. 19 pp.

Argues that employment of women in arsenals and plants
depends largely on the size and type of ammunition to
be handled; but the tasks women already perform vary
from plant to plant and indicate that women could be
used more extensively in operations still performed by
men in some plants.

AUTHOR INDEX

SUBJECT INDEX

Female-headed household. See Household, female head of
Female Labor Reform Associations, 169
Female sub-culture, 45
Feminism, 789, 856; and class, 297, 640-42, 646; and social-
     ism, 343, 344; 347; social, 298, 560, 695, 696
Feminity, 27, 32, 119, 133, 144, 145, 798
Fertility, 66, 67, 71-73, 101, 147, 251, 257. See also Motherhood
Fiction, 796
Fines, 455, 458
Fires, 463. See also Triangle Fire
Flint, Michigan, 380
Florida, 510
Flynn, Elizabeth Gurley, 24, 300
Food workers, 788
Fourteenth Amendment, 664
France, 662
Free enterprise, 290. See also Capitalism
French Canadians, 186
Fruit-growers, 511
Furriers, 638

Gannett, Deborah Sampson, 63
Garment workers, 87, 203, 206, 401, 458, 460, 461, 477, 498,
     505. See also Homework; International Ladies Garment
     Workers Union; Sweatshops; Unions
Gastonia, 599, 623
General Electric, 610
Georgia, 512
Germans, 84, 85, 236
Glorieux, Emilie L., 335
Glove workers, 309, 408, 493, 542
Goldmark, Josephine, 719
Government agencies, 663, 759
Government, federal, employment, 122, 129, 235, 428-30, 435,
     570; policy, 1003-05, 1010
Government, local, 235, 254, 605
Government planning, 643
Great Strike of 1860, 112

Hamilton, Alexander, 58
Handicraft, 370
Hanson, Harriet. See Robinson, Harriet Hanson
Harassment, 122, 594, 953
Hardships, 791
Hart, Schaffner and Marx, 345, 559, 615
Hat-makers, 618
Haverhill, Massachusetts, 197

Richmond, California, 859
Richmond, Virginia, 224, 431
Rights, 50, 210, 300, 890. See also Civil rights; Women's
    rights
Robins, Margaret Dreier, 21, 298, 717
Robinson, Harriet Hanson, 21
Roles, 29, 247, 306, 823, 1006
Roosevelt, Franklin D., 783
Rosie the Riveter, 947, 998
Rubber workers, 624
Rural areas, 224, 264, 370; sources of industrial labor force
    in, 142, 144, 171, 182, 186, 188, 189, 191
Russell Sage Foundation, 285

Safety, 374, 664, 687, 704, 740, 767, 857, 876
Sales workers, 419, 425, 432, 433, 945. See also Department
    stores
Sampson, Deborah. See Gannett, Deborah Sampson
San Antonio, 776
San Francisco, 123, 584
Sanger, Margaret, 274, 312
Sanitary board, 504
Sanitation, 457, 467, 468, 506, 510, 511, 619, 689, 693, 770
Savings, 64, 83, 438, 781, 817, 960
Scandinavia, 291, 296
Schneiderman, Rose, 24, 220, 313, 643
Scientific management, 218, 679. See also Efficiency
Scientific research, 360
Scots, 83, 236
Scudder, Vida, 346
Seamstresses. See Garment trades
Seattle, Washington, 382
Security, 114, 829
Seduction, 75
Self-confidence, 861
Self-determination, 813
Self-improvement, 26, 95, 158, 173, 174, 181, 182, 445. See
    also Education
Self-sufficiency, 120, 218, 233
Servants, indentured, 47, 55, 59, 61
Service occupations, 44, 263, 766, 787, 889, 912, 926, 998
Settlements, 302, 311, 346
Sex, 3, 6
Sex segregation, 209, 353, 501, 755, 850, 867, 997. See also
    Employment; Working conditions
Sexual equality, 33
Sexuality, 6, 71-73